IDLER

SLOW DOWN. HAVE FUN. LIVE WELL. NOVEM… ECEMBER 2024

libertas per cultum

NO. 99

IDLER NO.99 NOVEMBER–DECEMBER 2024

Idler is a bi-monthly published by Idle Ltd.,
Great Western Studios, 65 Alfred Road, London W2 5EU Tel: 0203 176 7907 idler.co.uk
Subscription enquiries: 01442 820 580 or subs@webscribe.co.uk

Editor: Tom Hodgkinson
Art Director: Alice Smith
Deputy Editor: Michael Meekin
Sub-editing: Cathi Unsworth
Typesetter: Christian Brett, Bracketpress
Programming Director: Victoria Hull
Assistant: Aliya Gilmore
Literary Editor: Cathleen Mair
Video Director: David Hunt
Publishing Advisor: James Pembroke

Advertising: renata@parkwalkmedia.com

Idle Limited Reg. No.5897340

Print managed by Adam Shaw Associates

ISSN 1351-5098
ISBN 978-1-7384998-4-7

Cover photography by Chris Floyd
chrisfloyd.com

Editorial illustrations throughout
the *Idler* (except where noted)
by Alice Smith
alice-smith.co.uk

Contributors: Dean Patterson, Royston Robertson, Nik Ramage, Paul Shadbolt, Jon Link, Mick Bunnage, Gray Jolliffe, Arthur Smith, Jon Glover, Mark Vernon, Alex Johnson, Stephen Bayley, James Thellusson, Robin Timmis, Mary Ruskin, Edward Thomas, Orlando Gili, Georgina Williams, Lee Osborne, Tim Richardson, Ella Berthoud, Stewart Lee, Georgia Mann, Guy Hayward, Graham Burnett, Bill Anderson, Kate Morris, Lindsey Bareham, Oli Meade, Cameron Murray, Joseph Piercy, Rachel Kelly, the Money-Saving Amateurs, Michael Gilmore, Virginia Ironside, Alex Bellos

Letter from the Editor

Dear Idlers

Welcome to our 99th issue. Our cover star Dominic West explains why evil is boring. We follow Kate Morris's week without WiFi on the North Devon coast, and learn about the crazy medieval life of writer Gervase of Tilbury. Troubadour Robin Timmis outlines the appeal of the busker's life to the idle at heart, and Alex Johnson encounters the sensational diaries of Vivian MacKerrell, the original Withnail. When Stephen Bayley proposed an "Odium" column on lobster, he elucidated: "It will not be a hate-crime against individual crustaceans, but an assault on a gastronomic category." Bayley has no objection to the lobsters themselves. It's the way they are eaten that irks him.

Stewart Lee puts the needle on the record, and Arthur Smith reveals his stoical technique for coping with diabetes – he calls it Dennis. Tim Richardson visits the mysterious Isokon building, Georgia Mann proposes a classical soundtrack for winter, Rachel Kelly cuts the crap and Virginia Ironside solves your problems.

The merry old season of Christmas approacheth, and we have modestly proposed a few gift ideas in a special festive section.

Thanks for reading. See you next time for issue 100.

Live well,

Tom

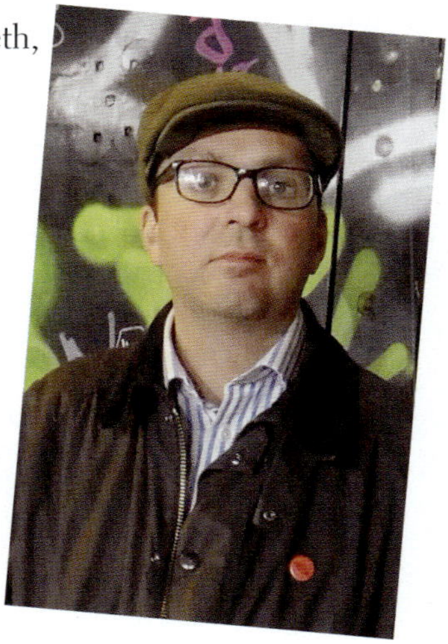

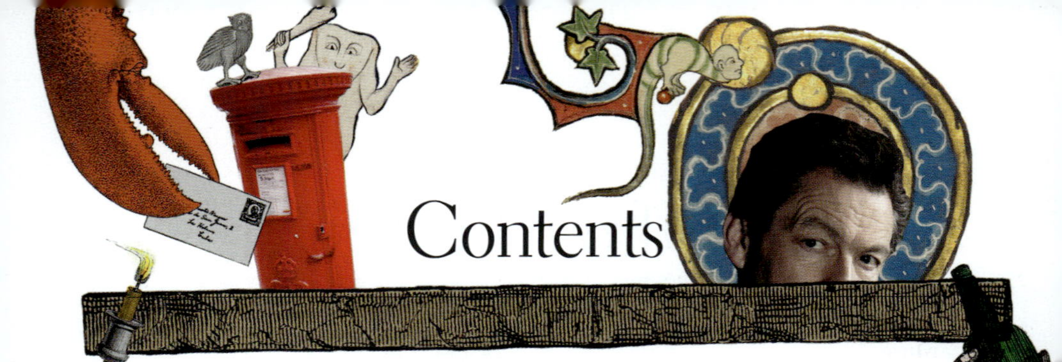

Contents

NOTES FROM THE COUCH

Idler's Diary 8

Arthur Smith
On his lifelong friend, Dennis the Diabetes Menace 14

How I Live
Jon Glover, Actor, Voiceover, Writer 16

Philosophy
An Ode to the Poet, that most magical of souls, by Mark Vernon 20

Idler Heroes
Raise a glass of lighter fluid to the real Withnail, says Alex Johnson 24

Odium
Why Stephen Bayley will not be having the lobster 28

FEATURES

Wire in the Blood
Actor Dominic West talks Tom Hodgkinson through the most rewarding – and disturbing – roles of his life 32

Going Postal
The little red boxes that unite our land celebrated by James Thelluson 40

All The World's a Stage
The life of the travelling troubadour by busker Robin Timmis 44

Here Be Monsters!
Mary Ruskin on Medieval Essex's foremost chronicler of the bizarre 48

Poetry
With Edward Thomas 52

STYLE

Hearth of the Matter
The art of the mantelpiece celebrated by Orlando Gili 54

Santa's Little Helpers
Our complete Christmas gift guide 60

Idle Home
Georgina Williams salutes mosiacist Carrie Reichardt's suburban subversion 66

The Good Stuff
Victoria Hull discovers an idle tipple, elegant tableware, the greatest gloves, funky coffee grinders and tequila made by bees 72

Slow Tech
David Bailey loved his Olympus Trip 35. Lee Osborne knows why 78

ARTS & BOOKS

Art Flâneur
Tim Richardson on the secrets of the Isokon, north London's modernist house of spies 82

Books: Lead Review
Clare Pollard is delighted by an illuminating map of the minds of poets 92

Books: Style & Design
Snoop around some enchanting country piles 96

Bibliotherapy
Make room for the mushrooms, says Ella Berthold 98

Music
Stewart Lee chases ghosts of post-punk dreamers and lonesome cowboys 101

Classical Music
Georgia Mann takes you on a musical sleigh-ride 108

IDLE PURSUITS

Pilgrimage
On the mystic peaks of the Black Mountains with Guy Hayward 112

Gardening
Build your own micro-arboretum with Graham Burnett 116

Beekeeping
It's bonfire night for bees, says Bill Anderson 119

Sheds
How to light up your inner sanctum with Alex Johnson 121

Travel
Kate Morris spends a week without WiFi in deepest Devon 124

Recipe
Cranberries are not just for Christmas, says Lindsey Bareham 128

MERRIMENT

Eating Out
Victoria Hull enjoys a trattoria treat in Florence 130

Beer
A tour of the hop spots of Windsor with Oli Meade 133

Ukulele
Remembering tons of fun with Tessie O'Shea by Cameron Murray 136

Spirits
Christmas gifts to raise the spirits with Joseph Piercy 138

SELF

Being Well
Your New Year's diet for better mental health by Rachel Kelly 142

Fun and Frugality
Why credit cards are a con, by the Money-Saving Amateurs 145

Easy Money
Make Christmas a more charitable occasion with Michael Gilmore 146

Problems
With Virginia Ironside 149

Readers' Letters 152

Puzzle
A portmanteau of possibilities from Alex Bellos 156

Idle Pets 160

Puzzle Answers 160

READER OFFERS ...

Page 31 Order your copy of XXX: *Thirty Years of the Idler*
Page 111 Get your Idler T-shirts
Page 157 Join the Idler Academy

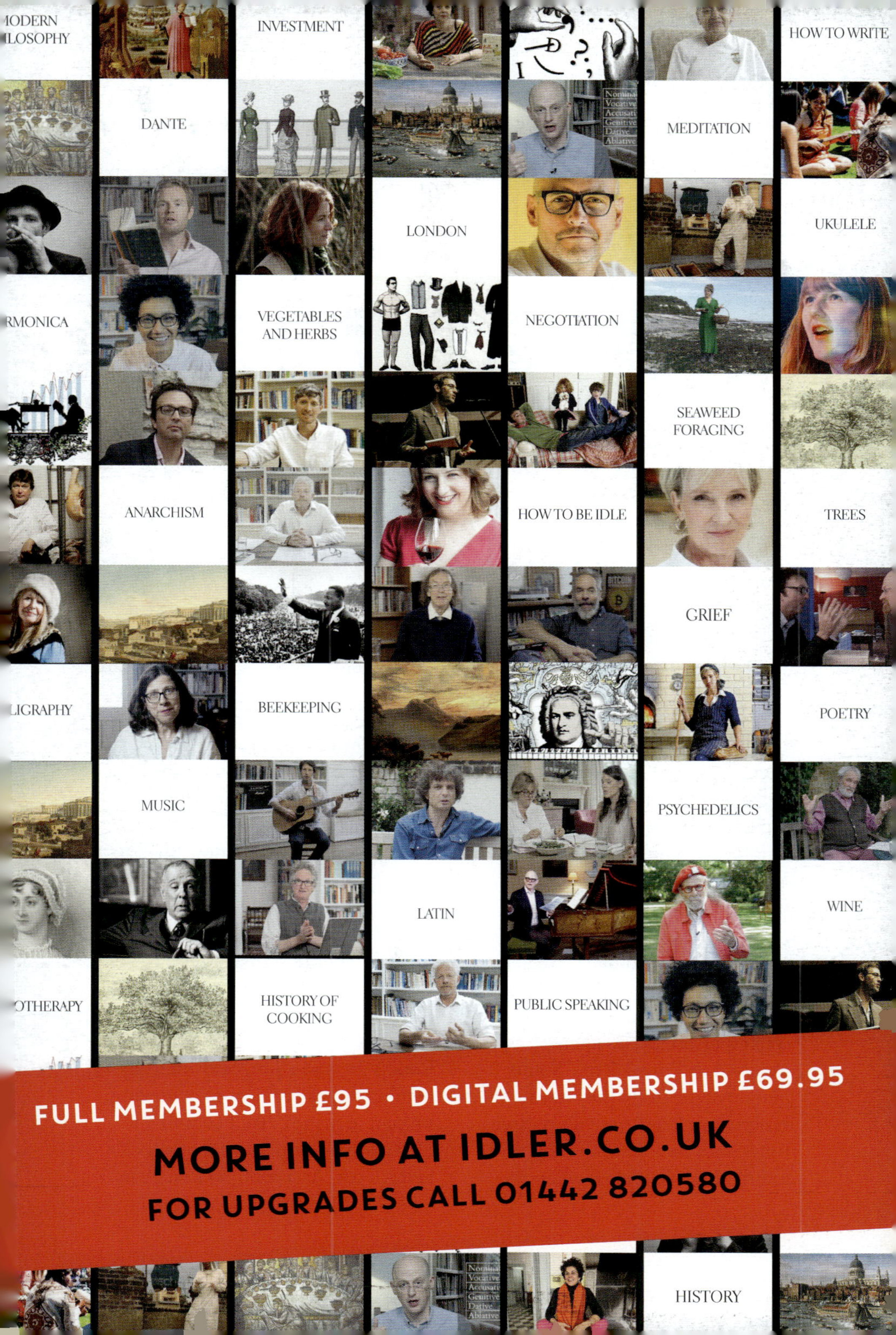
IODERN
ILOSOPHY
RMONICA
LIGRAPHY
OTHERAPY
DANTE
ANARCHISM
MUSIC
INVESTMENT
VEGETABLES AND HERBS
BEEKEEPING
HISTORY OF COOKING
LONDON
LATIN
Nominative
Vocative
Accusative
Genitive
Dative
Ablative
NEGOTIATION
HOW TO BE IDLE
PUBLIC SPEAKING
MEDITATION
SEAWEED FORAGING
GRIEF
PSYCHEDELICS
HISTORY
HOW TO WRITE
UKULELE
TREES
POETRY
WINE
FULL MEMBERSHIP £95 • DIGITAL MEMBERSHIP £69.95
MORE INFO AT IDLER.CO.UK
FOR UPGRADES CALL 01442 820580

NOTES FROM THE COUCH

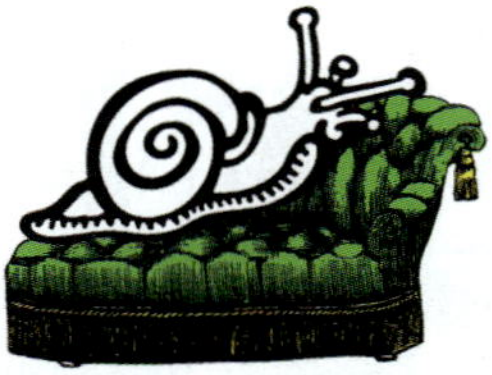

Idler's Diary

A roundup of the news in idling from across the world. Send your stories to us at mail@idler.co.uk

Hit It and Quit It

A new agency has opened in Japan dedicated to helping people quit their job – not always made easy by employers. The company, called Momuri – Japanese for "I can't take it any more" – charges clients 22,000 Yen (£120) to help them escape the nine-to-five. "We get calls from people crying, asking if they can quit their job," said a spokesperson for the agency, reported in *Private Eye*. "Some people come to us after having their resignation letter ripped up three times, and their employers not letting them quit even when they kneel down to the ground to bow." One client, Yuki Watanabe, said: "I used to spend 12 hours every day toiling in the office. I developed health problems, and knew I had to quit, but my supervisor ignored me and wouldn't let me resign. So I turned to Momuri for help." Maybe the *Idler* should start a similar service?

I, Robot

Robots are still a long way off from coming anywhere near to achieving human activities, like becoming a care assistant or playing football or being a car. According to René van de Molengraft, Professor of Robotics at Eindhoven University of Technology, that's because they work too hard. "Normal robots, such as self-driving cars, consider all of the information around them to be equally important. It doesn't work that way with humans," he says. "Humans are perfectly capable of ignoring, for instance, visual information that is not important to a task. Imagine yourself on a bicycle. You perceive all of the information that you do not require for safe participation in traffic, but you don't store that information. That person walking out of the supermarket you're cycling past: unimportant! A self-driving car cannot do that yet. It has 20 cameras running simultaneously, viewing and analysing each image. Everything is equally important, which takes a lot of computing power and a lot of energy. That needs to be improved." To that end, Van de Molengraft is carving out a new field of study: lazy robotics.

Classified Information

Ever wonder what happened to classified ads at the back of magazines? These ads used to supply a handy source of revenue to local papers and to mags like *Private Eye* and *The Lady*, and their equivalents all over the world. Then came Facebook and stole the lot. But now the plucky EU is cracking down, according to the *FT*: "Meta faces a hefty EU fine over its alleged efforts to dominate the

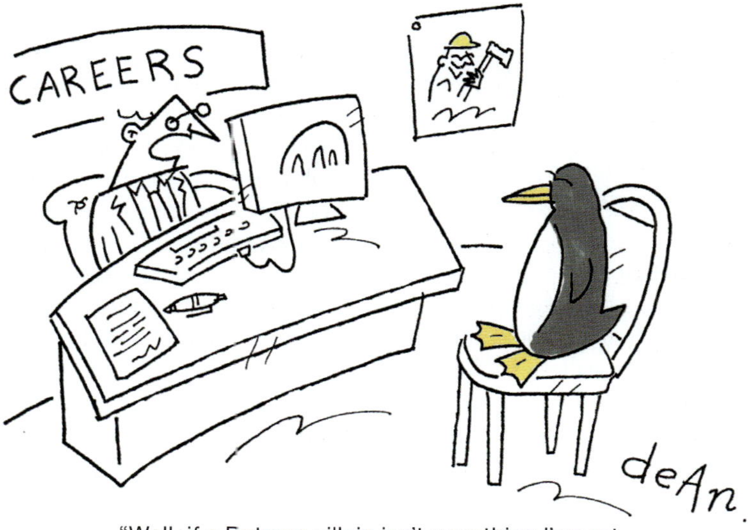

"Well, if a Batman villain isn't your thing I've got an opening at a chocolate biscuit factory?"

classified advertising market, as Brussels pushes to crack down on anti-competitive practices among the world's biggest technology companies. EU regulators will claim Facebook's parent company links its free Marketplace services with the social network in an effort to undermine its rivals, said people familiar with the matter." Last year Meta sold $145 billion worth of digital ads. Profit was in the $40–50 billion range.

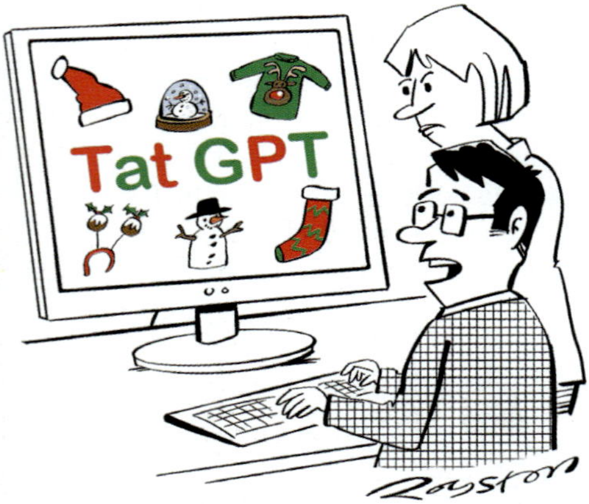

"It uses artificial intelligence to make Christmas present suggestions."

The Marshall Plan

Rich people hoping to launder their reputation and look cultured used to start art galleries. The Tate Gallery, founded by the eponymous sugar merchant, is a prime example. The Sackler family is another. Now rich people are buying old magazines and newspapers. In September, hedge fund manager and GB News backer Paul Marshall bought the *Spectator* magazine for £100 million. This crazy price tag looks to signal a return to vanity publishing for the 200 year old title. Under the stewardship of Fraser Nelson and Andrew Neil, the *Spectator* had transformed from a smallish, right wing cult into a very successful magazine with a circulation of 100,000 and around £5 million profit each year. Now it's a rich man's bauble again and has no need to make a profit, because the owner makes so much money elsewhere. For example, the London Economic website reported in July 2023 that one of Marshall's funds "netted paper gains of around £5 million on Wednesday after NatWest's share price slumped more than 3.7 per cent after the departure of its chief executive Dame Alison, which wiped more than £850 million off the value of the lender". That followed the Nigel Farage row. If you can make £5 million shorting stocks in a single day, then why struggle and suffer to make £5 million a year from a magazine? Another young loss-making but well-funded media company, Tortoise, is trying to buy another very old title, *The Observer.* Hum. Like both the *Spectator* and the *Observer*, the *Idler* claims kinship with 18th century periodicals. Maybe someone would like to buy us for £100 million?

Growing Pains

Striver of the Month award goes to Robin Sharma, hyperactive founder of the Five Am Club. He tells people to get up early for worldly success. If you sign up to his newsletter, you will get this sort of drivel on a daily basis: "You're smart so you know that the smartest investment you'll ever make is investing in your wisdom, courage, skills and mastery. The more you grow, the more you can create, achieve and lead." You can guess what this is leading up to. "If you'd like full access to my premium new online system carefully designed to help you live your richest life please keep reading.... for many, many weeks readers of my #1 global bestseller *The Wealth Money Can't Buy* have been deluging my team with requests for me to create an online course based on the book that is transforming so many human lives across the planet. And so I have." Ah, thanks Robin! So nice of you. "*The Wealth Money Can't Buy Method* is an extremely powerful and special online program that will help you live your richest life." For a mere $199!

The Prisoners
Australian mining firm boss Chris Ellison of Mineral Resources told investors that he wants to prevent staff from leaving the office. "We have a lot of different benefits that we have brought on," said Mr Ellison. They include a restaurant, *nine* staff psychologists and a gym. "Why have I done that?" he enquires. Could it be out of sheer altruism? Of course not! "Because when I get them first thing in the morning, I want to hold them captive all day long. I don't want them leaving the building. I don't want them walking down the road for a cup of coffee."

My Generation
Gen X complain about Gen Z's work habits. We never had "wellbeing" days, they whinge. But now the *FT* reckons that Z may have a point. In an age of smartphones, says columnist Pilita Clark, working hours should be reduced. "The health benefits are obvious. Working at least 55 hours a week led to 745,000 deaths from stroke and coronary heart disease in 2016, a 29 per cent rise since 2000, UN data shows. And long hours are not necessarily good for business either. Gallup research in June showed just six per cent of employees feel engaged at work in Japan, which has an entire word for death by overwork (karoshi)."

Correction Corner
Eagle-eyed readers will have spotted the glaring error in the last issue of this esteemed magazine: page 12, last line, should have read "bumbled" *not* "mubled".

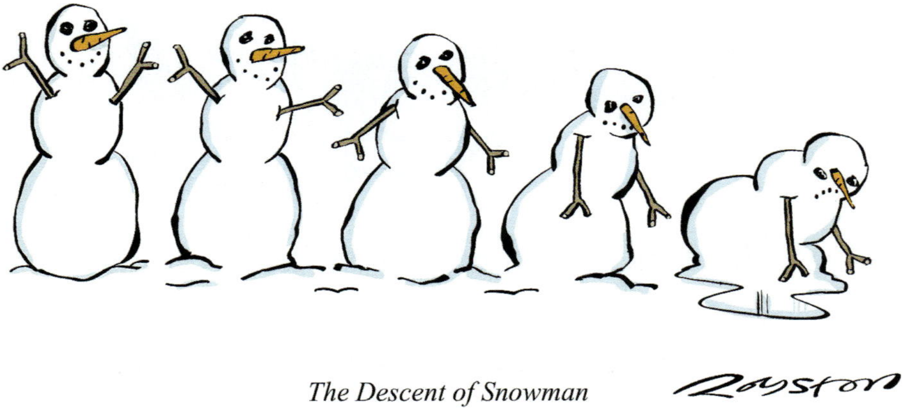

The Descent of Snowman

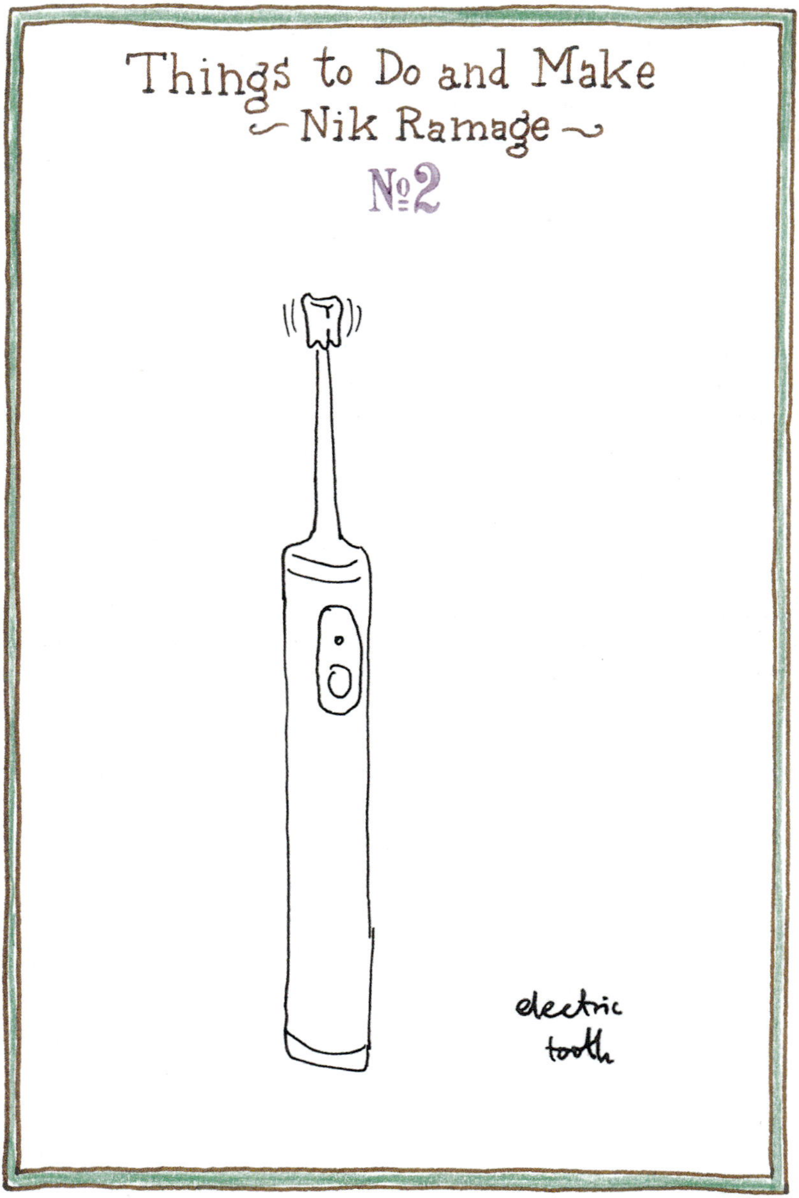

nikramage.com

Arthur Smith

Living with Dennis

You know the type – high-maintenance, always needing attention, impossible to get rid of. Still, even an annoying companion can have their upsides, says **Arthur Smith**

TWENTY-TWO YEARS ago I was becoming concerned about my health. Why were my eyes growing so hazy that the world was beginning to resemble an impressionist painting? Why was I guzzling two pints of apple juice every day? Why was I feeling so constantly – *yawn, think I'll have another lie down, darling* – tired? And the most worrying thing – why was I losing weight?

The year before, I'd ended up in the ICU at St George's hospital Tooting with acute necrotising pancreatitis caused by too much alcohol consumption. But now I'd given up the booze and become a more sensible person – so what was this? Back at St George's I heard the words: "You have diabetes and will have to inject yourself with insulin every day for the rest of your life." I spent another five days in hospital before passing once again through the unfortunately named Patients Discharge Lounge.

I think of diabetes as a friend called Dennis. Dennis needs to be considered at all times and prefers that I eat a balanced diet – he doesn't really like it if I have too much sweet stuff. Dennis used to require that I prick a finger three or four times a day just to check on how he's doing. These days he has a little round friend attached to my arm. It has a relationship with my mobile phone and likes to squeak if Dennis needs attention – which is quite often.

Even when I'm enjoying a deep sleep and having a lovely dream about being on holiday in Cannes with Emma Thompson and Miriam Margoles, Dennis might wake me up and insist I have some fruit juice to stop myself going into too deep a sleep. It's nice to have such a devoted friend but in truth I think I preferred it before I met him.

People don't realise that diabetes is not just a physical condition – it can affect your wellbeing too and make you miserable. If you're lucky, like me, you have a Beth. Beth is my long-suffering wife who, having lived with me for 24 years, knows more about diabetes, I suspect, than most doctors. She's often better at knowing how I'm feeling than I am myself and always ensures that, when we go away, I've packed all the right medications, and she reminds me to inject at the best time before I eat. She is alert to my mood, and her wit, beauty and tenderness keep me on an even keel. More than once she has raced to some comedy gig I'm at to bring me the insulin I'd forgotten. If we have a row and I'm dispatched to the doghouse, I am at least pleasingly distracted from worrying about the effects my diabetes is having on my kidneys, eyesight, circulation etc.

There are some positive aspects of having Dennis as a friend. For example, when you're in a restaurant you can pretend to be some wild man sixties rock star by saying, "I'm just going to the toilet to inject myself." Also, since most people who don't have the condition understand it so little, but know it can cause sudden problems, it provides the perfect excuse for getting out of any ghastly situation – "I'm sorry I can't stay for the last five hours of this opera because I think my blood sugar is a bit high and I need to go home and inject." Plus, when your blood sugars are very low, anything you eat tastes delicious. I've often thought you could open a restaurant where you injected non-diabetics with some insulin and then just give them some toast and marmalade and charge them 50 quid – the only downside to this is that you'd be arrested and thrown in prison.

Of all the popular, chronic, life-threatening syndromes, diabetes ranks among the least nasty since, if you can get your blood-sugar levels close to normal, it's more sinister complications can be avoided, or at least delayed. So Dennis is a lifelong friend who will only die when I do. Diabetes Type 1 has been recognised as a disease since Roman times but it only stopped being a death sentence in the 1920s when Sir Frederick Banting, aided by his student Charles Best, isolated insulin. So let me end this article by saying thanks to Fred and Charlie. If I had a cap I would doff it to you. And well done Fred on winning the Nobel Prize.

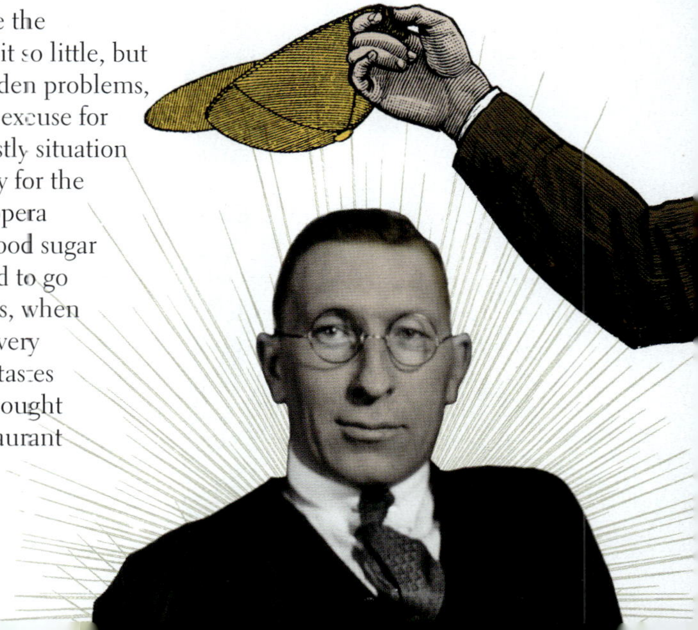

How I Live

Jon Glover, Actor, Voiceover, Writer

From trading cheeky one-liners with Leslie Phillips to playing Mr Cholmondley-Warner and Martyn Gibson in The Archers, **Jon Glover** *has lived many lives in the past half-century – here are just two of them*

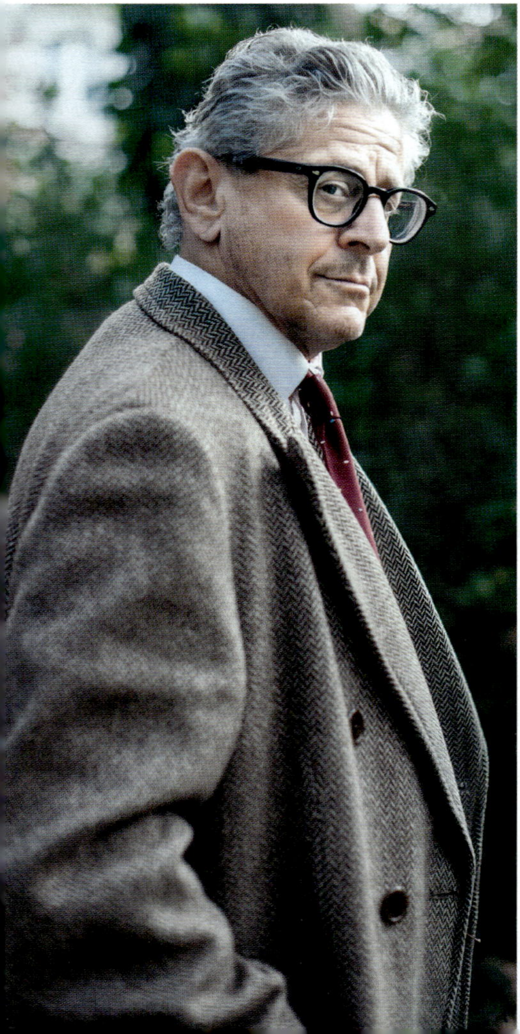

Portrait of Jon Glover by Etienne Gilfillan

MOST ACTORS live with idleness – or "resting" as it's known. Resting from what? Working? That's the easy bit. The hard part is getting the work, while not taking umbrage at those cheery *Downton* addicts. "Can't you get into that, Jon?" Yeah right, I'll just give Julian Fellowes a bell and tell him I'm free on Tuesday. Argh!

So why keep hoping? Well, nothing gives me so much pleasure as acting. I'm addicted to performing and, like any addiction, the non-supply of the drug leads to withdrawal symptoms – anger, self-pity, depression. Then the dealer calls. After submitting endless "self tapes" – one rarely actually meets anyone these days – I might land a part. An early start, but still – I get driven to the location, popped into a trailer and given a full English. After that, I put on a costume, go to make-up, try to remember a few lines, have a three-course lunch, a nap, afternoon tea… Finally, at 6pm, I deliver my lines and get taken home. The only stress is that, as I'm usually only employed for a day or two, I have to be spot-on.

How did I get into the *other* "oldest profession"? Well, being a show-off from an early age, I always knew I would. I wasn't academic and, as such, a disappointment to my father. Children in our family went into the professions – even though our immigrant grandfathers lived on their wits. I wasn't thick, but wasted time tinkering with cars, listening to radio comedies and playing in school productions – which turned out to be more useful than passing exams.

One of my Polish grandmothers told my parents not to worry – I could always run a garage. I compromised and did a teaching course at the Central School of Speech and Drama – or "Screech and Trauma" as we called it. But the idea of following a timetable was anathema.

After 50 years in the business, when strangers approach and tell me their daughter is just as good as that Julie [sic] Dench, I duly arrange a meet with the budding Dame. My first question is: "If you couldn't act, what would you do?" If they mention *any* other occupation – which is 99.9% of the time – I politely offer the advice: "Do that then." The 0.1% who say: "I can't do anything else", I help.

Show business is *the* most brutal industry. You need the hide of a rhinoceros and unshakeable belief in your talent. Not that talent is a requisite – the most gifted often never make it. But you need persistence. An actor is a travelling salesman – your product being YOU. Above all, you need luck.

I live in two parallel universes. A normal day starts around 7am, woken by one's wife Caroline – herself having been roused by our Burmese cats, who crave attention. Our oldest is Theo, an old chap who retired with a port and the *Times* about two years ago, having trained young buck Athos to do all his running about. Bella is Caroline's favourite. She has ataxia, which means her hind legs don't follow messages from her brain.

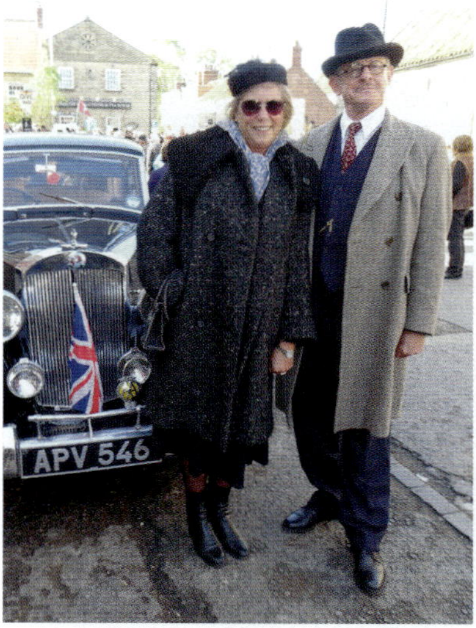

Jon and Caroline at the Pickering War Weekend

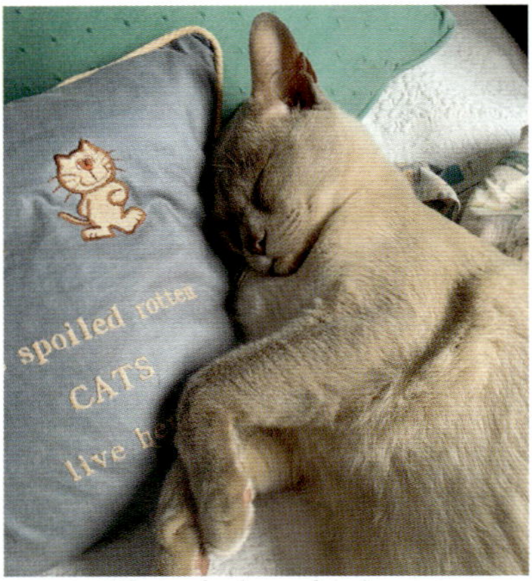

Athos, who loves sleeping…

Gracie is Athos's sister – a right little madam.

Breakfast is with the *Daily Mail* – horoscope first, followed by news of the Arsenal. Then it's off to my desk to see who I can bother for work – usually getting distracted by classic-car websites. This prompts me to give my 1968 MGC GT

…and fast cars

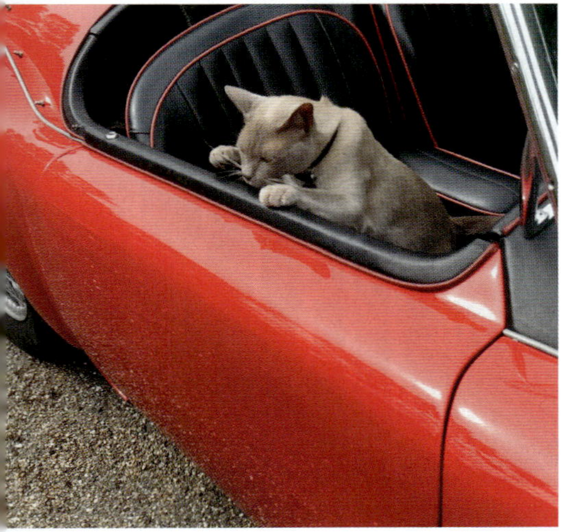

another polish. Then it's time for gardening. We've just moved to a village in Surrey and I spent last winter reviving a grass-covered 1950s vegetable plot and creating a rose garden. I even own my first greenhouse.

Lunch is taken shouting at *Loose Women*, then it's *Dickinson's Real Deal*. Before I know it, it's three o'clock. I check the phone in case any agents have emailed – which they inevitably haven't – and so at 6pm I switch it off. Caro goes to bed around nine. I read until midnight – the war, classic cars, Sarah Raven. I don't have to be up early the next day.

Or sometimes I do – if I have work. On those days, I get up at 6.30am, much to the cats' bemusement. I take a train to Birmingham and spend the day recording my character Martyn Gibson for *The Archers* ("Rumptee Tum" as it's known to the cast). Sometimes I have scenes with my old mate Simon Williams. Much has changed in Brum since I used to go there as a *Playschool* presenter (at Pebble Mill), and later when I was a voice on *Spitting Image* for producer John Lloyd (at Central Television). Central had no facilities for recording the voices of the "dollies", as the floor manager called them, so we would have to record the skits on a boom microphone in the *Crossroads* set (where you could see the cast's lines had been penned in the motel register as prompts).

For the second series, we were joined by Harry Enfield. We bonded at once through our love of forties and fifties British films. Our attempts at replicating them transmogrified into "Cholmondley-Warner and Grayson" on Harry's TV series. That *was* lucky. I still get asked to do "Chumley" as people usually call him.

BBC Radio is my first love. My father was a GP who started practising on the first day of the NHS in 1948. He felt television was harmful and rationed it to Sundays, but radio was unlimited. When I found I could replicate episodes of *Hancock's Half Hour* and *The Goons*, I sent off a tape to Edward Taylor, a producer whose name I found in *Radio Times*. He gave me some lines in live shows, with legends like Leslie Phillips and Jimmy Edwards. Good old Auntie Beeb!

After visiting their agents in the West End, actors used to meet in the Salisbury pub off St Martin's Lane.

"Anything doing, old love?"

"No, not a dickie. But they feel something big is just around the corner."

It's the hope that kills – just like the Arsenal.

Back to the greenhouse.

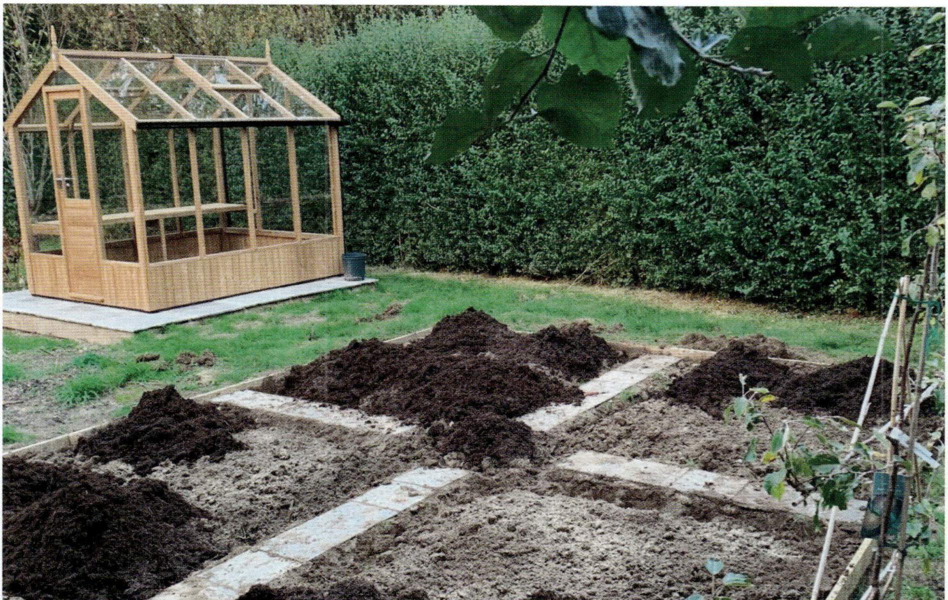

Digging for victory: work in progress in Jon's back garden

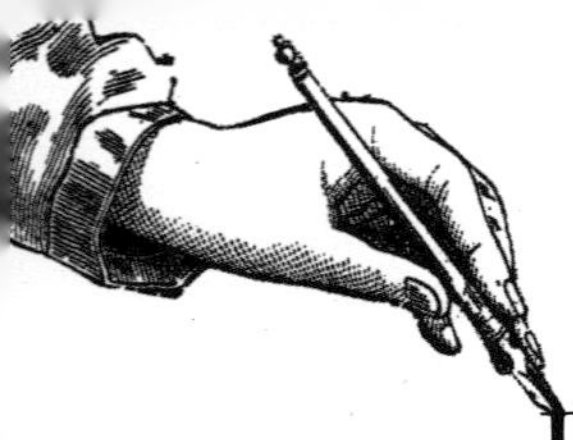

Rhyme and Reason

Poetry is history encoded in language, says **Mark Vernon** *– and those who practise it are the wizards of words*

HOW DOES POETRY WORK? What does poetry do to us? My favourite theory comes from Owen Barfield, the great friend of CS Lewis and JRR Tolkien. He has a proposal about the remarkable way that poetry functions, and it has to do with words.

The dynamic he describes so impressed Tolkien that the writer on wizards and hobbits underwent the great labours of creating an entire language and literature for the elvish people of his imagination. Only then did he feel he could convincingly enter the world of Middle-earth. So, what was Barfield's big idea?

At heart, Barfield insisted that words have soul; the sounds we breathe on the air carry a vitality and convey a living meaning. Words are not just physical vibrations shaped by our mouths and tongues, nor are they mere signs for the things around us: "tree", "rock", "cup". They bring experiences, echo histories, focus desires, release relationships. The poet works with this energy by positioning words in creative ways, so that the inner stories held by language can be re-released afresh. The reader of poems loves that sense of revelation and to read a poem is to travel inwardly, reach horizons, and peer into other worlds.

Take two words to gain a sense of this magic, as Barfield suggested: "old" and "prophets". First, consider the phrase, "old prophets" and ask what connotations come to your mind? For me, I think of bearded men and grizzled crones, times past and antiquated wisdom. Make a mental note. And now, second, read a different phrase: "prophets old". What associations emerge with that? The changed inflection, the poetic air conjured by the inversion of the words, prompts a different imagining. With "prophets old" my mind is now ready for timeless wisdom and forgotten insights. I think of figures I would like to hear; of guides whom I would repeatedly read.

Poets arrange words in unexpected, non-prosaic ways to express otherwise hidden

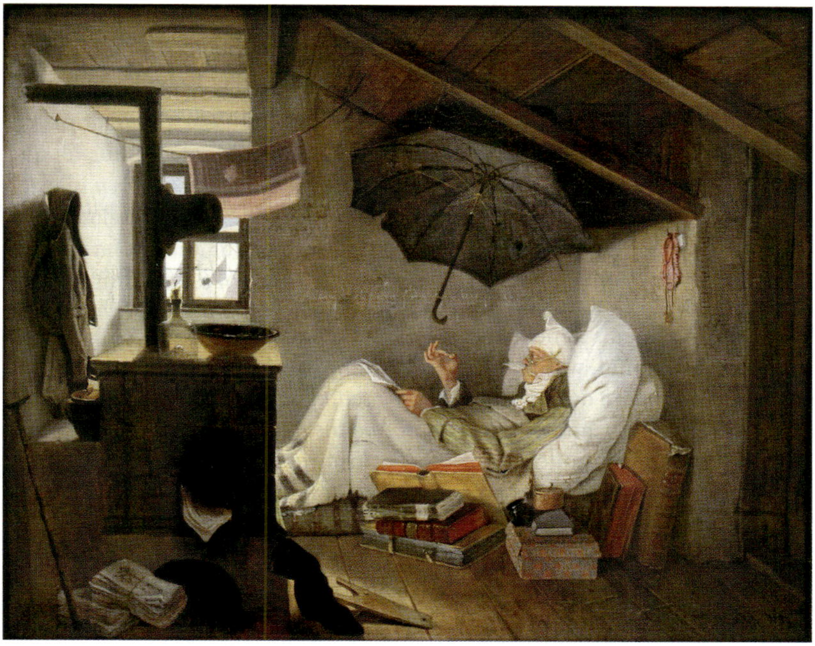

Carl Spitzweg *Der arme Poet* (Neue Pinakothek)

resonances, thereby unleashing spirits that can revive us. Barfield argued that when reading a poem, the important aspect to keep in mind is the energy of the lines, and only secondarily to be concerned with their meaning. To ask too soon: "What is this about?", is to break the spell. Instead, stay in the zone of not fully knowing, and you will receive unsought feelings, unexpected insights.

The genius of a great poem is not therefore, fundamentally, about novel aesthetics or clever linguistics; a great poem might quite literally save lives.

Take the case of the philosopher John Stuart Mill. A child prodigy, he was the subject of educational experiments at the hands of his fanatical father, who was a disciple of the utilitarian innovator Jeremy Bentham. The upshot was that Mill was reading Greek and Latin before most kids can tie a shoelace, and became dangerously depressed in his late teens. As he writes in his *Autobiography*, he faced a calamitous mental crisis because, with reaching that age "the whole foundation on which my life was constructed fell down". His learning had left him akin to an automaton; his advanced intellect had run way ahead of his emotional capacities,

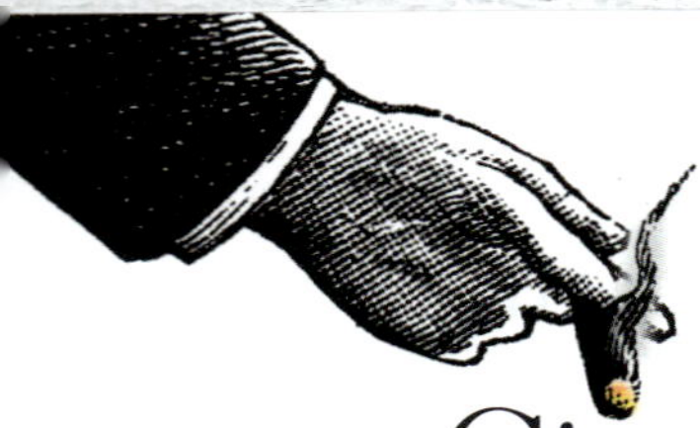

Idler Hero

Cigarettes and Alcohol

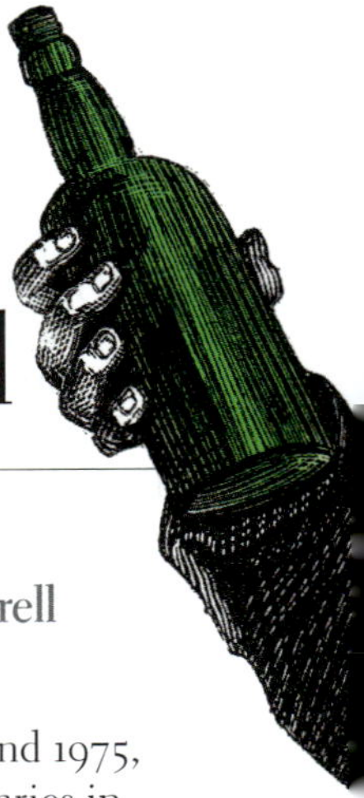

This slacker supreme was the inspiration for Withnail.
Alex Johnson *raises a glass of lighter fluid to* **Vivian MacKerrell**

ALTHOUGH THERE'S a lot going on in Bruce Robinson's 1987 film *Withnail and I* – an exploration of friendship, a dissection of despair, an examination of the terrifying responsibility of moving from twentysomethinghood to thirtysomethinghood – there is also a lot *not* going on. The two (anti) heroes muck about in their flat, then muck about in a rural cottage, then come back home. Which of the pair is the finer idler is open to debate, but there is certainly some impressive slacking on show.

However, it's neither of the fictional lead characters that concern us here, but the real chap who inspired Richard E Grant's hard-drinking thespian, Vivian MacKerrell. In the seventies, MacKerrell (1944–1995) shared a house on Albert Street, Camden Town with Robinson and songwriter Lord David Dundas (who would go on to have a No3 hit with "Jeans On" in 1976, and later co-write the score for *Withnail*). Here they lived in bohemian squalor not dissimilar to that depicted in the film. At the same time, between 1974 and 1975, MacKerrell kept various diaries in which he mentions that Robinson was beginning the new writing project that became *Withnail and I*. Unseen by the public, MacKerrell's diaries were due come up at auction at Sotheby's in July 2024 but were withdrawn before they went under the hammer. (The lot – which also featured photos of MacKerrell from his personal archive, including unseen negatives from a *Vogue* photoshoot – had an estimate of £12,000–£18,000).

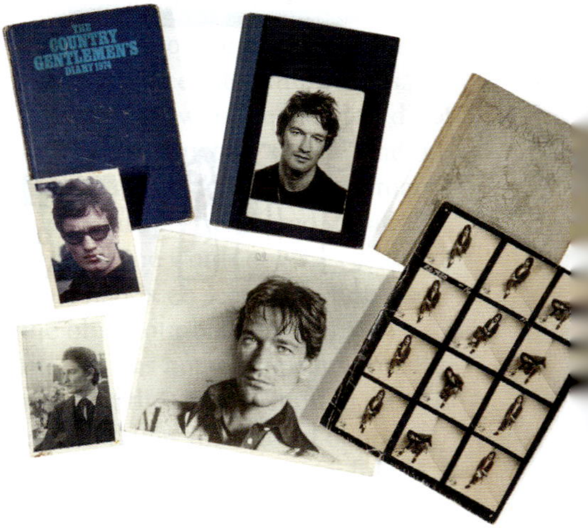

[Images courtesy of Sotheby's]

As Gwendolyn brags to Cecily in *The Importance of Being Earnest*, "I never travel without my diary. One should always have something sensational to read in the train." And these diaries certainly live up to expectations. Here is a typical example:

16 March 1975: "I had intended to kip on the couch and nearly away – when I felt this scratching and pattering on my head – a mouse – on the couch I told it to fuck off and it disappeared thank god. The buggers are spreading and no poison can deal with them"

Devotees of *Withnail* will immediately link this with the mouse-ridden flat in the film. Other entries will also ring bells, such as the ones about imbibing lighter fluid, and visiting the wolves in Regent's Park – as well as bittersweet notes about watching friends moving on with their lives.

In Robinson's introduction to *Withnail and I: the Original Screenplay* he wrote: "There isn't a line of Viv's in *Withnail and I*, but his horrible wine-stained tongue may well have spoken every word. Without Viv, this story could never have been written."

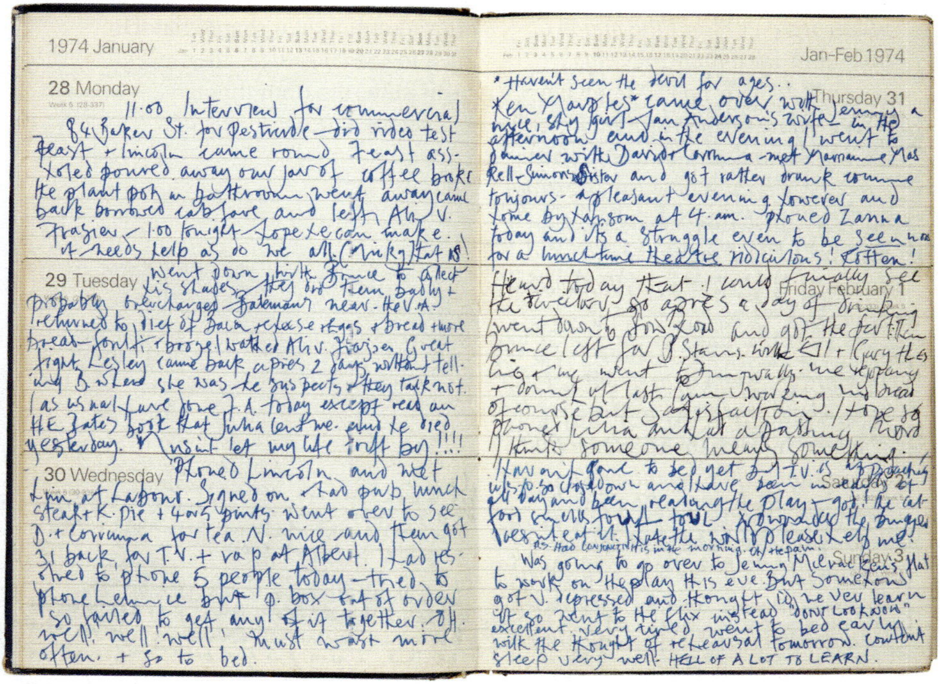

Idle riches: the auction lot had an estimate of £12–18K

The film ends when the "I" character (whose name is actually Marwood) moves out, but the diaries continue after Robinson left and show that MacKerrell continued living the same kind of rackety lifestyle. To give you a flavour, here are some more excerpts:

26 January 1974: "I drank some lighter fuel – got frantic & burst into tears – walk in the park & bed at 5am"

21 August 1974: "we had some wine and then went over to see the wolves"

2 May 1975: "O Lord the march of time in its inexorable grey cloak – we're into May now! No job, no chick and no bread – still nil Carborundum. And what is worse – as I peered into the dusty intestinal hall no Bunce [unemployment benefit] *I had a fag and coffee and hastened out to a blustery but hazily sunny day"*

27 March 1974: "Up at about 9.30 to go down to sign on with B[ruce]. *The labour* [exchange] *seemed fuller than usual – they've cutdown on staff – the buggers. After a pint … I read and corrected more of 'Withnail and I', his book and when he came back we opened the bottle of Pouilly-Fuissé that L had put out in the windowbox to chill"*

29 March 1974: "Up bedtime and over to Spread Eagle for wine then another. Then changed into suits + B + I went for a large Pernod as a double bunce arrived for him … down to the Little Theatre to see Chick she said if B + I were to do the play she'd be worried about us being stoned – Christ I said – How dare you – and persuaded her that we had discipline at our fingertips … Back home by tube and so to kip with copy of men only. God what a fate. Must work work work."

MacKerrell's acting career never flourished, but he did continue drinking unwisely after Robinson moved out of their shared flat. He died in 1995, aged 50, after several years suffering from throat cancer.

[image courtesy of Sotheby's]

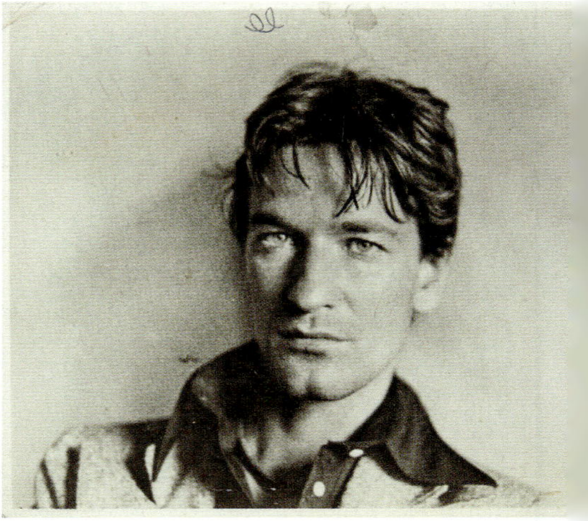

Vivian MacKerrell

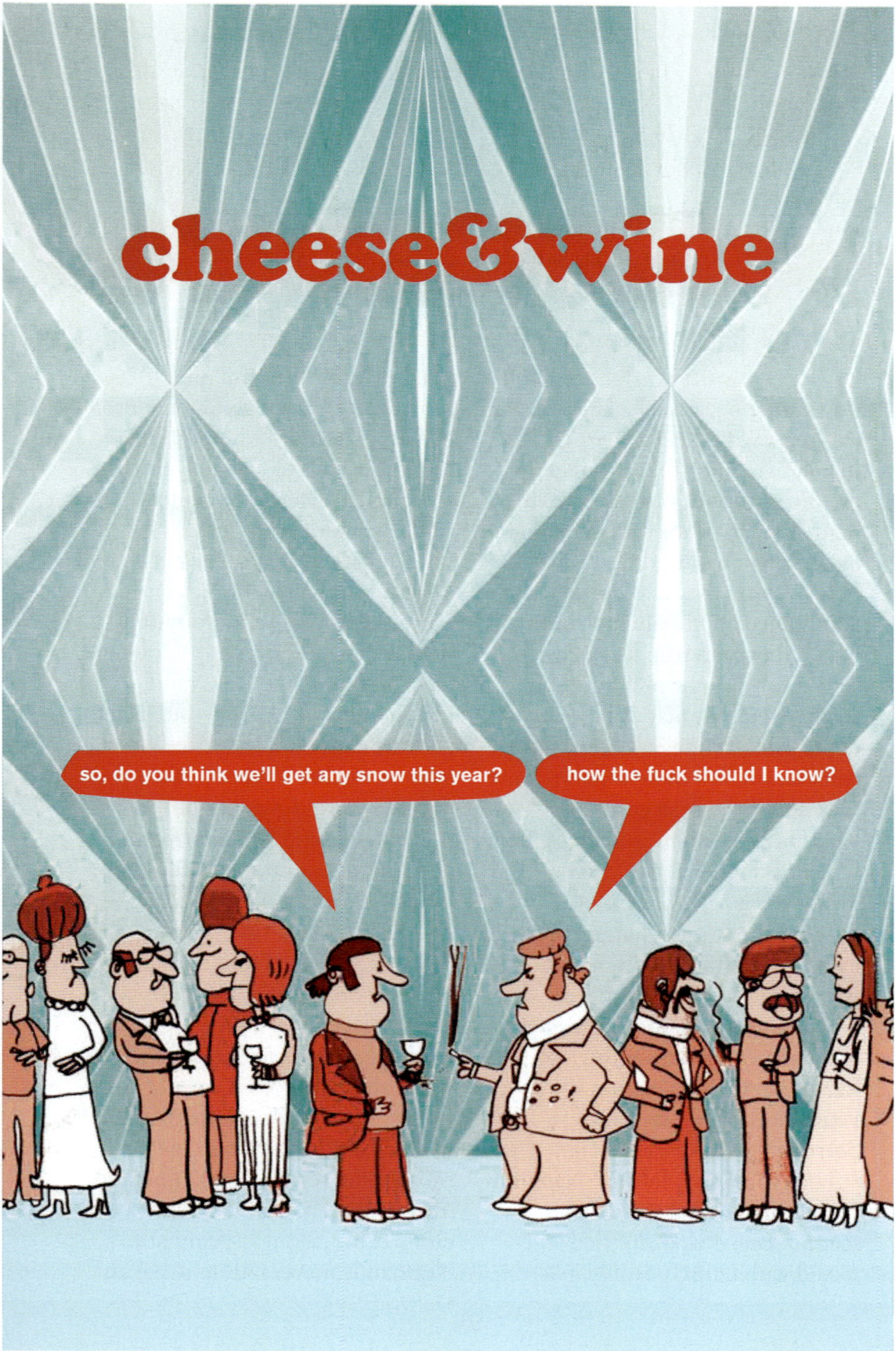
cheese&wine
so, do you think we'll get any snow this year?
how the fuck should I know?

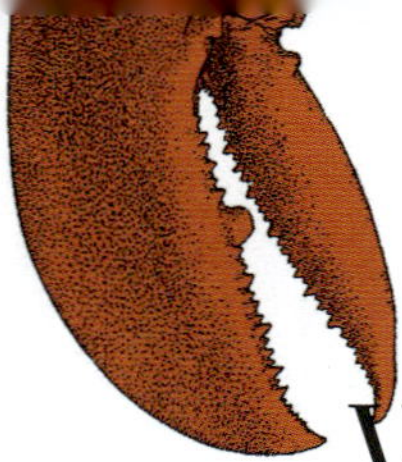

Why I Hate Lobster

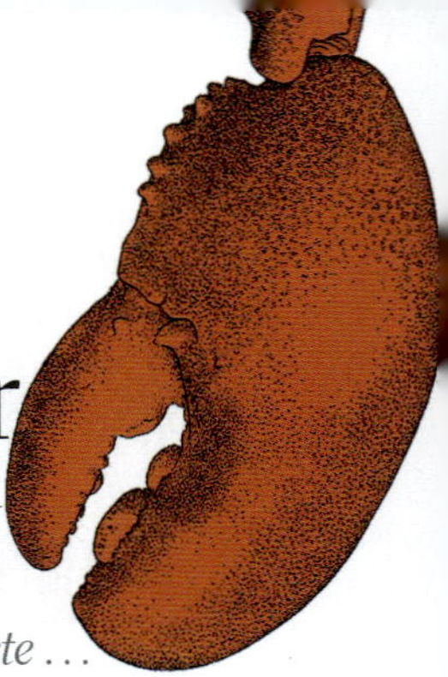

It's not the flavour of this deluxe crustacean that **Stephen Bayley** *objects to – it's more a question of taste . . .*

THE TALMUD says lobsters aren't kosher because, lacking fins and scales which aid manoeuvrability, they dwell at the bottom of the sea where filth settles. Same goes for oysters. It's said that oysters are an aphrodisiac, but that's only because they're often eaten in conditions of intimate sociability which may lead who knows where. And surely the slurping sound is suggestive of lubricious pleasures to come. Meanwhile, a lobster, if you can crack it, is a more reliable route to venery as its flesh contains Vitamin B12, which stimulates the sex hormones.

And the lobster has history. Apicius, the Roman Jamie Oliver, calls it "locusta", a word which settled into modern European languages as *aragosta*, *langusta* and, of course, *langoustine*. You also find lobsters in the feast scenes of Petronius's gloriously bawdy *Satyricon*.

The Norwegian lobster (*Nephrops norvegicus*) is what we know as scampi. Breaded, deep-fried and served with chips, possibly in a "basket" at a Berni Inn on a provincial bypass a generation or two ago, scampi – with portion-control sachets of fake mayonnaise – became a gateway to genteel sophistication.

And that's why I hate lobster.

Alexandre *Three Musketeers* Dumas *père* (not to be confused with his *fils*, the author of *La Dame aux Camélias*) wrote a *Grand Dictionnaire de Cuisine* (published posthumously in 1873, three years after he died in Dieppe). It's 600,000 words long, has only two illustrations, and is "an engaging and impressive jumble" according to Alan Davidson, author of the standard work on fish, *North Atlantic Seafood*. Dumas, in his 600,000 words, finds things to say about lobster. His recipe for *Homard à la broche* (lobster on a spit) calls for a stout skewer, a hot fire, a sprinkle of Champagne and melted butter. You char the exoskeleton, extract and chop the meat and then dribble it down your chin. "This ragout . . . peculiar to Normandy, never fails to make an impression."

Lobsters are all about impressions. Enthusiasts revel in the difficulty of prepping this multi-legged invertebrate. Dumas says of *Homard à l'américaine*: "We beseech our readers, and above all the ladies, to pay great attention, as the dish is very complicated … One must be a real cook … in order to attack it." There was evidently no *MoiAussi* Compliance Officer in 19th-century Normandy.

Madame Prunier's Fish Cookery Book of 1938, written by Ambrose Heath, has 36 lobster recipes, surely a record. It was sponsored by Lady Melchett and a prominent member of the late Queen Mother's family, giving a clear idea of its whereabouts, socially speaking. Madame Prunier opened her St James's restaurant in 1934. Regulars – perhaps anticipating the 36 variations of lobster – included the Prince of Wales and Wallis Simpson, on lunchtime strolls from their nearby palace.

Thus lobster encourages both vulgar social-climbing in the serving, and meretricious elaboration in the preparation. While once served as prison food in the United States, lobster acquired its social status because it goes off quickly: an implied indulgence and demonstration of showy urgency.

Lobster Thermidor is the ultimate. This is a recipe calling for eggs and brandy and requiring the dish to be finished with an oven-browned cheese crust. Thermidor was the 11th month in the French Revolutionary calendar and the title of a popular *fin-de-siècle* play. A dish to celebrate the theatricals was prepared at the Café de Paris by an apprentice of the great chef Escoffier. Absurdly, Escoffier had made his reputation with the insistence that cooks should "Faites simple!" The exclusive, laborious rarity of the dish, its demented indulgence, gave rise to the old joke, "What are the two things you never get at home? Lobster Thermidor and a blow-job." Although perhaps Escoffier had both.

Something about lobster encourages smut. Peter Cook and Dudley Moore's sketch about "The Worst Job I Ever Had" described the task of extracting lobsters from Jayne Mansfield's bum. Thereby confirming the association of lobsters with bottom-dwelling.

Yet I enjoy clever recipes and crazy menus. On the Greek island where we have use of a house and, therefore, visit often, an ambitious taverna advertises its edgy cosmopolitanism with garbled names. "Chicken in pain" is a favourite of mine. *Pain* meaning bread in French. You get a piece of fried chook in a baguette. I haven't seen a "Porn cocktail" advertised yet, but I'm sure they're working on it. And, for the gullible and spendthrift, they offer "Spaghet with lobster". By the standards of the Western Aegean, this approaches (at least in concept) the gastronomic ultimate. People off yachts order it.

My hatred is based on cultural taste, not the gustatory sort. But I'm not an inverse snob about expensive foods. I adore foie gras and caviar. I'm sure I would enjoy ortolans too, but they're dreadfully difficult to come by, even in Clapham. I hate lobster because of its associations. It's a lazy gesture by a host or hostess and shameless evidence that money is being spent to impress you. I'd be much more impressed if someone baked a loaf of bread or foraged nettles for a gnocchi dressing. And had made the gnocchi themselves. (It takes just minutes.)

My moment of enlightenment in the matter of lobster hatred came some years ago when Sotheby's of Bond Street opened a café. I may not need to gloss on the type of customer it attracted: women who wear sunglasses indoors, men with no socks in winter. Both types sneering at the poor, not realising that fine-art sales is a conspiracy to make them look stupid.

Anyway, its signature offering was a "lobster roll", a staple of the Long Island Hamptons and the ugly rich people who live there when not lunching in auction houses. Still today, the insufferably smug cooking pages of the increasingly lunatic *New York Times* valorise the lobster roll as evidence of civilisation and status.

I think I may be diffident about fish in general, although I do enjoy a paper cone of *crevettes grises* or an honest-to-God fish finger. But let's face it, in a blind tasting, how many people can distinguish one fish from another? Sure we could all tell an anchovy from salmon. But, turbot apart, isn't all white fish much the same? And only interesting when turned into a challengingly foetid concoction like bouillabaisse?

The poet wrote, "Oh sea, the only love to whom I have been faithful". I never much loved the sea, nor fetishised its contents. Even if I do enjoy looking at it. But I concede that lobster has inspired lyrical poetry, making the snippy crustacean comparable in its way to Keats and his nightingale. The fast-evolving genre of rap has made the equation, as Petronius did, between shellfish and lust. In a striking lyric, as sensitive as it is memorable, Beyoncé says: "When he fuck me good, I take his ass to Red Lobster". Red Lobster being a chain of US restaurants where he, and his ass, might enjoy a little surf 'n' turf – lobster and steak – after his rumpty-tumpty.

As I say, my hatred of lobster is a matter not of its taste, but its associations.

FEATURES

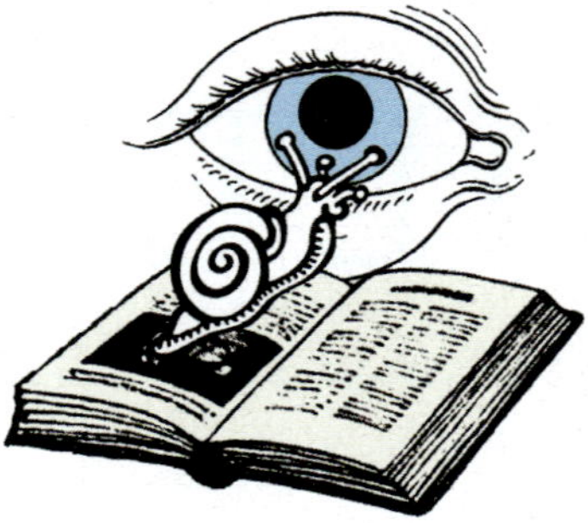

Interview: Dominic West

Of Kings and Killers

From Prince Charles to Fred West, **Dominic West** *has shapeshifted into the gods and monsters of our times.* **Tom Hodgkinson** *finds out how he does it. Photos by* **Chris Floyd**

SPRINGING TO FAME as McNulty in *The Wire*, Dominic West is one of our finest actors. He can play American, French or English Royal. Remember his Valjean in Les Miserables, and his Prince Charles in The Crown? He can do evil. He's played Fred West and Vicomte de Valmont in Les Liaisons Dangereuses. He's funny too. And when he's not away for months or years filming legendary TV shows like *The Wire*, he likes nothing better than to tread the boards with a troupe of travelling players in Blighty. But, he says, he's done with evil characters. I chatted to the charming troubadour at the 2024 Idler Festival, when he was halfway through a run of Arthur Miller's A *View from the Bridge* in the West End.

TOM HODGKINSON An actor was telling me the other day that you can get Americans like no one else.

DOMINIC WEST Well, I hope so. I was in *The Wire* for five years, and then *The Affair* for another five years, and people still go, "Oh, it's amazing. I didn't realise you're English." And I think, well, if you had realised I was English,

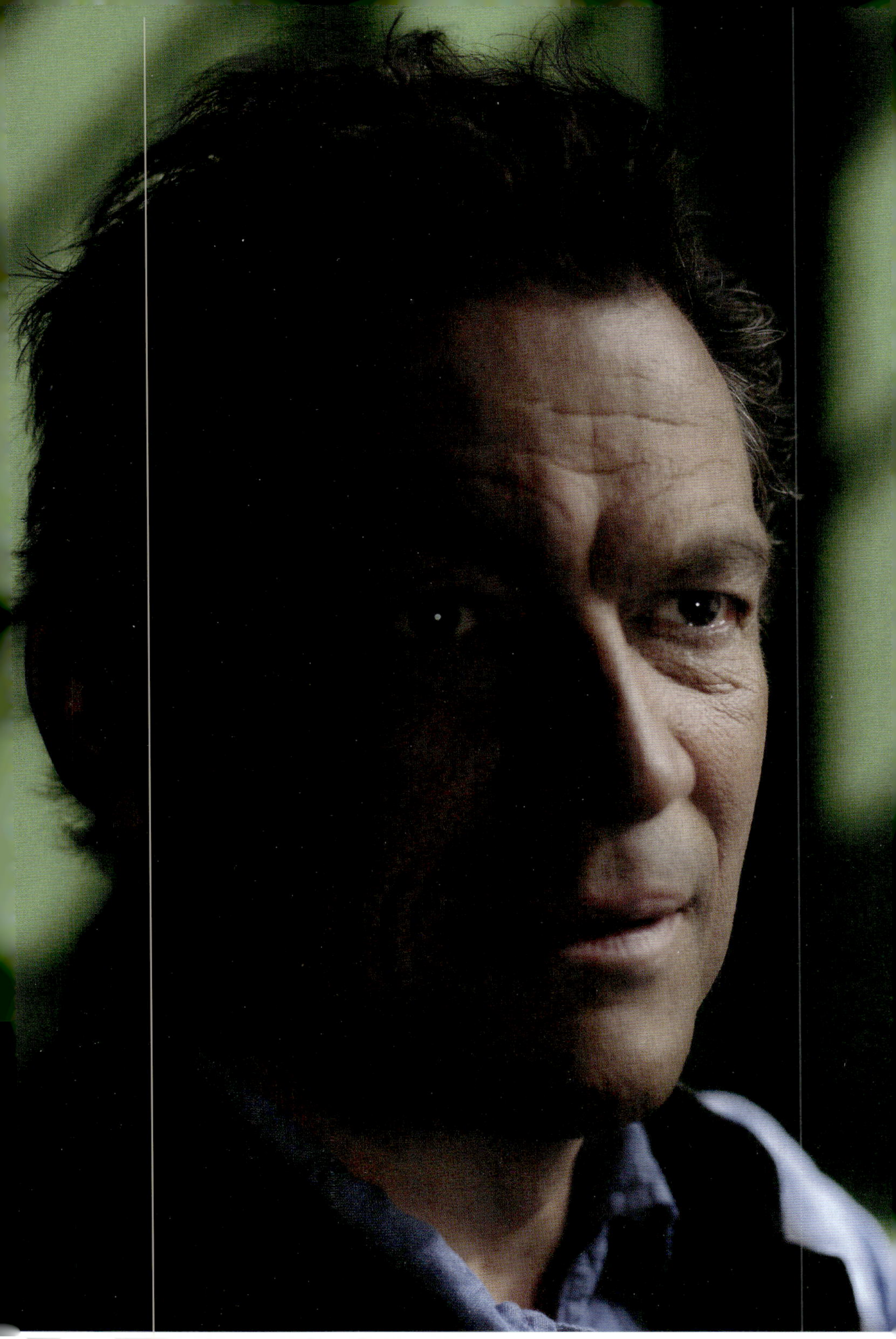

TH Well thank you Dominic for coming along today, and more generally for supporting the *Idler*.

DW I adore idleness. A lot of actors worry about where the next job comes from, but you need a lot of downtime, and to do other things, otherwise you become burnt out. I've just done a chainsaw course. And I'm desperately trying to learn about gardening so that I can talk to my wife [garden designer Catherine FitzGerald] about it. Every time I attempt to and I say, "That's a lovely petunia!" she goes, "Oh, don't even try." I keep pigs, and we've got lots of lovely kids too. So plenty to do.

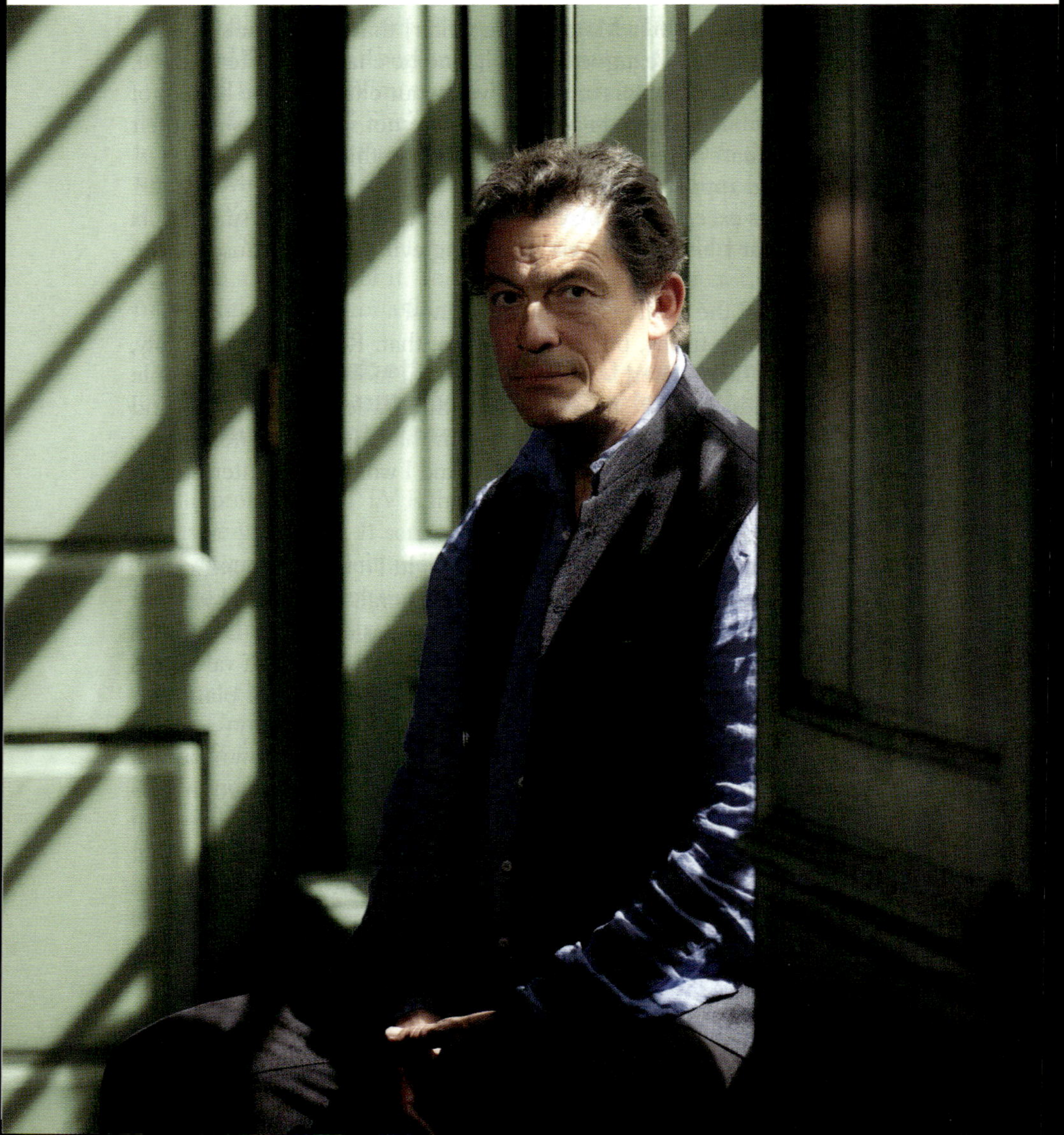

Essay

Pillars of the Community

Our Great British post boxes aren't just convenient public utilities, they're historic pieces of the landscape that deserve to be celebrated, writes **James Thellusson**

In all created nature there is not ... anything so completely ugly as a pillar-box ... [yet] there it stands ... disguising one of the most beautiful ideas under one of the most preposterous of forms.
GK Chesterton

A PROLIFIC LETTER WRITER, GK Chesterton may have hated the aesthetics of post boxes, but he loved the exchange of ideas, affections, and opinions they facilitated. Architecture critic and author of *Pillar Boxes* Jonathan Glancey says they're a "glorious piece of public design". But they can also be politically significant. The IRA have used them to plant bombs in. And when the Royal Mail placed the first post box bearing the Royal cipher of the newly crowned Elizabeth II (EIIR) in Edinburgh, nationalists challenged its legitimacy on the grounds that the Queen was Scotland's *first* monarch named Elizabeth, not its second. Protest anthems were sung and the box was blown up. Since then, Scottish post boxes don't carry regnal letters and use the Scottish crown instead of the English one.

Post boxes are more than a utility. They have symbolic value and can arouse violent passions. In this age of click-and-collect however, we never give them a second thought. Or a second glance. But we should pay more attention. There are around 115,000 working post boxes in the UK, with about 800 variations in shape, colour, material, and history. That's more varieties than species of British birds. By statute there should be a working post box within half a mile of 98% of us. That means there's one within a fitness-building 1,000 steps from your front door. Flâneurs should add post boxes to their promenades. With so many interesting ones nearby, why drive to a National Trust site for your dose of heritage?

Ironically, post boxes were designed to stop people having to walk. Before they

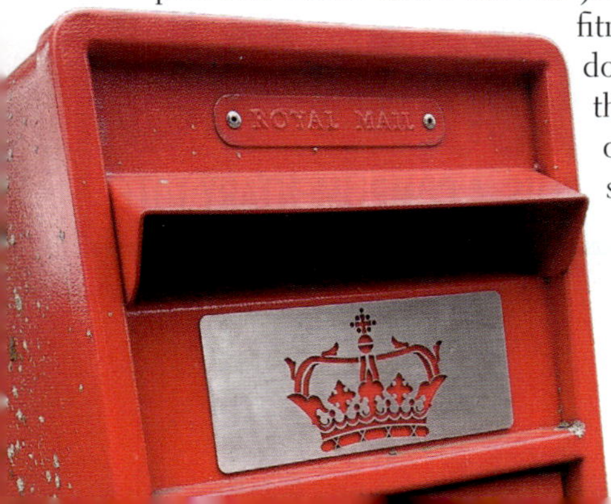

Scottish Crown lamp

were introduced in 1853, you had to deposit your letter at a Receiving Office (which, if you were lucky, might have been your local pub) or wait for a Bellman – a fellow in a uniform who rang a bell to attract attention and collected letters from the public. But by the mid 19th century this system was creaking. Bellmen weren't always honest and the boom in personal and business correspondence forced the General Post Office to rethink how to meet demand.

They sent Anthony Trollope, then a GPO employee, on a tour of the Continent to see how things might be done better – France had introduced post boxes as far back as 1829. When Trollope returned he recommended they be introduced here, and the first British post boxes were trialled in Jersey in November 1852. This was followed by a roll-out nationwide in 1853, with Carlisle getting the first post box on the mainland. The next 50 years saw a boom in the installation of post boxes driven by urbanisation, increasing literacy and the desire to communicate over long distances. Self-adhesive stamps and the Penny Black helped Britain move from a "pay to receive" to a "pay to post" system.

George Vermillion

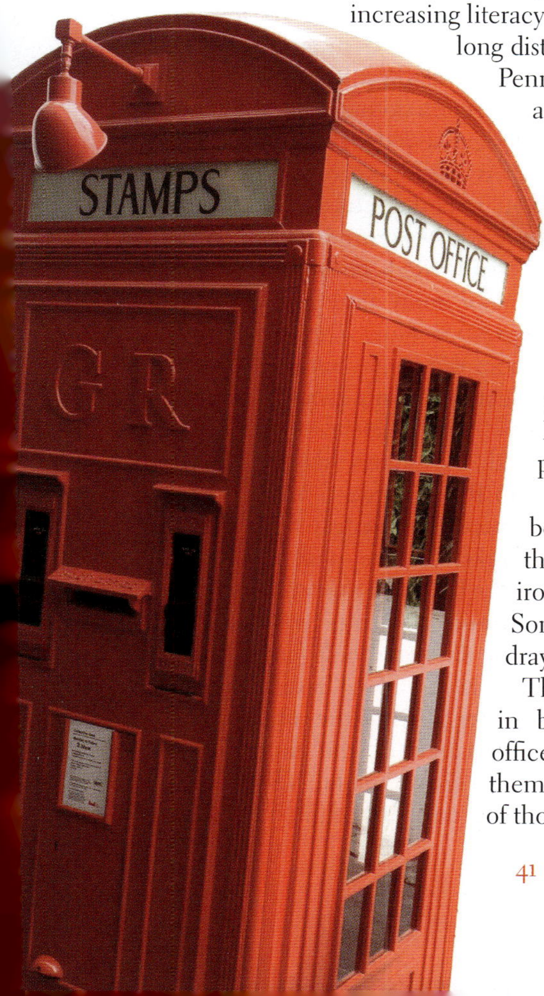

Each post box can tell you something about its history – you just need to know what to look for. Luckily, the Letter Box Study Group, which maintains the only comprehensive database of post boxes in the UK, has recently produced a Beginners' Guide to Letter Boxes. The *Idler* was given a preview. Take note …

There are three main types of post box. Pillar boxes, as Chesterton called them, are those red chunks of cast iron you'll find on most streets. Sometimes double fronted, they're the dray horses of the British postal system.

The second – wall boxes – are found in building walls, often outside post offices. A few are painted black, making them rare as a hawfinch. If you find one of those it's a red-letter day.

The third variant is the lamp or pedestal box. This is mounted on a lamp post or telegraph pole and is the smallest type of post box. It's now the most common and has four designs. My favourite is the Hovis, which has a rounded top like a loaf of bread.

Shape-wise, pillar boxes are often cylindrical – although rectangular, oval, or even hexagonal variants exist. Most are cast iron because this material has proved the most durable. But sheet steel (preferred for new boxes), wood and plastic boxes also exist. The delightful and rare Ludlow, however, has an enamel fascia.

You should never look a gift horse in the mouth, but a letter-box expert will always inspect its aperture. A sizable mouth indicates a newer box because mouths have got bigger to cope with larger packages. If the mouth is vertical, the box is probably a rare pre-1880 edition, after which vertical mouths were discontinued because they let in more rain than horizontal ones. Verticals can still be admired in Warwick, Banbury, and Eton.

Another clue to your post box's pedigree is the black stripe around its base. Here you'll find the name of the firm that made it or the architect who designed it. The roof of the post box is also worth noting. The rare hexagonal Penfold design has a delightful bud on top.

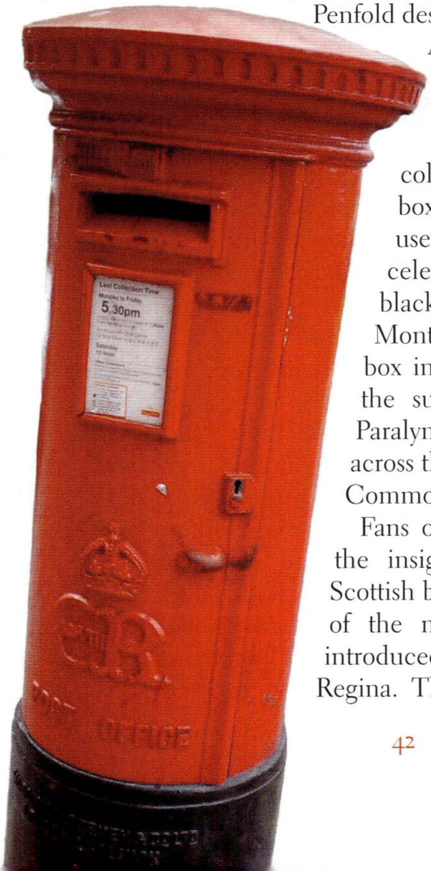

Edward pillar

As with bird watching, colour is important. In 1853, all boxes were painted green (in Ireland they still are). Red became the standard colour from 1874 but in Guernsey boxes are blue. The Royal Mail also uses different coloured boxes to celebrate various events. For example, black boxes celebrate Black History Month. Gold ones, like the Ben Ainslie box in Restronguet, Cornwall, celebrate the success of British Olympians and Paralympians. Five pink ones in cities across the UK mark the launch of the 2022 Commonwealth Games in Birmingham.

Fans of Royalty should pay attention to the insignia on post boxes. Apart from Scottish boxes, each carries the Royal cipher of the monarch at the time they were introduced. For example, VR for Victoria Regina. The rarest Royal cipher is Edward

VIII's. Only 150 post boxes bear the abdicator's mark because his reign was so short. Cockfosters, Coulsdon and Catford are all good places to find them. King Charles has no post boxes yet because the Royal Mail is still thriftily working through the stock left over from his mother's reign. Nevertheless, one can imagine the excitement when the location for Charles's first box is announced.

Post boxes play an unacknowledged role in our culture. Think of the films *Looking for Eric*, about a postman from Manchester, or the recent *Wicked Little Letters*. Or Postman Pat. Elvis sang "Return to Sender" of course. And while they're seldom the focus of a play or novel, they often have important roles in them: whenever a letter is written, a post box is there, ready to do its duty to drive the plot forward. As the poet Aidan Andrew Dun says, post boxes are a "halfway house in the affairs of human beings".

Post box lovers know how to let their hair down, too – like the 80,000 members of the Post Box Toppers Facebook group. These funsters (also known as yarn bombers) knit or crochet bonnets, which they drape over their local boxes to celebrate something, for example NHS staff during lockdown.

Post boxes also feature on stamps, and people collect miniature versions of them. At Christmastime some boxes sing carols and deliver children's dearest wishes to Santa Claus at the world's most exclusive address – Santa's Grotto, Reindeerland, XM4 5HQ. What other public utility is so vital to such important a cultural myth?

Their importance also means there's a market for vintage letter boxes. A double-cast Elizabeth II box might be worth over £11,000. Sadly, this leads to thievery. "Older lamp boxes are prone to being stolen and wall boxes can be vulnerable too," says the Letter Box Study Group. "Please don't help thieves by posting a location or grid reference of an old lamp box on the web or social media," they add.

The red phone box has died off almost as quickly as the Dutch elm tree. The future of the post box is more secure. There are laws to keep them in place. But I can't help feeling their fate is dependent on us. It could be a case of "use them or lose them".

David Cameron once urged us to hug a hoodie. I think it's time to hug your post box. Pick up your pen and write. Join the Letter Box Study Group. If you don't help preserve these icons of the streetscape, how will your child's Christmas wish list ever get to Santa?

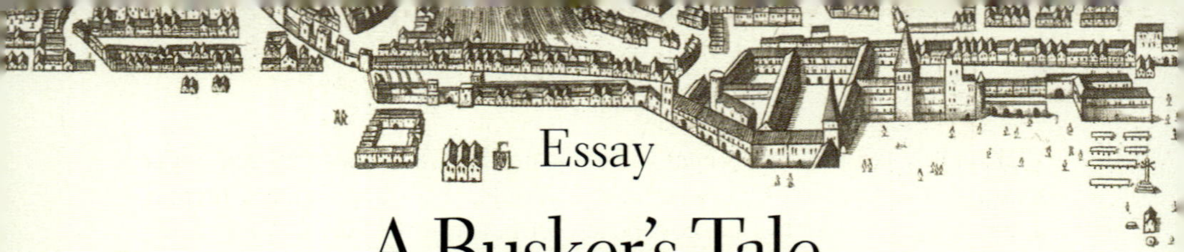

Essay

A Busker's Tale

Ever wondered what it's like to make a living from performing music whenever and wherever you like? Musician **Robin Timmis** *has spent the past few years living the life of a troubadour*

Ever since we've had streets, we've had street performers – musicians, jugglers, clowns, acrobats, magicians and other entertainers persuading passers-by to part with their cash in an activity we now call busking. The word "busk" derives from the Spanish *buscar* – to seek. Which, as a busker myself, begs the question: what is it that I'm seeking? Are my fellow buskers and I just idle chancers chasing a quick buck? Or are we seeking something deeper? Here are some thoughts based upon my own experiences and on conversations with other practitioners of the ancient art of busking…

My journey as a busker began when Covid restrictions led to me losing my face-to-face violin teaching and music performance work in the UK. I also became increasingly disillusioned with British politics, so I decided to escape yet another bleak winter in Leeds and left for Portugal in October 2020. Once there, I lived out of my car and began travelling around the country playing music on the street to make ends meet. Fast-forward three and a half years and busking is still a significant part of my income. It's also taken me far and wide. From Portugal to Bulgaria and back to Leeds, busking has allowed me to travel and live a life of freedom unparalleled to anything I've experienced before.

But a life of freedom isn't always straightforward. Often when we choose freedom we sacrifice stability. Full-time buskers are at the mercy of the elements, addicted to the weather forecast, chasing the elusive pocket of sunshine that allows us to take to our stage. Busking can be a life of highs and lows. One day you might feel rich in pocket and free in spirit; the next you might be penniless, washed-out in the rain and stranded in a place you don't know.

Josefa, a busker and DJ living in Lisbon, told me busking is "the hardest school there is, you have to be musically dead on, consistently for long periods, which requires a stamina and skill that's not the same as doing an hour's live show". Similarly Phoebe, from the busking and street theatre duo

Old Time Rags, also explained how the streets can be a hard stage to conquer. "You don't have a theatre and lights to hide behind. It's the most raw you can be as a performer."

But I think the rawness of the performance is also part of the appeal – both to the audience and the artist. The fact that there is nothing to hide behind means it becomes more interactive and alive than a show restricted to a conventional stage. For example, when I was on tour in Bulgaria recently, I ended up busking in a park with a Russian clarinet player, a Ukrainian keyboardist and a Polish guitarist. An international and spontaneous line-up. The clarinetist was a classical graduate from the St Petersburg Conservatoire who'd moved to Bulgaria to flee the Putin regime. The keyboard player was of gypsy descent and had been fighting in the war for Ukraine before leaving for Bulgaria. The guitar player got stuck in Sofia during Covid and never left. We played a mixture of *klezmer* and traditional Balkan music, improvising and harmonising with each other as we tried to feel out what shared repertoire we had.

The impromptu coming together of musicians from different backgrounds is something I seek from busking as much, if not more, than the money I receive. All of us were from completely different backgrounds and would have been unlikely to meet any other way. Yet we found an instant camaraderie through our love of music and performance, which we took to the most public and accessible of stages, the streets.

Robin with his klezmer band outside the Castelo São Jorge in Lisbon

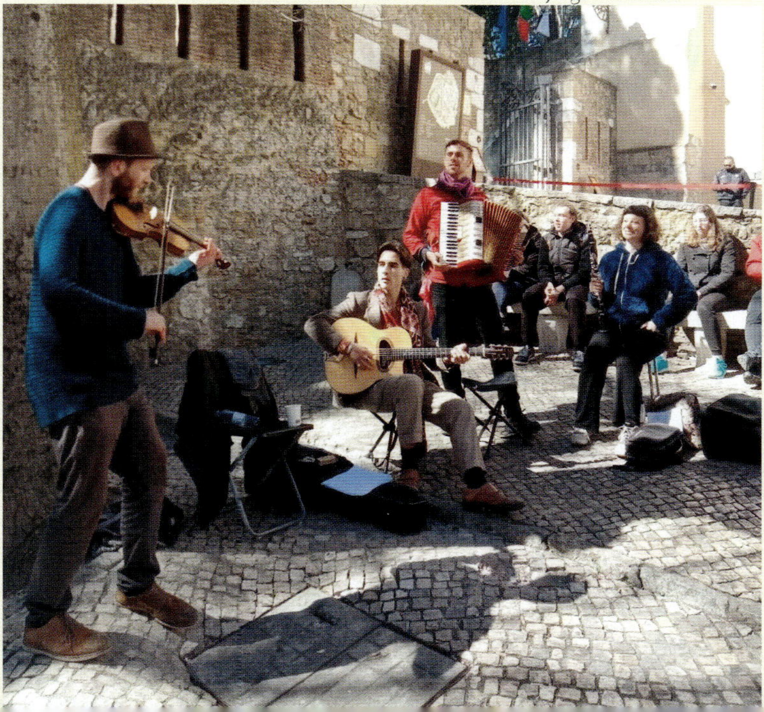

Although busking can be a freeing experience, you also have to operate within a chaotic labyrinth of unknowns – not just the weather but the background noise, street sellers and dwellers, the general public and the law. As a busker who often performs in countries where I don't speak the language that well, I often operate in a somewhat grey area legally speaking, never entirely sure of the busking etiquette, laws and restrictions. I find if I just start playing I normally figure them out quickly enough, one way or another. Personally, other than the odd occasion where a policeman or shopkeeper has asked me to move on, I've never had any serious problems. Not speaking the language can sometimes be a blessing in disguise, as the authorities don't want the hassle of trying to communicate with you. However, I have witnessed buskers having problems with the police. One time after I'd finished playing in Sofia, two gypsy musicians took over my pitch. I had a coffee and stayed to listen, but within ten minutes two police officers who'd walked straight past me earlier without batting an eyelid, came back and whisked them away in a police car. I can't help but think a certain amount of discrimination was at play.

Similarly, in Portugal I have had friends who've had their amps and instruments confiscated by the authorities, which they then have essentially to buy back through an expensive fine. In fact, in Lagos, on the south coast of Portugal, which used to be a haven for street performers, the council recently banned busking with amplification. One time, when some friends and I were busking acoustically there, we ran into a bit of trouble with one of the local policemen, who was un-affectionately known among the busking community as "brute pig", due to his large appearance and intolerance towards street entertainers. We tried to explain that we were playing acoustically so it wasn't breaking the rules, but he replied saying, "If you continue to play, I will start to play with my truncheon." We didn't fancy sticking around to test his cudgelling skills so gave up the game for the night.

Surprisingly, the UK has some of the laxest legislation concerning busking. Other than a few specific spots in London and the Underground, you're unlikely to have any issues with the law. According to Laurence, a busking buddy I know from Portugal and Leeds, "The 2012 Live Music Act in the House of Lords declared busking in the UK as an unregulated activity and that you can do it. It's freedom of speech and if you're not causing an actual disruption, then they [the authorities] should keep their nose out."

But even though legal battles are unlikely, there are still those frequent struggles with the cold and rain to contend with. Loopholes and sweet talk can often get you out of issues with the authorities, but the elements are not so forgiving.

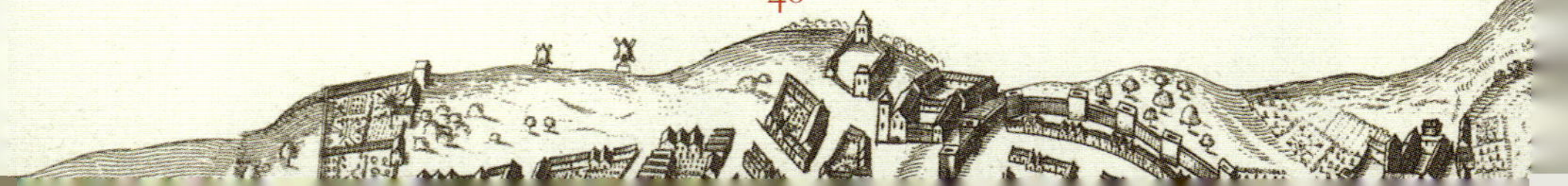

The unpredictability of busking due to the weather and being reliant upon the generosity of the public can make it hard to rely upon economically. However, it can also be lucrative. Some buskers are reluctant to give away any specifics on what they earn, but I'll let you in on the secret. When things are going well in Portugal or the UK, in a good spot with plenty of foot traffic (preferably tourists), I can average around a hundred pounds in three to four hours, normally split into two sessions. However, in Bulgaria I make much less, but also the cost of living is considerably cheaper, so in a way it balances out. As for the future of busking in an increasingly cashless society, we will have to wait and see. I've seen buskers with card machines but somehow for me this loses part of the magic. I prefer to busk at bustling market towns or tourist hotspots where the passersby are from an older generation who still tend to carry some coins in their pocket.

Over the course of my busking years I've met and performed with countless people from all walks of life. To name but a few: disgruntled doctors, drug addicts, lawyers, ex-convicts, and professional musicians displaced due to war. Although I think we've probably developed a bit of Pavlov's dog syndrome, receiving a dopamine hit from the clink of coins falling into a case (sometimes thrown off the scent by the jangle of a loose keyring in a pocket), I believe that what we're seeking is more than just a handful of change to see us on our way.

Most buskers I've met are optimists. We always round up when counting our earnings, we enthusiastically interact with the public and other performers, and we're forever searching for the perfect busking spot. Through busking we're seeking a sense of organic freedom and autonomy which is often hard to find in a bureaucratic and digitalised world. Kuba, a Polish busker in Bulgaria, told me that "the tempo and bureaucracy of the modern world makes it very hard for people to share any unplanned moments" but the beauty of busking is the ability "to bring people together for that moment". Whether this connection is a shy smile, a thunderous round of applause, or a child dancing, these small interactions are what makes busking an amazing heart-warming experience.

I can think of few other jobs where you get to thrive in a flow of meaningful interactions, while choosing your own hours, your own stage, your own or others' company – and you never have to send an email. You can work internationally or on your local high street, as little or as much as you like; captivate a crowd of hundreds with a slickly designed street show, or whistle an idle tune into the wind and watch the world go by. The beauty of busking is that you choose when and what you do and how you want to share it.

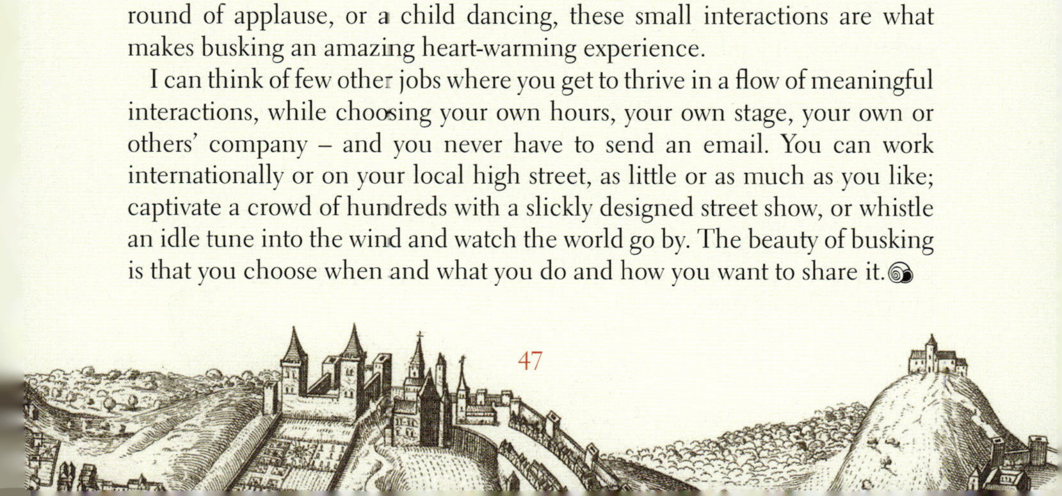

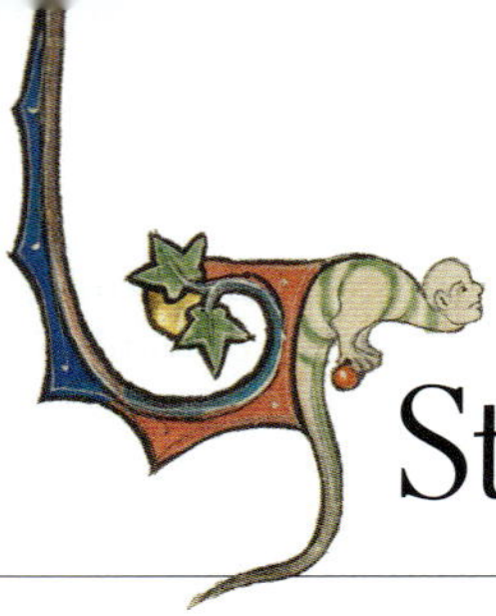

Essay

Strange Days

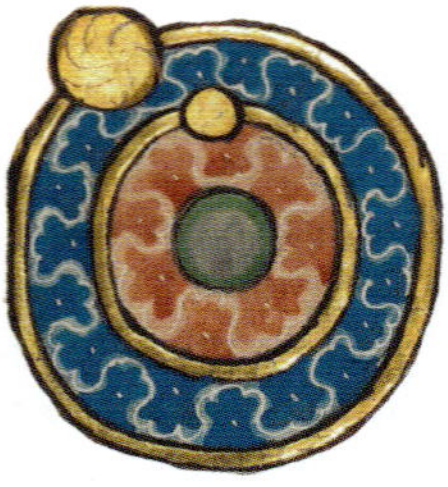

Not your typical Essex boy, 12th-century scholar Gervase of Tilbury travelled Europe writing a collection of weird and wondrous tales for the amusement of an Emperor. **Mary Ruskin** *salutes this medieval marvel*

TAKING THE TRAIN from London to Southend, on a rare-surviving branch line through the industrialised lower reaches of the Thames, it might be hard to believe that one is passing the birth place of one of the most interesting and well-travelled writers of the High Middle Ages (roughly AD 1000 to 1300). Present-day Tilbury is dominated by the Ford factory, the QE2 Bridge and, in the oddest of juxtapositions, a brand-new terminal for luxury liners.

It was in this most unlikely of places, on the marshy shores of the tidal Thames, some 25 miles from the City of London, that Gervase of Tilbury, diplomat, lawyer, historian and folklorist, was born in around 1150. His Essex-boy credentials were, however, slight: he seems to have spent very little time in his home-town and soon found his way to the court of Henry II. Later, he studied, and then taught, canon law at the University of Bologna. His biography is tantalisingly scant, but he crops up variously at Rheims, Arles (where he married and joined the upper echelons of Provençal society) and Sicily. It's possible he ended his days in Essex, in a *Premonstratensian* Monastery.

Around the year 1211, Gervase wrote the masterpiece that would ensure his fame throughout the Middle Ages and beyond, the wonderfully named *Otia Imperialia*, a three-book compendium of geography, history, Biblical studies and marvels, intended to while away the leisure hours of the Holy Roman Emperor Otto IV, who was then his employer. The title, which could be translated as *The Emperor's Spare Time* or *Imperial Idling*, paints an enticing picture of hours of story-telling and merriment at the Emperor's sumptuous travelling court. The *Otia Imperialia* can be compared with the arguably more famous *Courtiers' Trifles*, written for the diversion of Henry II and his court by a similarly prolific raconteur, Walter Map. Both Walter and Gervase illustrate the importance of storytelling as a pastime for the upper classes of the High Middle Ages.

All illustrations from Hugh of Fouilloy's De Avibus, circa 1280
Courtesy of J. Paul Getty Museum, Los Angeles

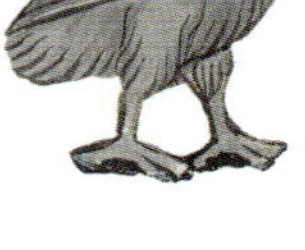

It might seem surprising that an Emperor who found time to go crusading with Richard Coeur-de-Lion, to be excommunicated by Pope Innocent III, to fight his way through Italy to Sicily and to be an ally of the ill-fated King John, would have had much leisure time, but was he perhaps a closet idler? It's our good fortune that he found such a splendid writer as Gervase of Tilbury to entertain him.

Book Three of the *Otia* is a collection of stories of *mirabilia* (wonders), of strange beings and strange things. Many are set in the British Isles, others are located in the Rhineland, Italy or France. The Middle Ages had inherited from antiquity a taste for such stories, but – for an orthodox Catholic such as Gervase – such wonders were strictly part of God's rational creation; it's only our ignorance that causes the wonder.

There are 130 stories in the standard edition of Book Three, ranging widely in subject. Some seem to take their cue from Isidore of Seville's encyclopaedic approach and describe such "marvels" of nature as magnets, balsam, vermillion and silk worms. Some are overtly Biblical, if somewhat Apocryphal: there are, for example, discussions of the Veronica (the veil said to bear the face of Jesus), the tomb of Moses and the cross of the Good Thief. Others seem akin to Herodotus's version of ethnography, as when Gervase tells us about men with no heads, women with the teeth of wild boars, and men with eight feet.

For me, however, the most interesting are the stories involving supernatural beings – pixies, fairies, lamias, mermaids and werewolves. Gervase is one of the most important sources for a little-known species of sprite called the Portuni. Old, wrinkled and tiny, the Portuni are fairy "home helps" who work all night in domestic drudgery for exhausted peasants. They're forbidden by nature from doing harm, but may – and do – cause mischief: one of their favourite nocturnal tricks is to lead horses into marshy ground and run off chuckling. They must surely be distant ancestors of Puck. Gervase also tells us about the Grant, a peculiarly English sprite, shaped like a colt, which

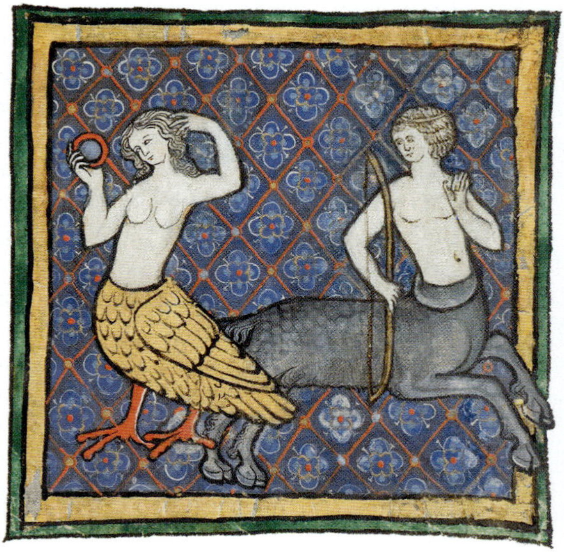

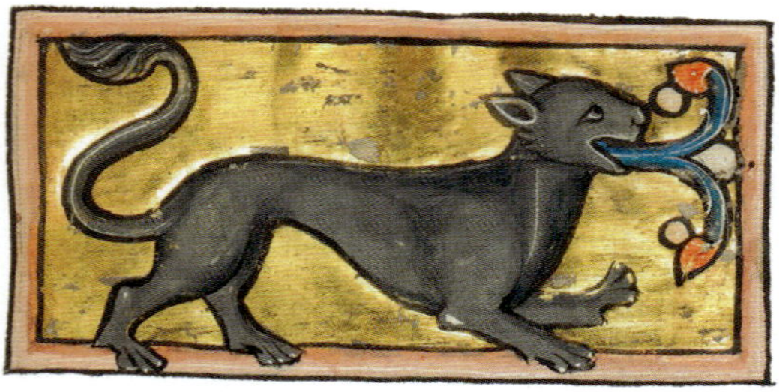

prances on its hind legs and has eyes that spark with fire. Despite its terrifying appearance, the Grant is considered an obliging spirit as it's a warning of a fire – its appearance allowing the townsfolk to take the necessary precautions.

The *Otia* also contains longer narratives for the edification and entertainment of Otto. One of my favourites is set in the Peak District, in a cave called the Devil's Arse. The cave was justly famous there for the blasts of wind it almost constantly emitted (presumably the Devil's farts). One winter's day an idle swineherd lost sight of a valuable pregnant sow. Having searched all over the peaks for her, he decided she must've wandered into the Devil's Arse. By chance, no wind was blowing from it so the swineherd entered the cavern without difficulty. Having crawled through the dark cave for some time, it suddenly became light and he found himself in a bright and sunny country at harvest time. He found the sow surrounded by a litter of healthy piglets, and somehow managed to transport all the animals back out to the Peaks, where it was, crucially, still winter. This is one of the more famous of the Medieval Antipodean stories – tales which speculate about the existence of a land on the other side of the world. Others from the period are more elaborate, such as the Green Children of Woolpit, in which a green-skinned boy and girl from an unknown land suddenly appear in a Suffolk village, with not wholly happy results.

Some of the stories have a more obvious moral intention. For example, Gervase tells us about a glade in a Gloucestershire forest where weary huntsmen may cry, "I am thirsty!" and a merry-faced, richly attired butler will come forth to offer him a drink from a golden bejewelled horn. The drink is a magical nectar of such potency that it immediately banishes all thirst and tiredness. Many huntsmen experience this supernatural largesse before, one day, a greedy trickster steals the horn and offers it to his master, the Earl of Gloucester, who promptly has him executed.

Similarly moral is Gervase's story about a law-court of swans in his native Essex. In Ongar, Richard de Lucie, the Lord of the Manor, witnesses a group of swans apparently giving evidence against an adulterous female swan. The evidence is compelling and the guilty pen is stripped of her feathers and left to die. There are many other marvels of the animal kingdom recorded in the *Otia*: one of the best is a description of squirrels crossing water by using leaves as rafts and their tails as sails.

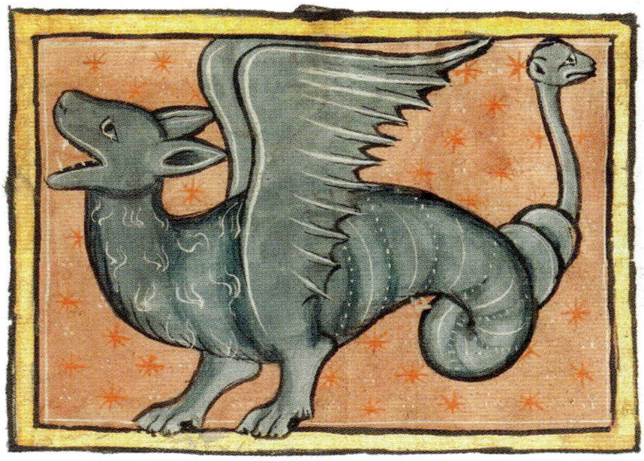

Other stories seem to lack a moral, but are simply entertaining. At Wandlebury, just south of Cambridge, was a magic clearing in a wood in which a spectral knight, upon hearing the words "Let knight come against knight!", would joust with all-comers. A certain Osbert Fitzhugh, lodging at a nearby castle, heard the story and decided to put it to the test. At the prompt, the spectral knight duly appeared. A fight ensued in which Osbert unseated his opponent and took his horse, but received a terrible wound in the thigh from his opponent's lance. The stolen horse, entirely black, was too spirited to be stabled and vanished back to the wood. Osbert's injury, however, remained as proof of the tale, an incurable wound opening up each year on the anniversary of the magical tourney.

And what are we to make of the story of Saint Simeon's horn? A knight, out hunting in the forests of Carlisle, loses sight of his companions and is suddenly overcome by a terrible storm. In the midst of the thunder and lightning, he glimpses a terrifying fire-breathing hellhound. Suddenly, out of the storm, a second knight appears saying, "Fear not! I am Saint Simeon, on whom you called for protection. Take my horn: it will hereafter protect you and your family from any storm." The knight takes the horn and Saint Simeon speeds off in pursuit of the dog. In vain. The dog has already entered the house of a priest and burned it down; his entire (illegitimate) family perishes.

We've only touched the surface of this amazing piece of literature, but the good news is that there exists an excellent English translation, with facing Latin text, of the entire work. Edited and translated by SE Banks and JW Binns, it's called *Gervase of Tilbury: Otia Imperialia, Recreation for an Emperor* (Oxford University Press). Enough stories, surely, to while away many a dreary commute from London to Southend.

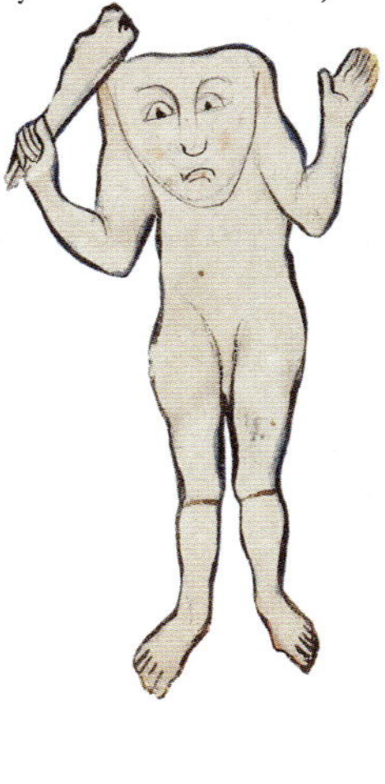

Mary Ruskin is a teacher and translator of Classical, Medieval Latin and Neo-Latin.

Poem

The Owl

By **Edward Thomas**

Downhill I came, hungry, and yet not starved;
Cold, yet had heat within me that was proof
Against the North wind; tired, yet so that rest
Had seemed the sweetest thing under a roof.

Then at the inn I had food, fire, and rest,
Knowing how hungry, cold, and tired was I.
All of the night was quite barred out except
An owl's cry, a most melancholy cry

Shaken out long and clear upon the hill,
No merry note, nor cause of merriment,
But one telling me plain what I escaped
And others could not, that night, as in I went.

And salted was my food, and my repose,
Salted and sobered, too, by the bird's voice
Speaking for all who lay under the stars,
Soldiers and poor, unable to rejoice.

From Poems *(1917).*

Photography Feature

Master Pieces

Mantelpieces used to be focal points showcasing beautiful and interesting possessions. Today they've become rather redundant – a place to plonk your post or spare change. But happily some householders are keeping the old tradition alive. Photographer **Orlando Gili** *captures a few here*

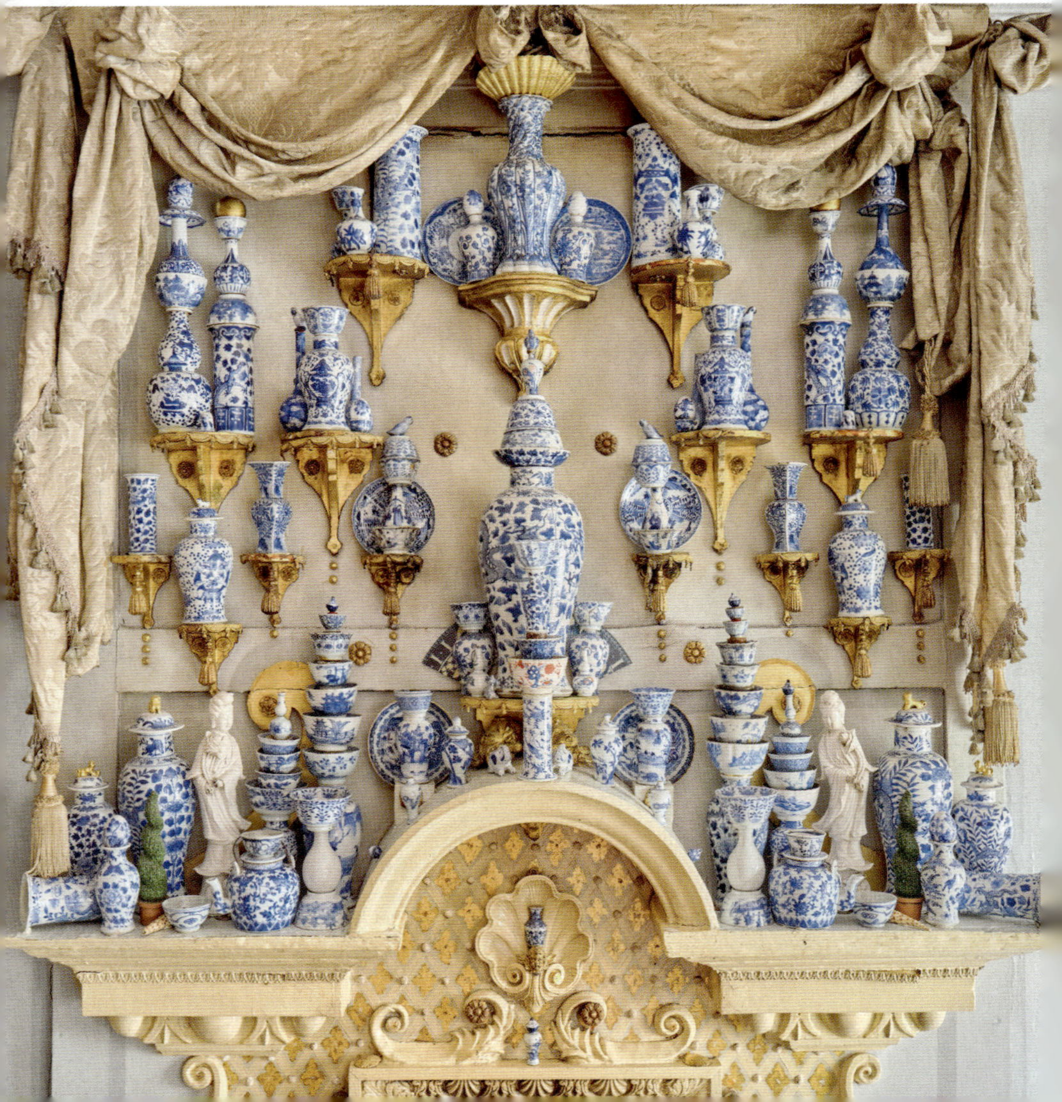

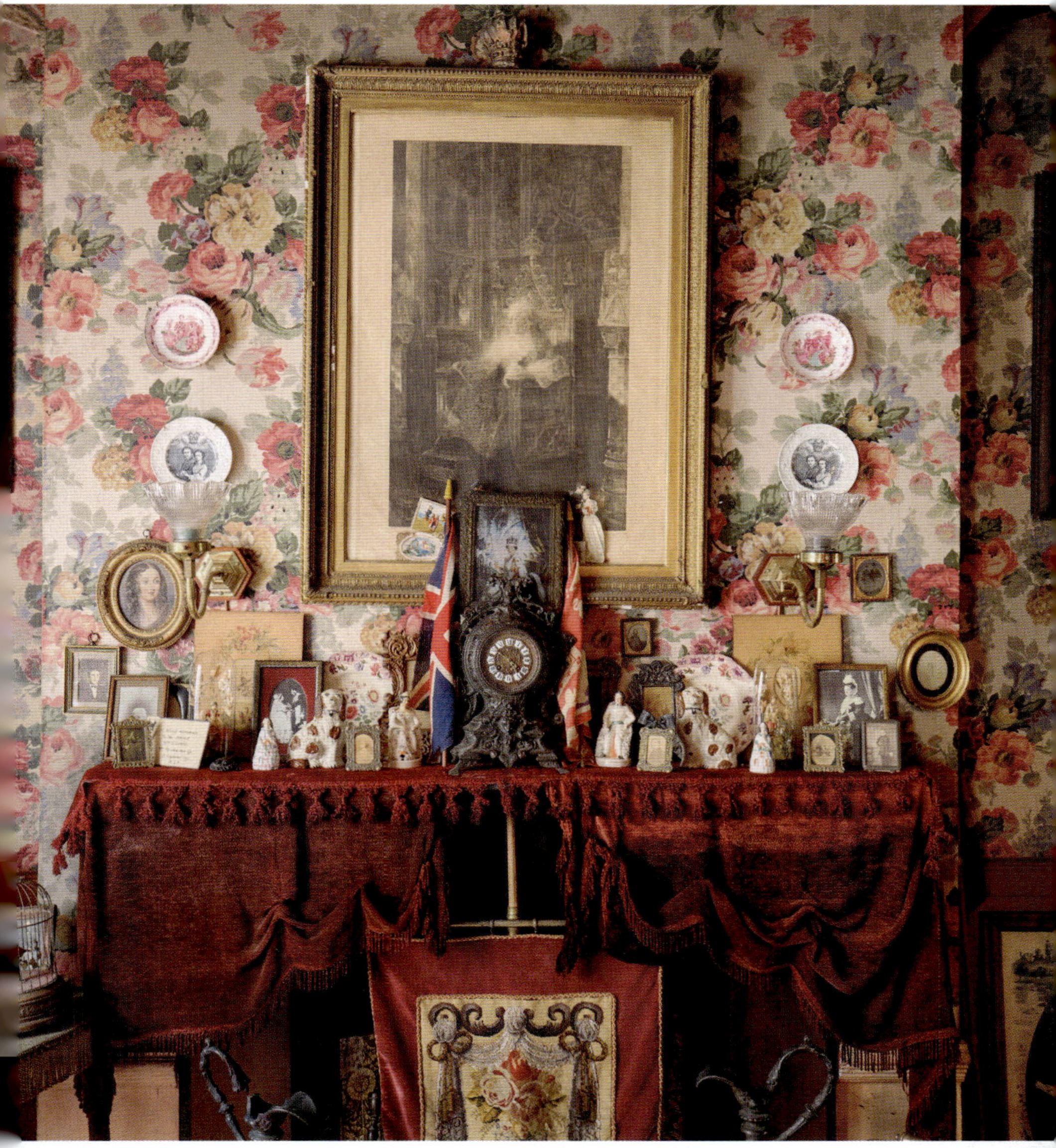

Dennis Severs, artist and curator
[images left and right]

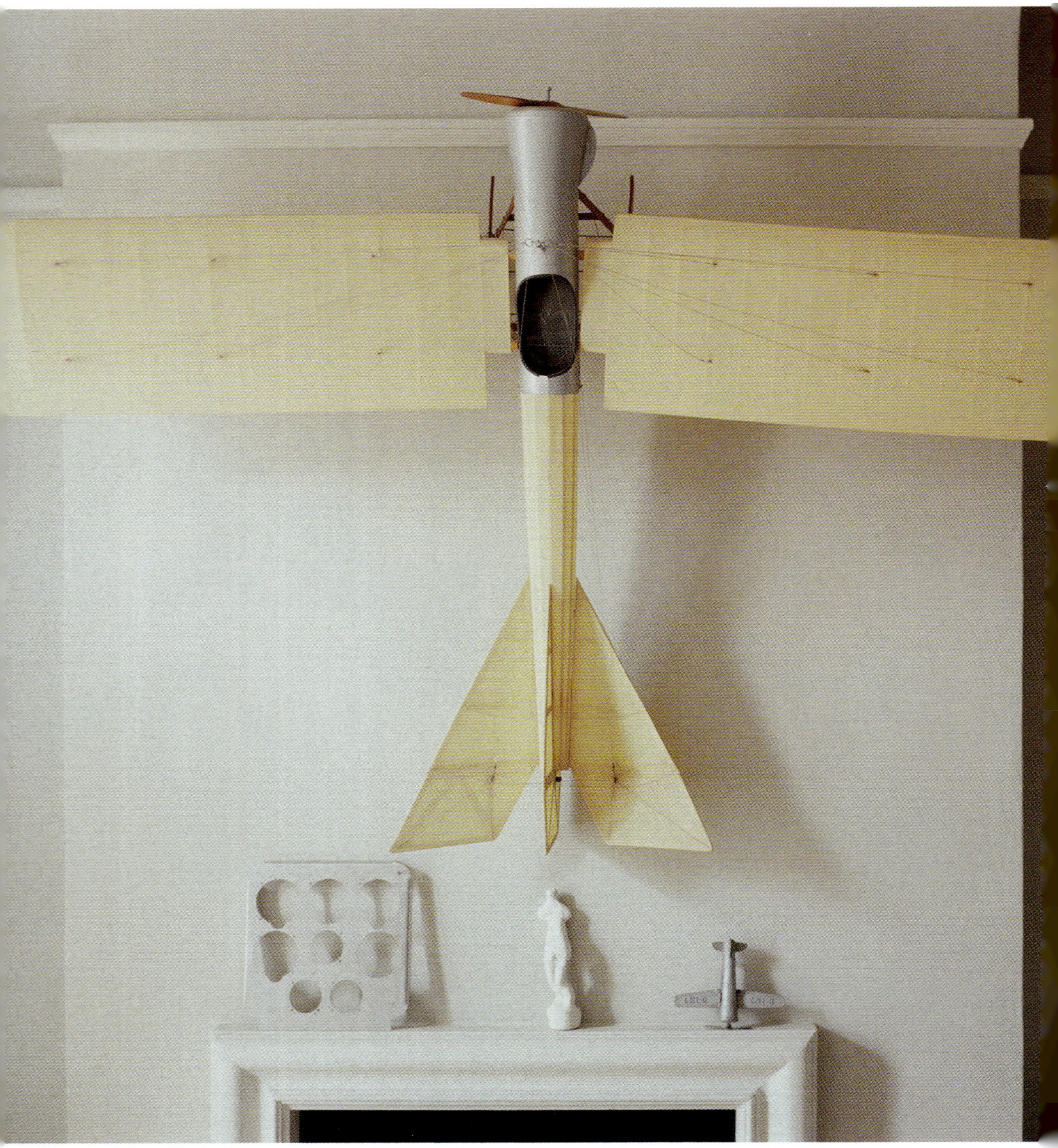

Stephen Bayley, writer and design museum founding CEO
(and author of this issue's Odium column)

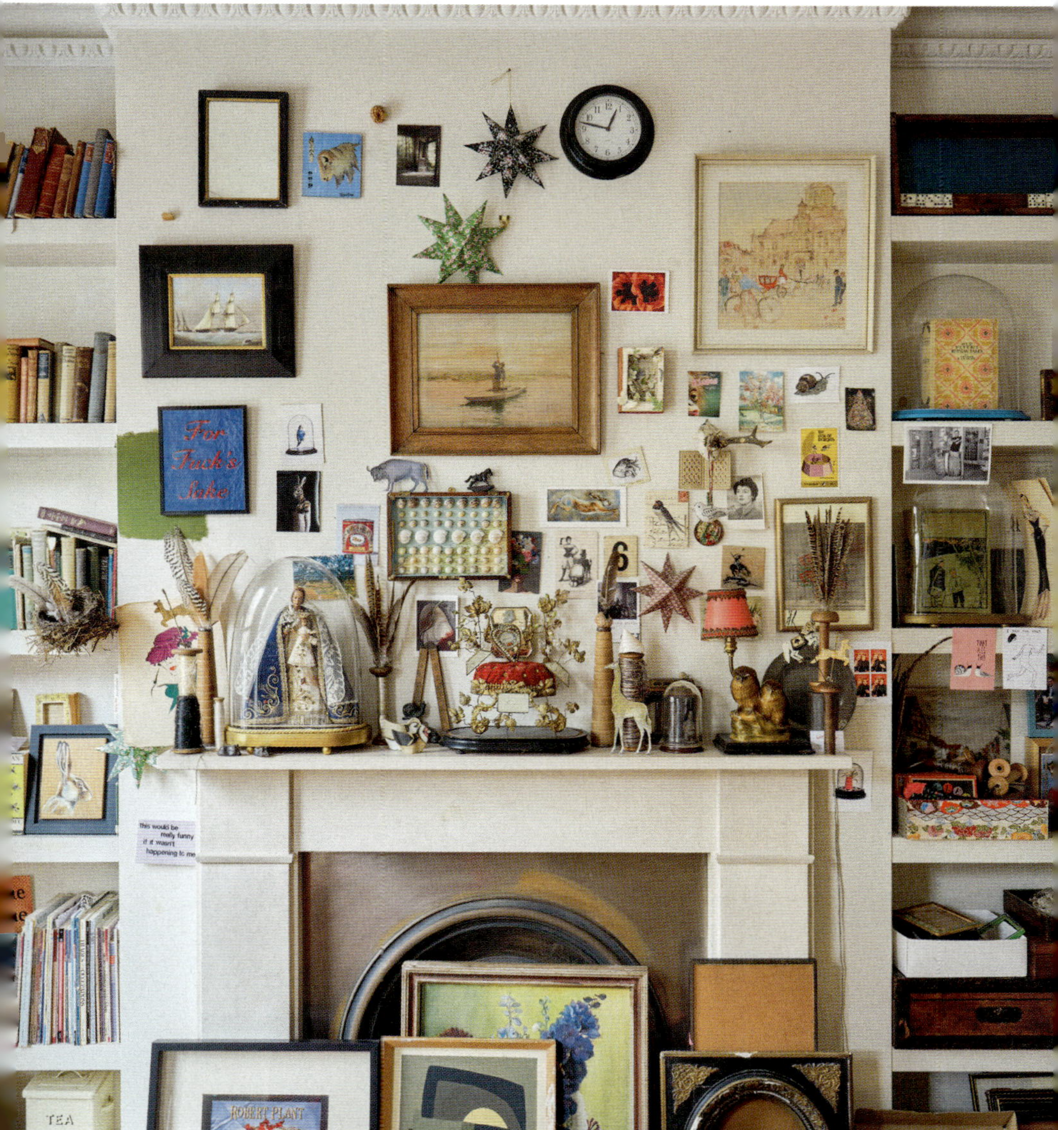

Sophia Langmead, artist

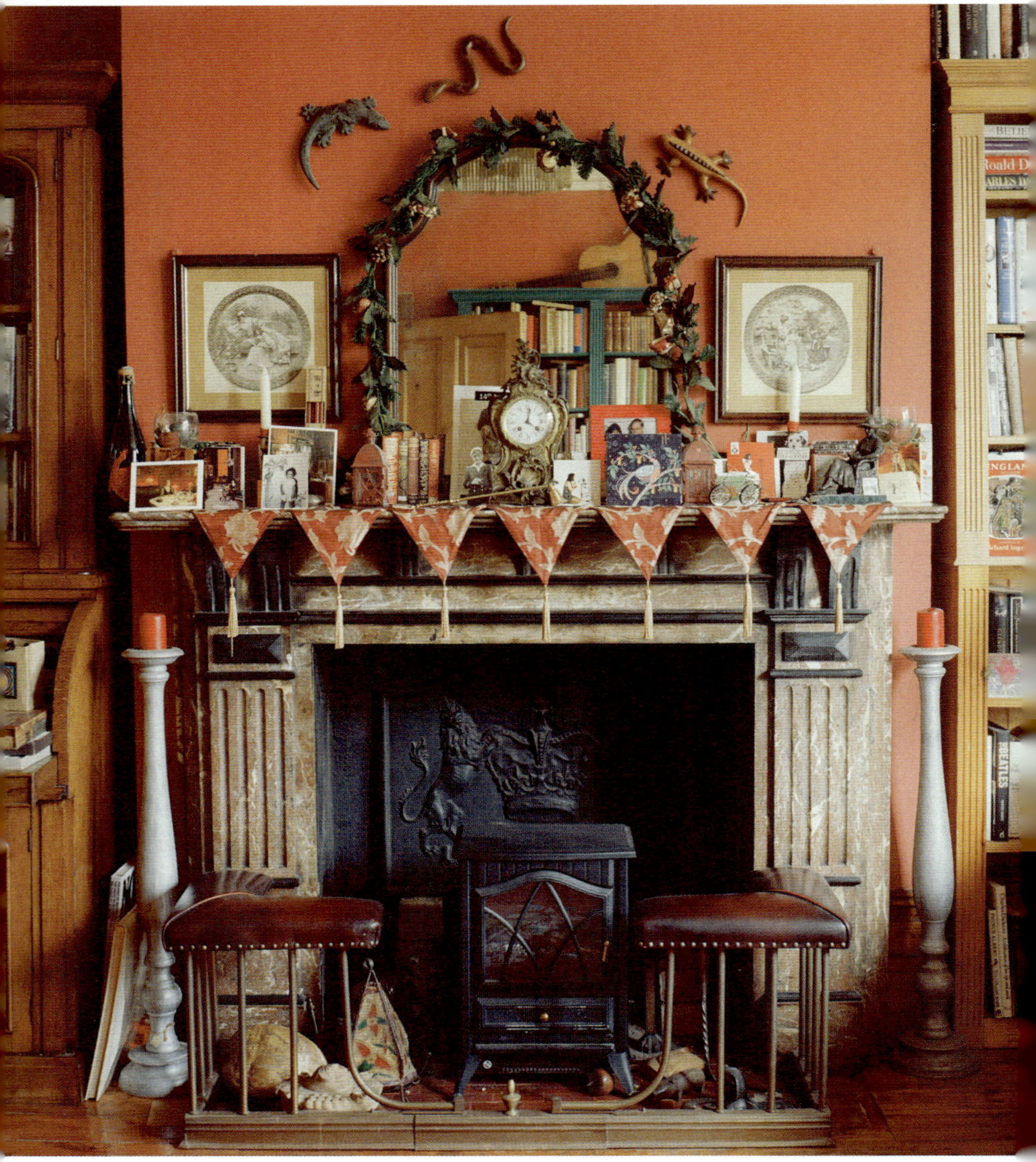

Valerie Grove, writer and journalist

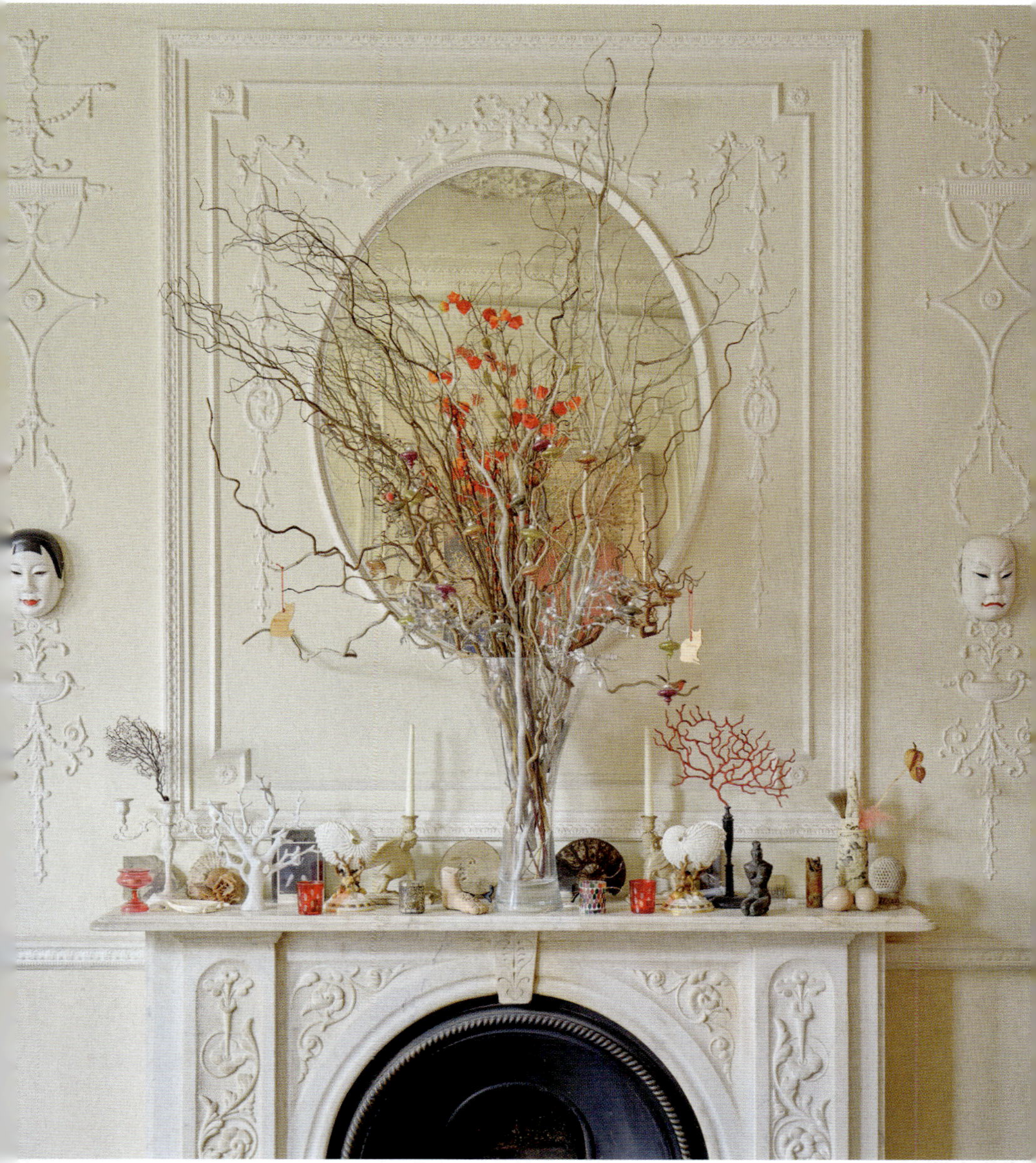

Jonathan Ross, gallerist

Gift Guide

Make your Christmas merry and bright with the perfect presents from our favourite indie retailers. With thanks to Holly.co

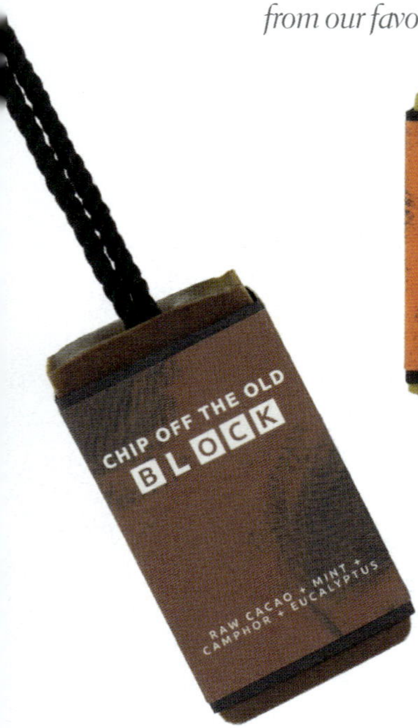

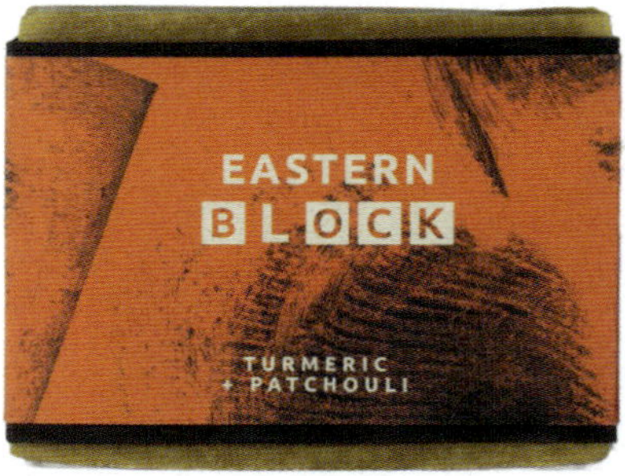

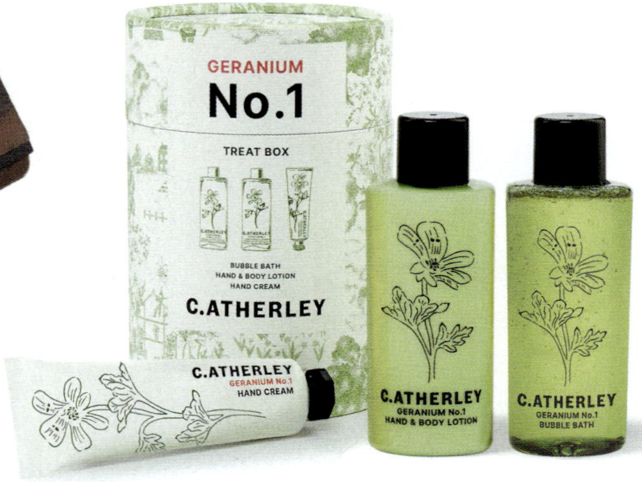

[top] Chip off the Old Block
soap and rope, £12, civilblock.co.uk

[bottom] Geranium No.1 Treat Box: travel size hand cream, bubble bath, and hand & body lotion, £45, c-atherley.com

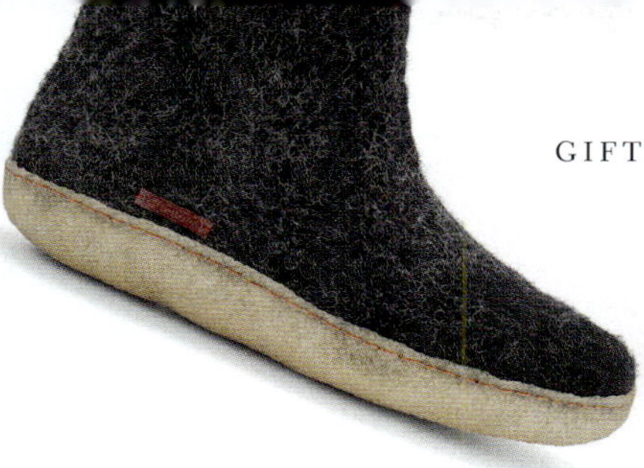

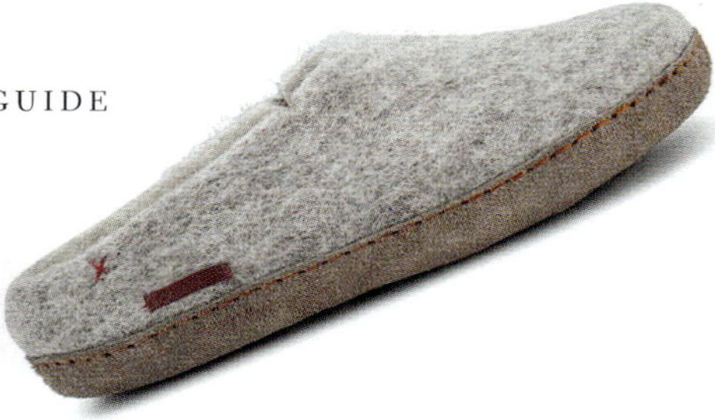

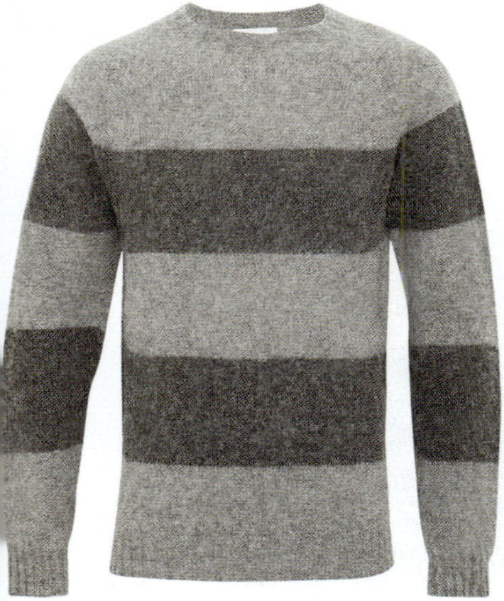

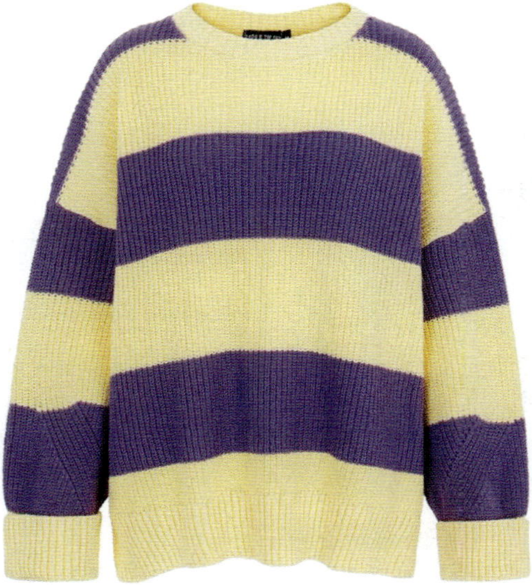

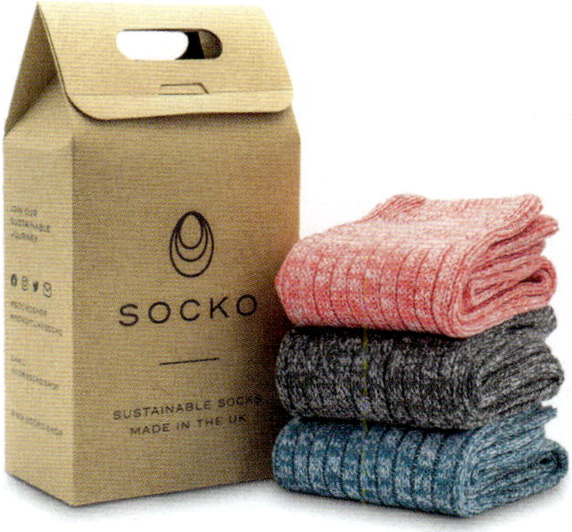

[top] High Boot Slipper in black with rubber, £69; Classic Slipper in grey with leather, £55, betterfelt.co.uk

[middle] Rhiannon Recycled Cotton Mix Chunky Stripe Jumper in purple, by Cara & the Sky, £74.99; Alford Brushed Wool Stripe Sweater Grey Melange, by Genevieve Sweeney, £180. Both available from holly.co

[bottom] Three pairs of 100% recycled socks, sizes 4–12, £50, socko.shop

[top] Organic French wines in 2.25-litre boxes, from £38, bobowines.co.uk

[middle] Chocolate Bars in a Cracker!, £12.50–£19.60; Christmas Chocolate Selection, £12–£47.50, chocolours.com

[bottom] A Cup of Life Gift Set: loose tea selection of English Breakfast, Glacier Green, and Lemongrass & Ginger, £22.95; Loose Leaf Sampler Collection, £12, karmateaco.com

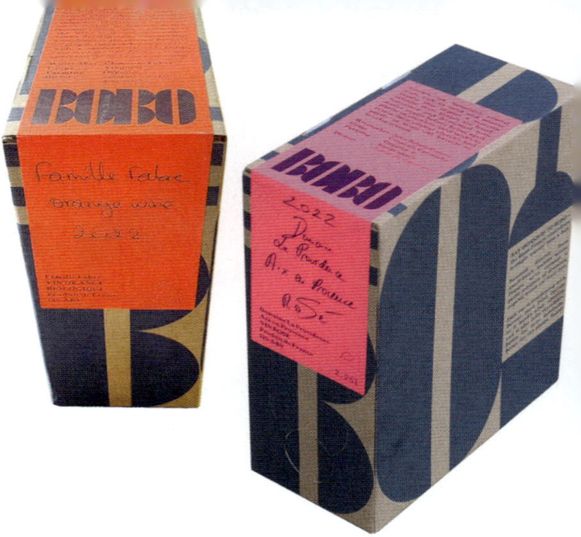

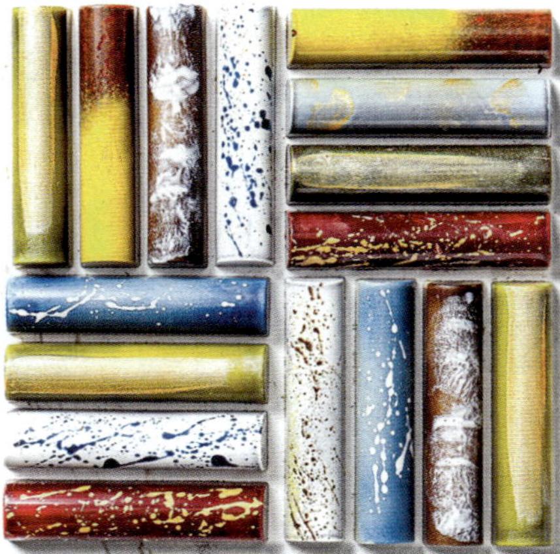

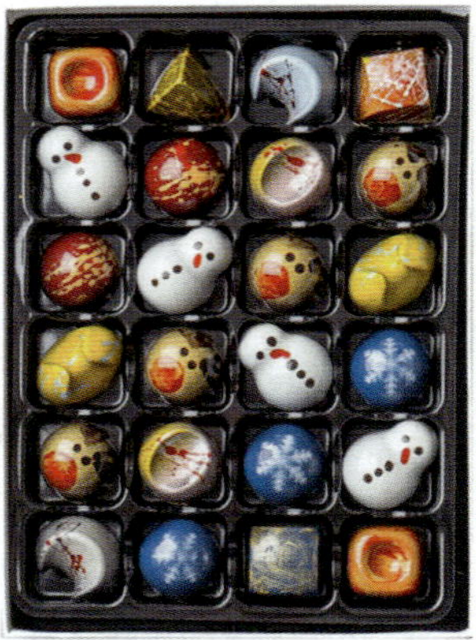

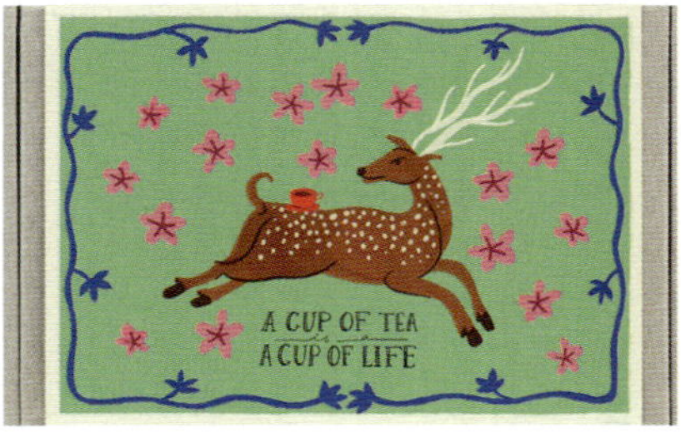

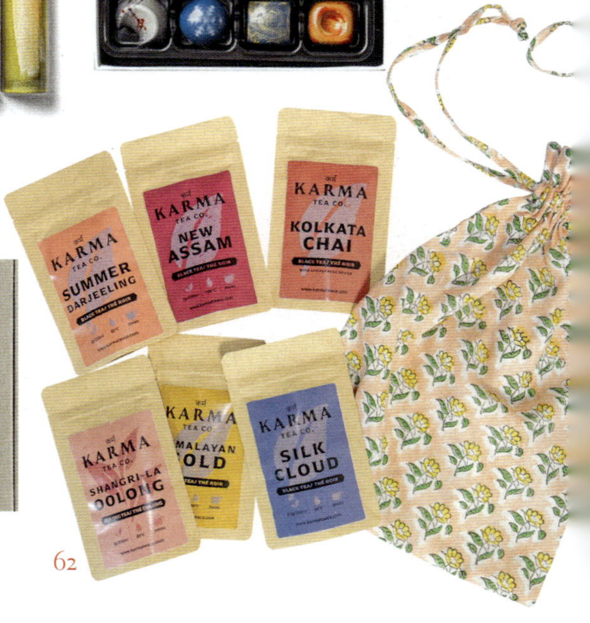

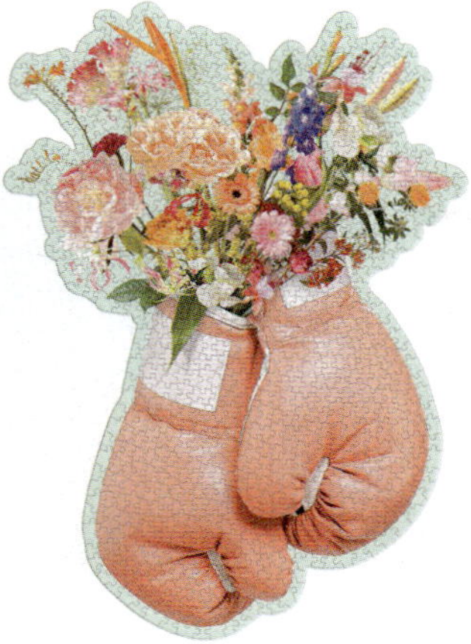

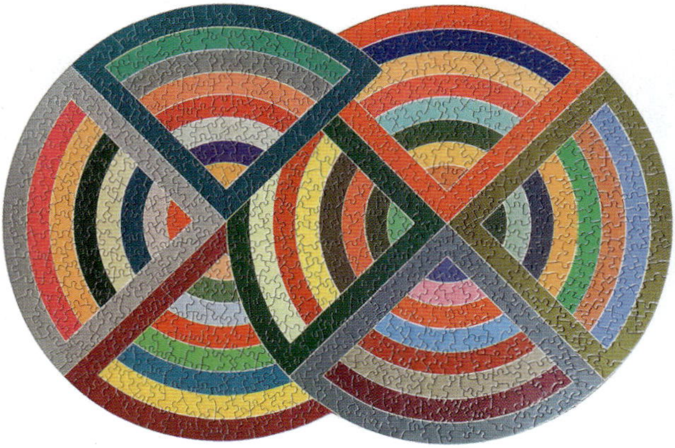

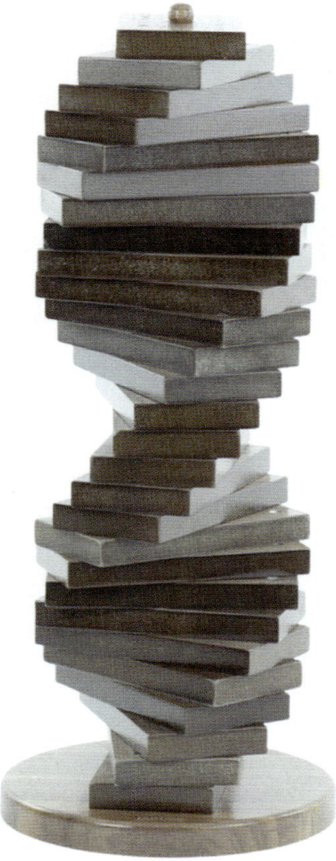

[top] Flower Power Shaped Jigsaw Puzzle, £25; Frank Stella Firuzabad Unique Shaped Jigsaw Puzzle, £24.99, both 750 pieces, restinpieces.co.uk

[bottom] Dominoes Tower, £29.99; Original Quoits, £19.99, jaqueslondon.co.uk

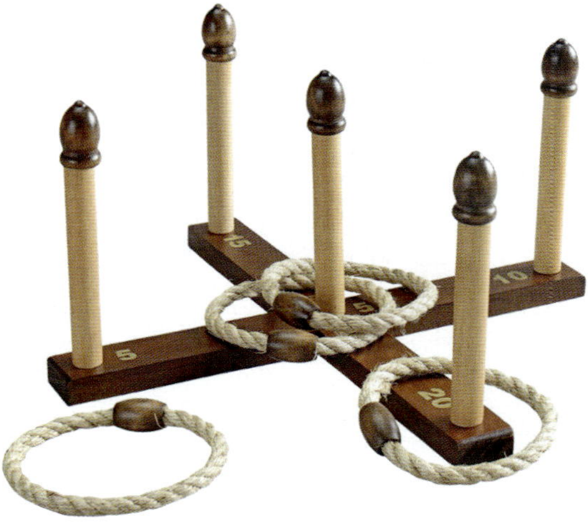

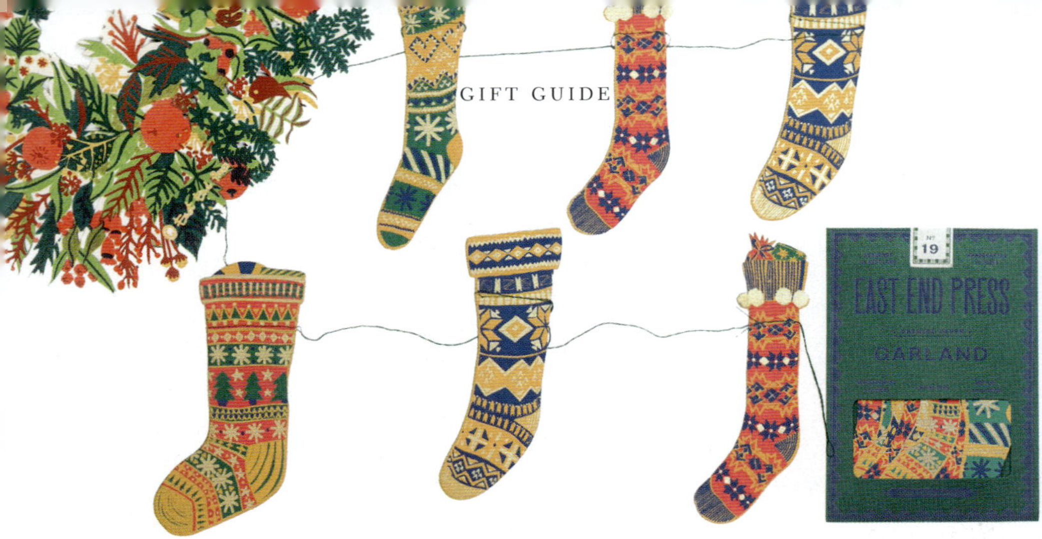

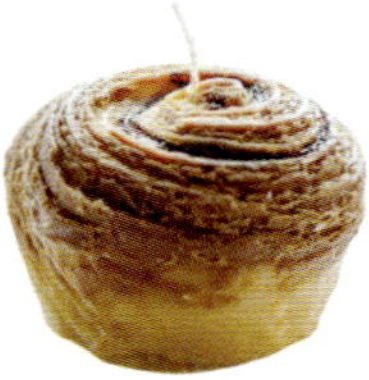

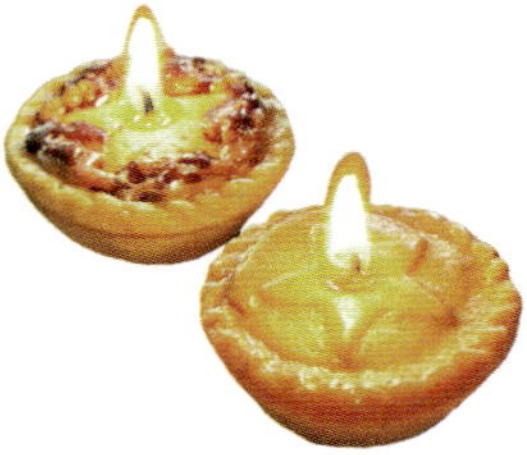

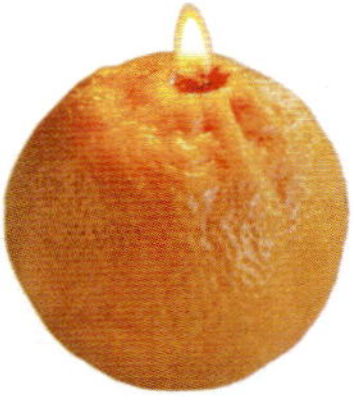

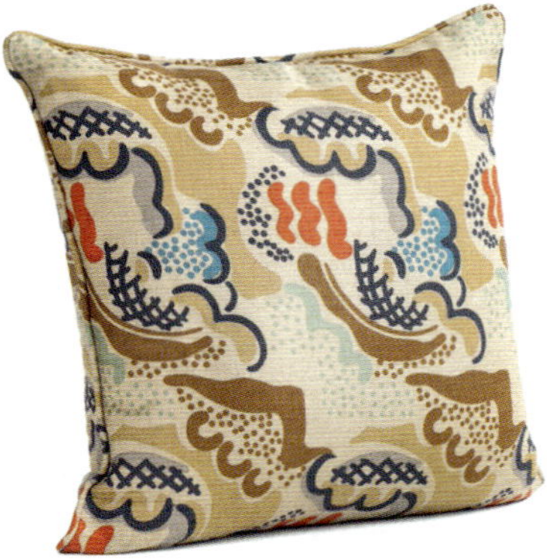

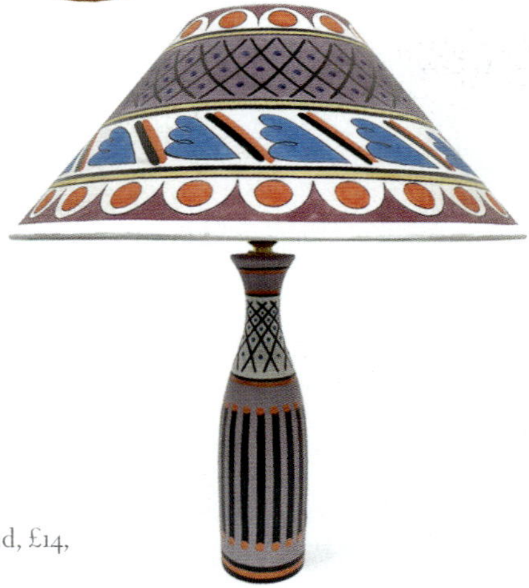

[top] Wreath, £20; Stockings Printed Paper Garland, £14, eastendpress.com

[middle] Cinnamon Bun Candle; Mince Pie Candles (set of 2); Christmas Orange Candle, £19.95 each, by Not Another Candle, available from holly.co

[bottom] Clouds Cushion Cover, a fabric designed in 1931 by Duncan Grant, £65; Cressida Bell Exclusive Lamp, purple, £420, shop.charleston.org.uk

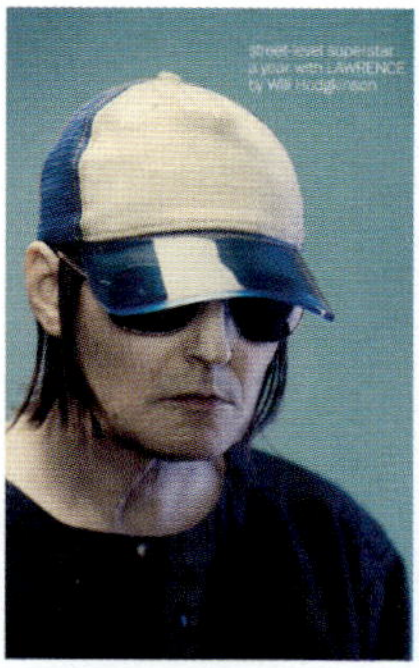
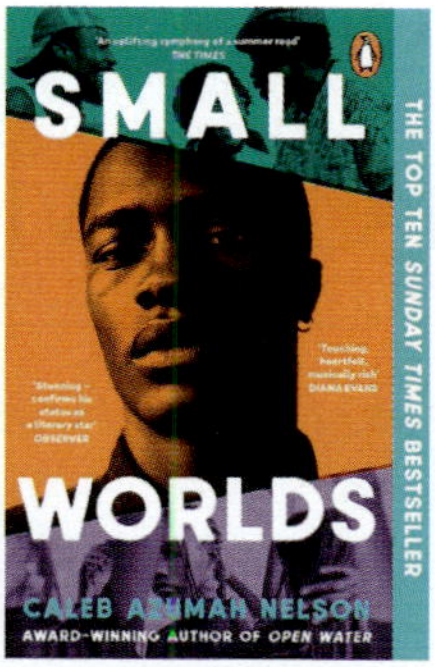

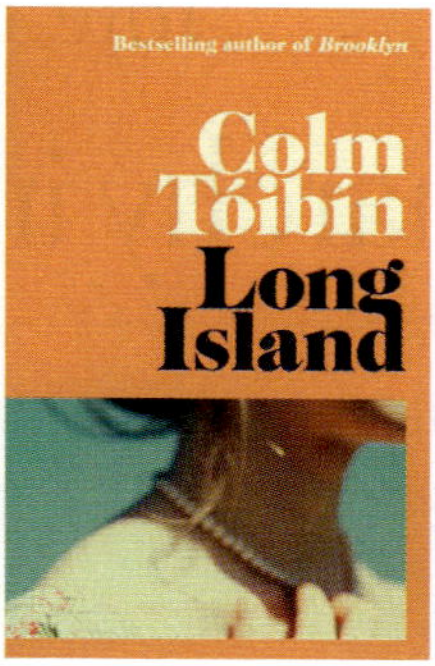

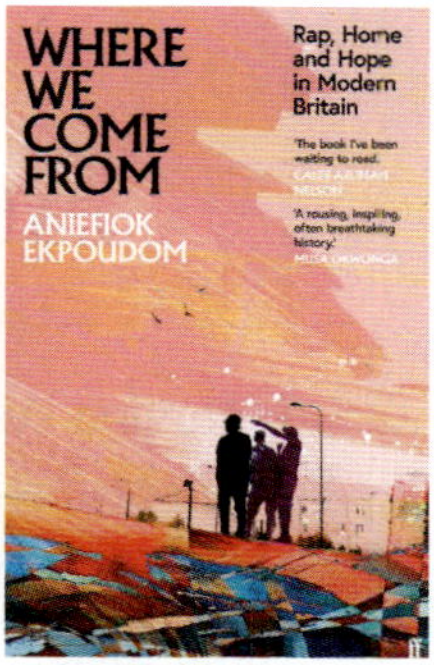

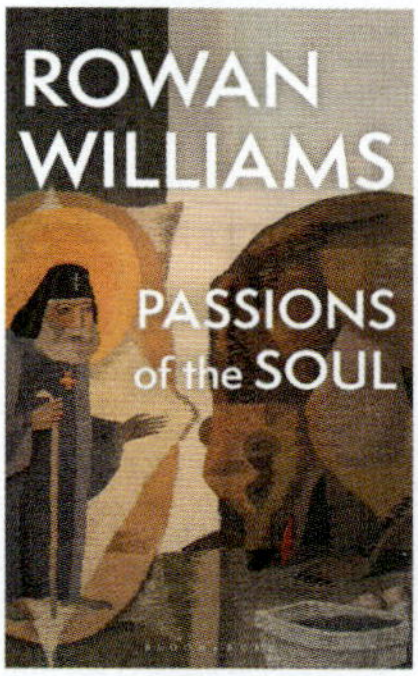

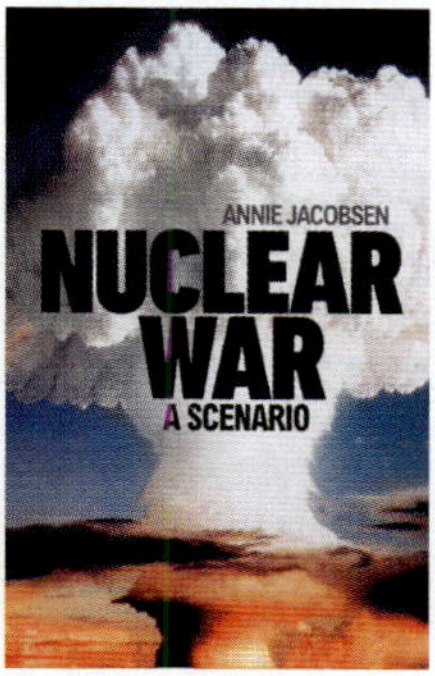

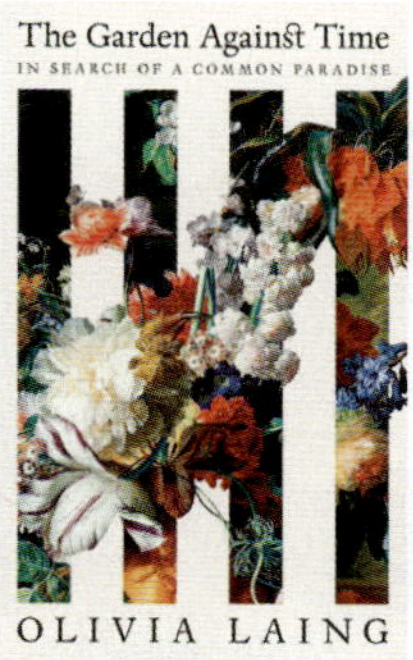

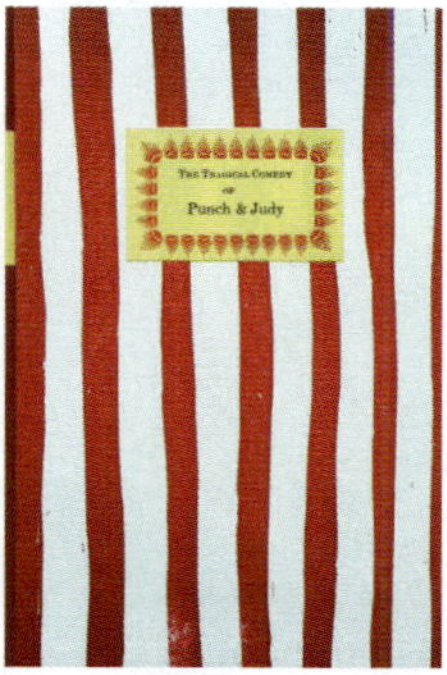
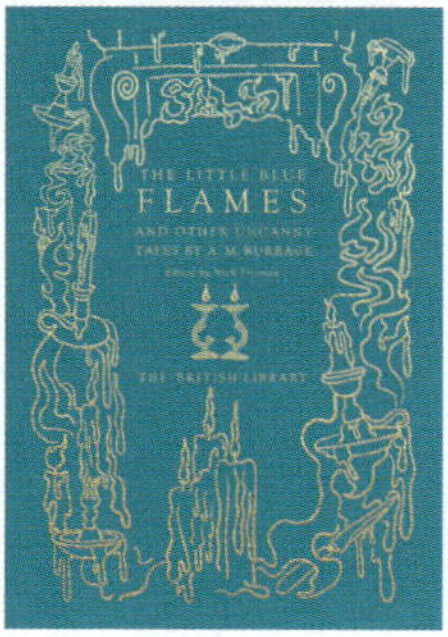

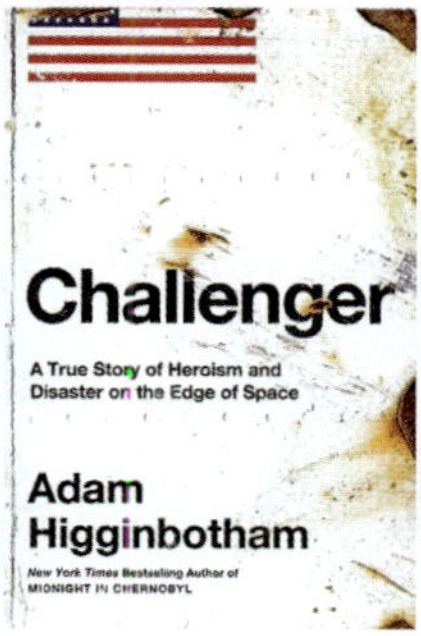

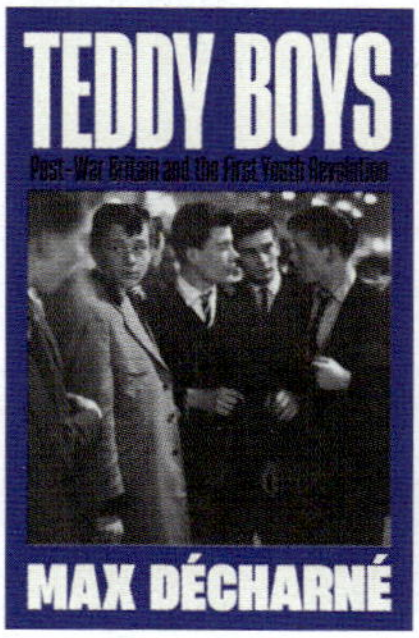

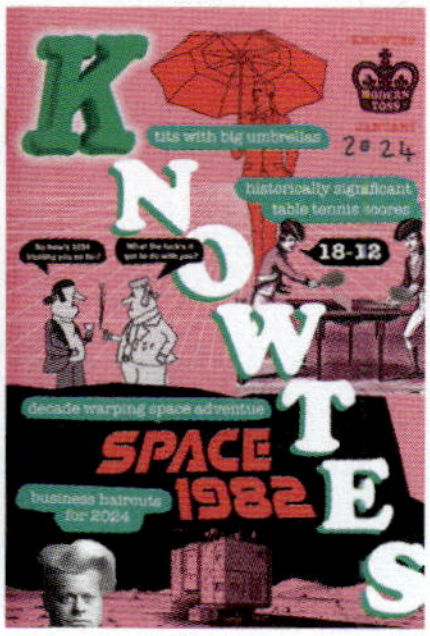

Idler Book Recommendations:

Street-Level Superstar by Will Hodgkinson [Nine Eight Books]; *Small Worlds* by Caleb Azumah Nelson [Penguin]; *Long Island* by Colm Tóibín [Picador]; *Where We Come From* by Aniefiok Ekpoudom [Faber & Faber]; *Passions of the Soul* by Rowan Williams [Bloomsbury]; *Nuclear War* by Annie Jacobsen [Torva]; *The Garden Against Time* by Olivia Laing [Picador]; *The Tragical Comedy of Punch & Judy* illustrated by Helen Moss [Incline Press]; *The Little Blue Flames and Other Uncanny Tales* by A.M. Burrage [British Library]; *Challenger* by Adam Higginbotham [Viking]; *Teddy Boys* by Max Décharné [Profile]; *Knowtes* [Modern Toss].

Idle Home

Anarchy in Chiswick

Georgina Williams *highlights the work of mosaicist* **Carrie Reichardt**, *who has turned her west London home into a glorious work of art and activism*

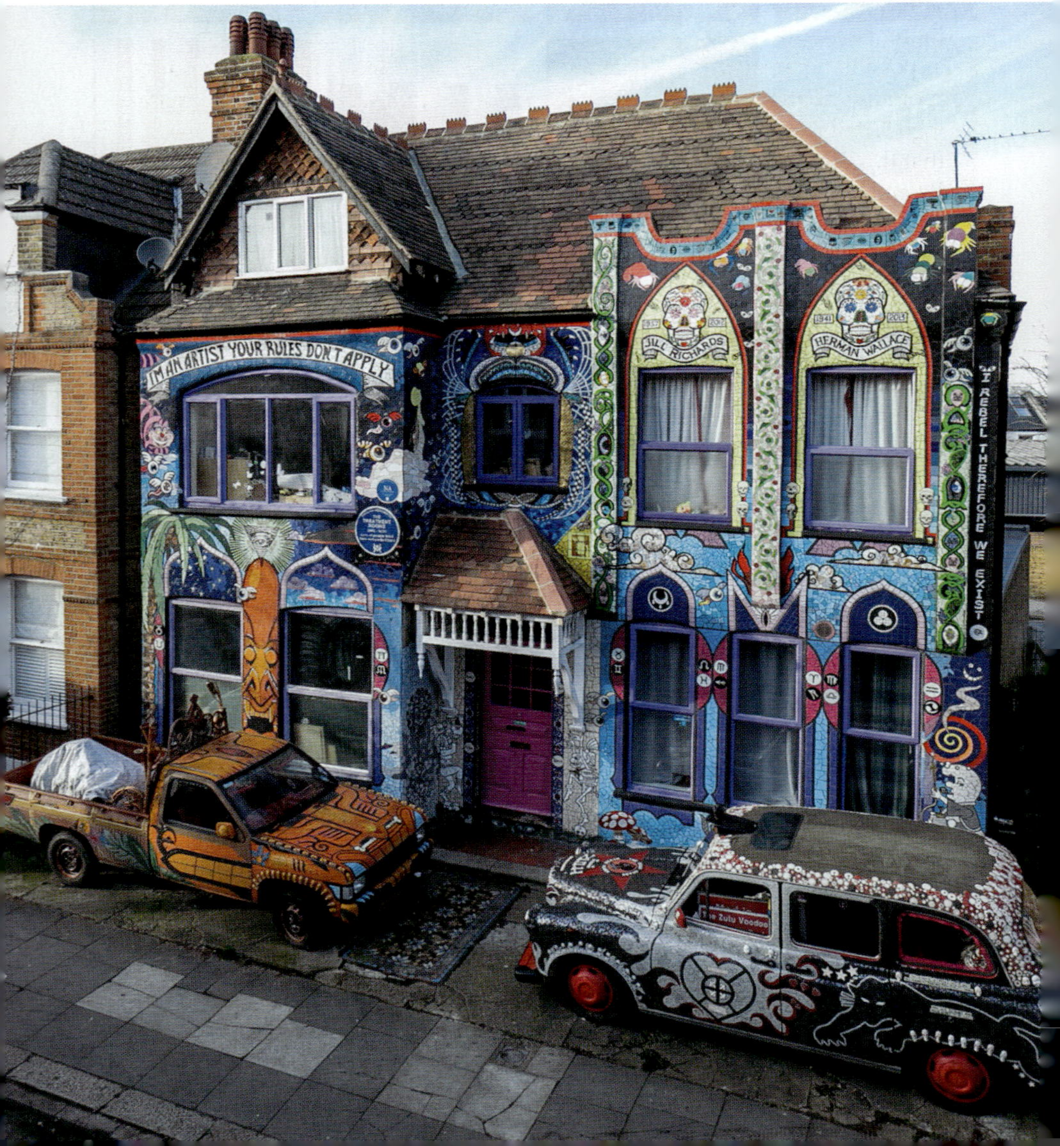

Earlier this year, trying to evade the traffic in Chiswick, west London, I took a right down a quiet residential street. It turned out to be fortuitous. Although it looped me back to the main road, I discovered the most staggering mosaic-covered house at the end of it – an audacious punctuation to the otherwise uniform Victorian villas there. Hovering outside for as long as possible in an attempt to glean more information, I noticed the logo "Mad in England" and realised that this must be home to an artist I'd encountered some years before, the anarchist and activist Carrie Reichardt.

Since graduating from Leeds with a degree in Fine Art in 1991, Carrie has worked across many media including film, performance and sculpture but her work has evolved to a more crafts-based practice and she's best known as a ceramicist and mosaicist, working internationally on large-scale murals. A deep thinker with strong opinions, her work is equally layered and profound, reflecting subjects that are important to her, in particular social injustices and mental health issues.

The house in Chiswick has become the ultimate canvas for uncensored work by Carrie and her artistic collaborators. It's an extraordinary work of art that has taken more than 20 years to complete; a confection of unbridled joy, serious political protest and a sincere celebration of life in many forms. Originally bought by Carrie's father Roland back in the 1950s, the house has long been both home and studio to Carrie as well as to many of her friends and fellow artists. The original red brick facade was once covered with a drab pebble dashed render but there is no trace of this now. It's been transformed into a place of wonder, adorned in its entirety with dramatic mosaic symbols and declarations.

Carrie began mosaicing in 1999, encouraged by her former partner James Newell to work in mosaic and to create a design in the back garden. She loved the process and found the practice totally absorbing, so much so that she moved to the front of the house where she began to mosaic a design around the front door. As the years passed, so the mosaics increased, often prompted by incidents that were significant to Carrie such as the death of her friend Luis Ramirez, a prisoner on death row in Texas who was executed in 2005. They had corresponded for years and his death led her to spend eight months mosaicing the back wall of the garden, incorporating a striking memorial to Ramirez.

There is a further tribute to prisoners of the state on the back of the house: above a bedroom window are intricate portraits of the Angola Three – Black Panthers in

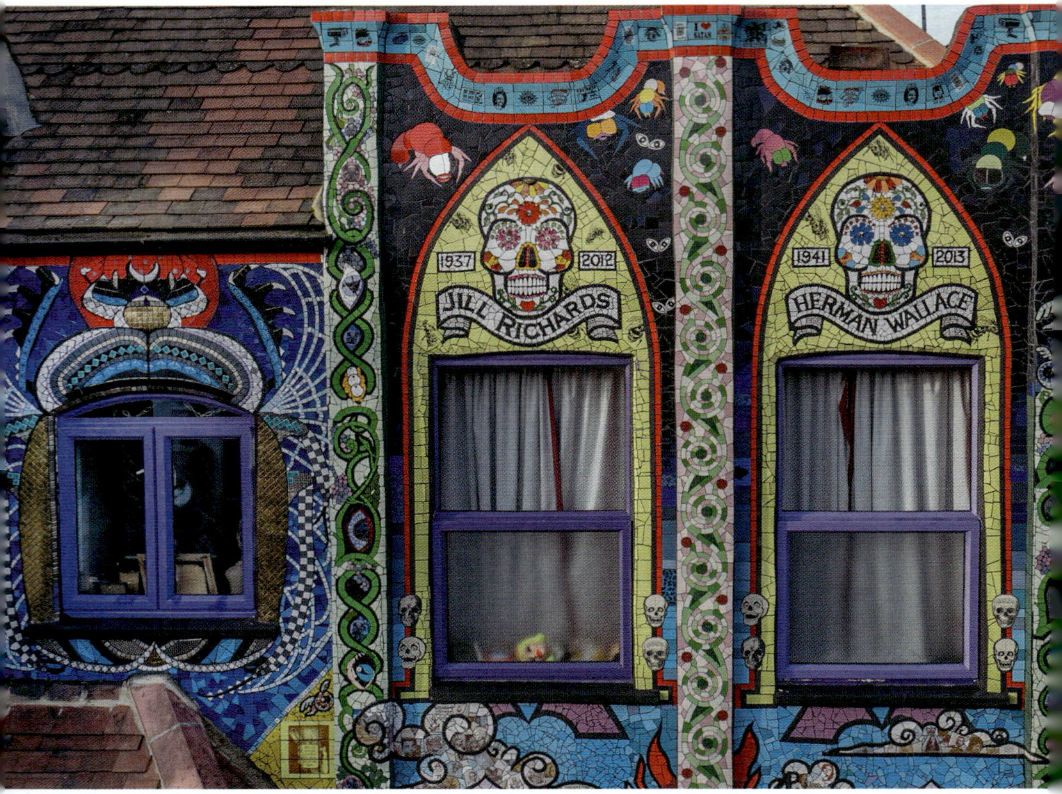

[above] Tributes to Carrie's mother Jill and the Angola Three's Herman Wallace
[right] Adding the Treatment Rooms plaque

the sixties who were incarcerated in Louisiana for over 40 years. In 2013 they were finally freed and two of them – Albert Woodfox and Robert King – later visited the house. However their compatriot Herman Wallace died from ill health just two days after being released and Carrie has created a striking memorial to him at the front of the house, next to one for her mother, Jill Richards.

Alongside these epitaphs Carrie uses the space to express her serious concerns about the environment – a stunning recreation of *The Great Wave off Kanagawa* by Hokusai is depicted engulfing totems of the City of London including the Gherkin, St Paul's Cathedral and Canary Wharf; topping the rear garden wall is a series of pyramid sculptures depicting a cycle of the moon (cast out of Ferrero Rocher boxes) under which is a quote from Bill Hicks: "Here's what we do. You know all that money we spend on nuclear weapons and defence every year? Instead if we spent that money feeding and clothing the poor of the world, which it would pay for many times over, not one human being excluded … not one … we could as one race explore space, together both inner and outer, for ever, in peace.

Amid the symbols of angst for the world and the repressed there is also much joy portrayed. Beside the wave, a giant lotus flower bears magic mushrooms. At the front of the house, lovers embrace and two glorious sections have been created by Carrie's long-time friends and collaborators to depict rebirth and life, a shimmering scarab beetle by Chilean mosaic artist Isidora Paz Lopez and a double helix by Karen Francesca. These pieces were among the many created by a host of international mosaic artists after Carrie put out a request asking for help to finish the house in 2017. Those who were unable to make the trip were invited to send flying eyeballs and these can be seen as a unifying theme all over the building, pulling the disparate subjects together.

Two blue plaques from the English Hedonists add a final witty stamp. One of them celebrates the artist collective that Carrie is part of. It's inscribed: "The Treatment Rooms 2002 – Now: Lots of people lived here and partied hard". The Treatment Rooms collective is named after a sign that Carrie sourced from a mental institution and which she fixed to the studio door. It alludes to the solace that she and many others have found in their practice and has become a fitting name for the community of artists who have worked at the house.

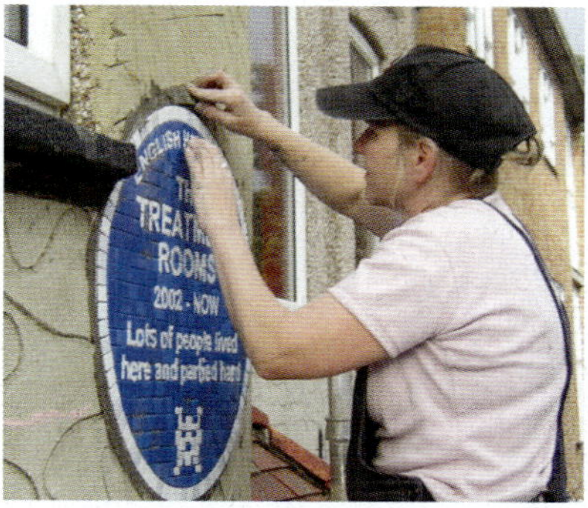

With the house finished and the scaffolding down, Carrie has turned her considerable energy to other projects in the public realm. She's currently working on a brilliant and bold art project in Merseyside: the Strong Women project, which highlights untold stories of local women from the communities of St Helens and Knowsley. A cathartic piece of art for many of the participants and one that truly represents them, it's been exhaustively researched and pulled together by Carrie under a very apt quote from Ada Lovelace: "Here's to strong women. May we know them. May we raise them. May we be them."

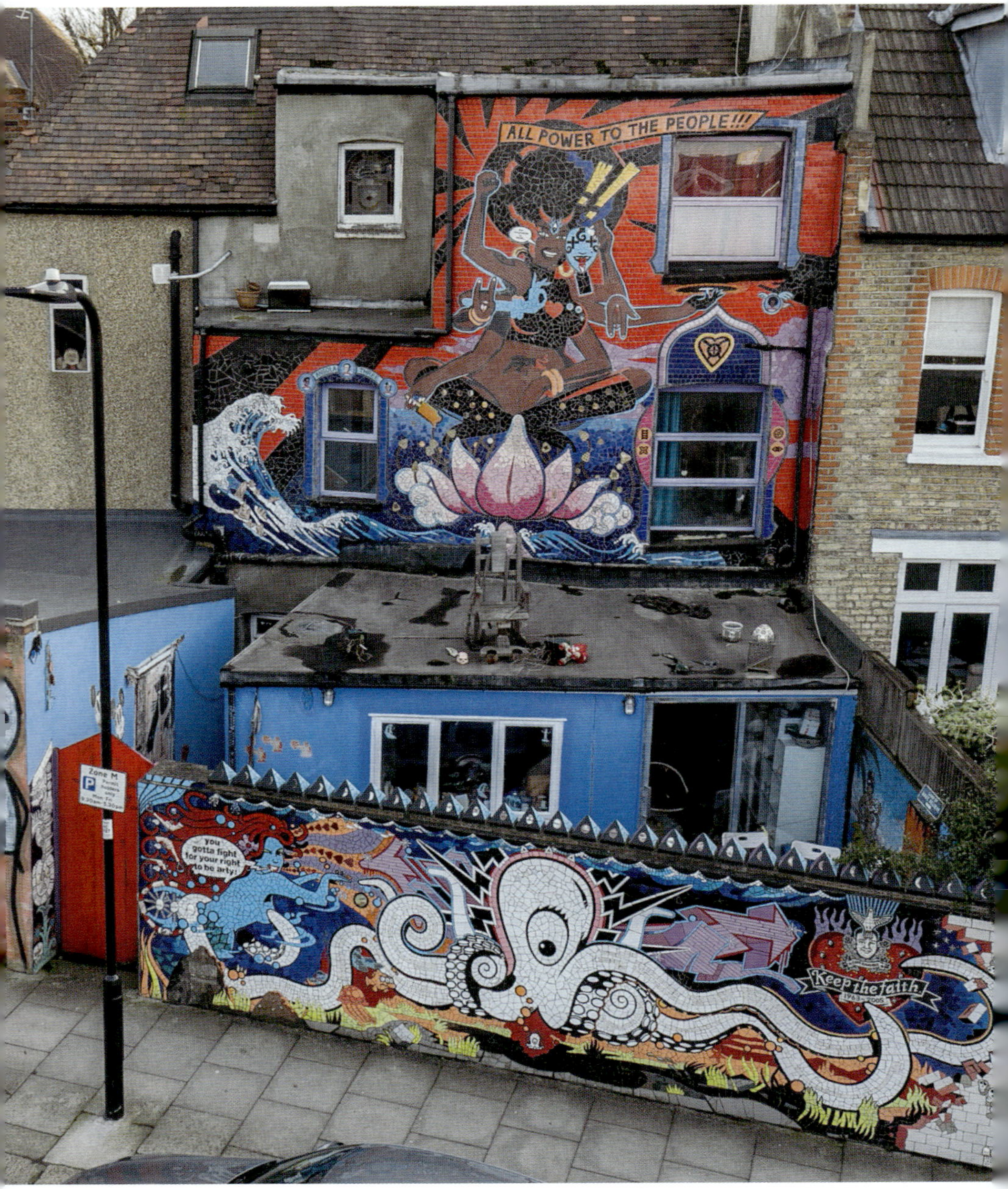

The final word: a caption on the rear wall reads: "You gotta fight for your right to be arty!"

Buy George

Visit
Pop along to the Mosaic House in Chiswick and feel free to take pictures – but remember it's a home and not a museum. *@mosaichousechiswick*

Discover
Find out more about Carrie's work and that of the Treatment Rooms Collective at her website, *carriereichardt.com*

Past Projects
- *Elm Tree of Life* mosaic at Finsbury Park Station, 2020, by Carrie Reichardt, Karen Francesca and ATM. The mosaic stands at the entrance to the station and incorporates stories from the local area.
- *The Voodoo Zulu Liberation Taxi*, 2015, by Carrie Reichardt and The Treatment Rooms Collective. A classic London cab transformed with mosaic to highlight the plight of Kenny "Zulu" Whitmore. See Carrie's interview with Whitmore in *Idler* 42.
- *Mary Bamber: A Revolutionary Woman*, 2011, by Carrie Reichardt and Nick Reynolds. A sculpture of Mary Bamber, bold orator, militant suffragette and social revolutionary – now on permanent display in the Museum of Liverpool.

The Strong Women Project
Carrie has been working with the Merseyside-based community arts organisation Heart of Glass, and mentee Claire Eddleston, to make two new pieces of large-scale street art for neighbourhoods in St Helens and Knowsley. They have collected untold stories and memories from hundreds of women within the community and turned them into a ceramic tapestry, interweaving 540 tile hearts made by local people, dedicated to strong women who inspire them, with local, historical detail. *heartofglass.org.uk*

Disobedient Objects, V&A
Curated by Gavin Grindon and Catherine Flood in 2014, this exhibition demonstrated how political activism drives design ingenuity and collective creativity. Carrie and The Treatment Rooms Collective exhibited their *Tiki Love Truck*, 2007, which was originally commissioned by Walk the Plank and constructed for the first Art Car Parade in Manchester. The *Tiki Love Truck* is a mosaic mausoleum and is dedicated to the memory of Carrie's friend John Joe "Ash" Amador. For details on the exhibition and to download some of the How to Guides on making some of the disobedient objects exhibited, visit the V&A website *vam.ac.uk*.

Try Mosaicing
The Mosaic Workshop was founded 30 years ago and sells materials for beginners and pros as well as listing resources and courses online. *mosaicworkshop.com*

Read
Femina by Janina Ramirez. This ground-breaking reappraisal of mediaeval femininity reveals how women have been written out of history and why that matters today. Published by Ebury. *hive.co.uk*

ROK On

Product designer and coffee enthusiast Patrick Hunt wanted to enable people to make their own high-quality espresso at home and so created the ROK manual coffee machine, which launched in 2004. ROK's range of espresso makers and coffee accessories are stylish and sustainable. Their products are non-electric and use ground coffee instead of capsules, meaning they won't wear out or send heaps of plastic pods into landfill. ROK sell replaceable parts so you'll never have to throw your machine away. They're also enjoyable to use. You create pressure yourself by slowly pressing down the levers with your hands, making a perfect espresso with a deep crema and rich taste. Without the whirr of an electric motor, the process of pulling your own coffee with a ROK machine is a silent and gentle pleasure.

Presso Smartshot, £149, rok.coffee

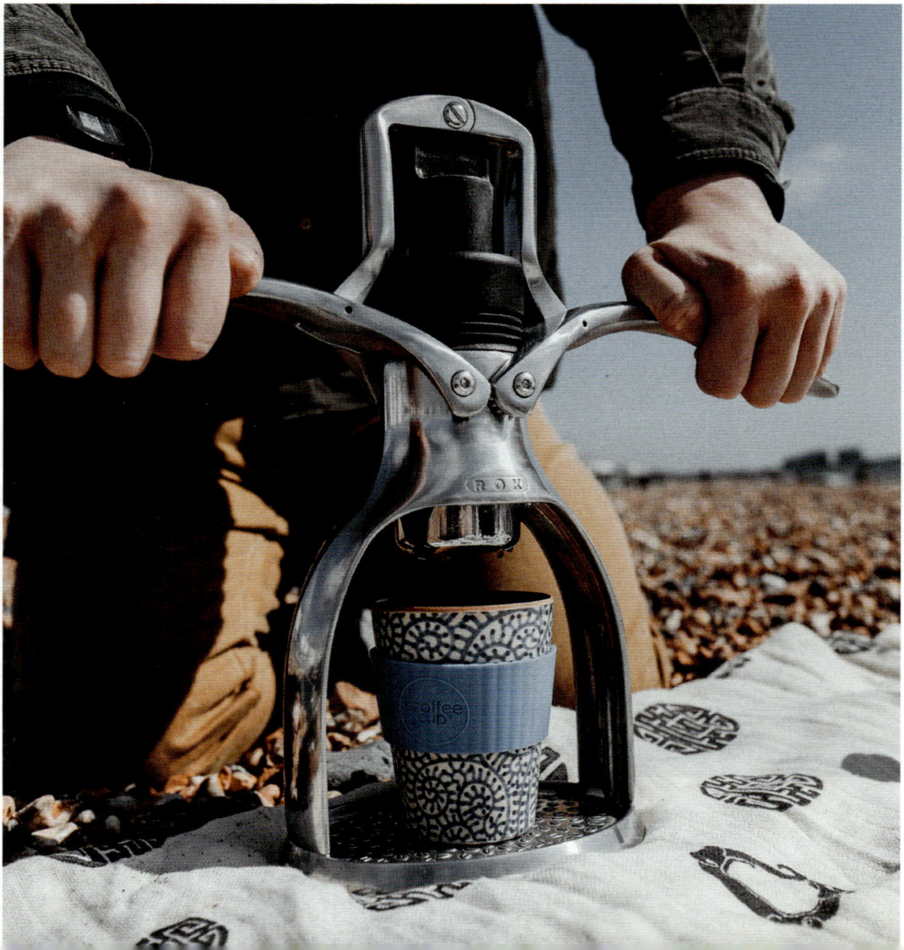

Slow Tech

Day Tripper

Launched in 1968, the Olympus Trip 35 was designed with the holidaymaker in mind. Today's budding David Baileys might find them just as useful, says **Lee Osborne**

ANALOGUE PHOTOGRAPHY continues its renaissance, with lots of people keen to shoot film for the first time. Just recently, a major manufacturer has launched a brand-new 35mm film camera, the Pentax 17, with a range of beginner-friendly features. I hope to review one soon, but at nearly £500, it's not a very affordable venture into the world of film photography.

Thankfully, there are lots of vintage cameras out there that are great for beginners, and can be found at much more affordable prices. Here, I'm going to look at a well-known classic that's simple to use, reliable and capable of great results. They're easy to find, and easy to repair if things go wrong. Welcome to the fun and enjoyment that can be yours with the Olympus Trip 35...

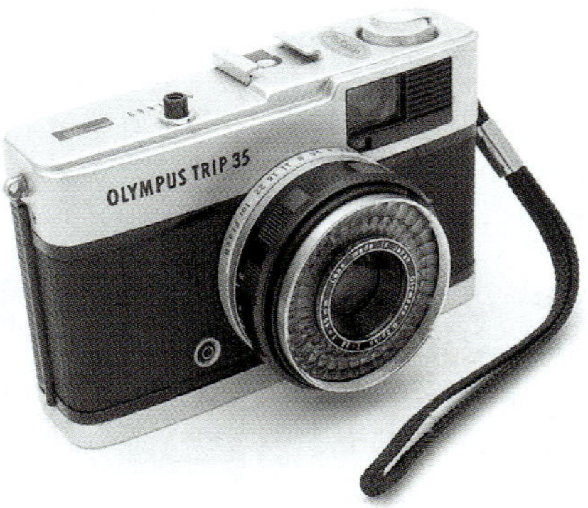

Launched in 1968, a whopping ten million were made until production ceased in 1984. It's a beautiful little camera that's ideal for those who haven't touched film before. If you're a bit intimidated by the whole business, this camera does all the complex stuff for you, and doesn't even need any batteries.

As the name suggests, Olympus had holidaymakers in mind when they designed the Trip. It hit the market when package holidays were booming, enabling many people to travel overseas for the first time. Of course, this led to a strong demand for compact, simple cameras that would produce great holiday snaps without needing lots of technical expertise, and Olympus hit a winning formula with this beautiful little machine. Solidly constructed with a largely metal body, it's compact and easy to handle, with a very high-quality lens. A TV advertising campaign extolling the virtues of these cameras featured David Bailey alongside a very young Phil Daniels (https://youtu.be/gngau9EqLgU).

The killer feature is an ingenious auto-exposure system that uses a light-sensitive selenium cell on the lens barrel. The current generated by the cell automatically selects a shutter speed and aperture for the right exposure every time. Based on largely mechanical components, it's very simple and reliable in operation. If the light levels are too low for a good exposure, a red flag appears in the viewfinder, and you can attach a flashgun if required.

The lens has four focus settings, from individual portrait through to landscape, and manual apertures for use with flash. It's generally all pretty foolproof if you make sure you get the settings right. This includes selecting the film speed when loading the camera. This is a slightly fiddly business at first, but once you've done it a couple of times, you'll find it quick and easy.

I've had an Olympus Trip for a good few years now, and it's my go-to film camera if I'm travelling light. It fits very easily into a small bag or even a coat pocket, and as it doesn't need batteries, you can use it pretty much anywhere.

I find it's best for landscapes, but it's a bit less predictable when using the closer focus settings – I tend to get slightly blurry images at close range. It might just be that I'm rubbish at judging distances, but as the camera selects a smaller aperture in bright light, the focus is a little easier to get right on sunny days. Those are the conditions where this camera really excels, giving sharp, colourful and contrasty images with very few duds.

It's often possible to find Trips at car boot sales and in charity shops, although do be careful as a lot of these can be in poor condition. I've yet to find one that doesn't work at all, but if the light-sensitive cell has been exposed to bright light over long periods, it can degrade and provide less accurate results. If you're after a reliable one for regular use, buy from a reputable second-hand camera dealer, who can provide a well-serviced example that looks immaculate. Expect to pay from about £100 for one of these; a battered one that works, but may be less reliable, will cost quite a lot less. Do make sure you use a lens cap or a case when the camera isn't in use, to make sure the light-sensitive cell stays in good condition.

Be careful about the model, too. There were subsequent ranges of greatly inferior snapshot cameras that bore variations on the Trip name – if in doubt, give imposters a miss.

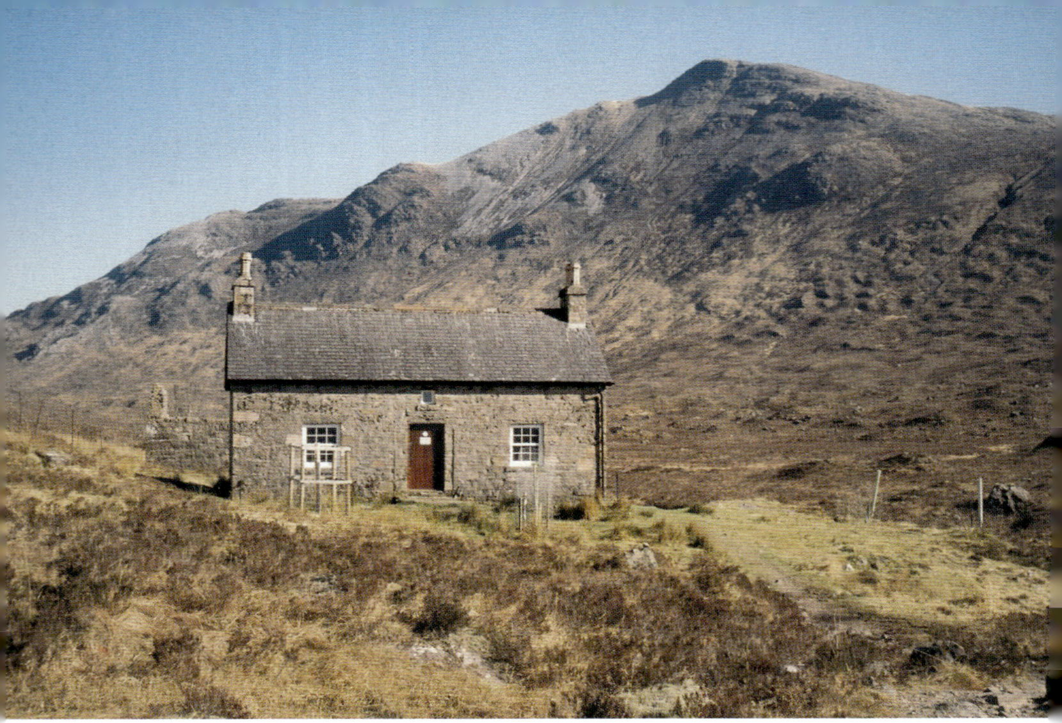

Coire Fionnaraich Bothy (taken with a Trip)

Finnieston Crane and the Hydro, Glasgow (taken with a Trip)

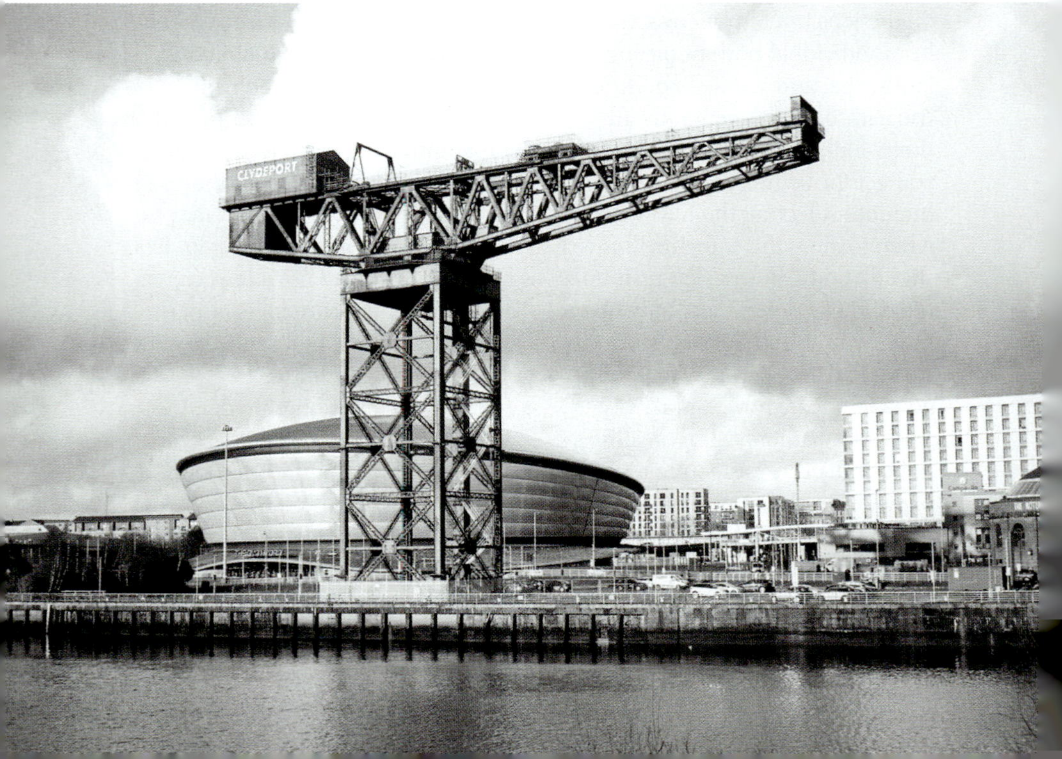

As you can see from my sample shots, this camera is very capable. If you want a lot of creative control over your pictures, you might find it a bit limiting, but for point-and-shoot photography in good light, you really won't go far wrong, and you'll get vibrant, sharp pictures every time. Given the cost of film, that's hugely important.

The camera is equally at home with colour or black-and-white film. I'd suggest using ISO 400 film for best results, as this helps sharpness by allowing faster shutter speeds and smaller apertures. For black-and-white film, I can strongly recommend Ilford XP2, which is widely available and easy to get developed. For colour, Kodak Ultramax or Fuji Superia are good choices.

The camera is a sixties design classic too, with an iconic appearance that has dated very well. You could come up with a wonderful range of period accessories and outfits to go with it! Due to its long production run, there are a few variations. Earlier models had a silver metal shutter button; later models had a black plastic one. There's also a rarer version with black metal parts at top and bottom, instead of silver. The black mock-leather finish on the body can often wear out – if you fancy, it can be replaced in a range of bright colours for a funkier appearance.

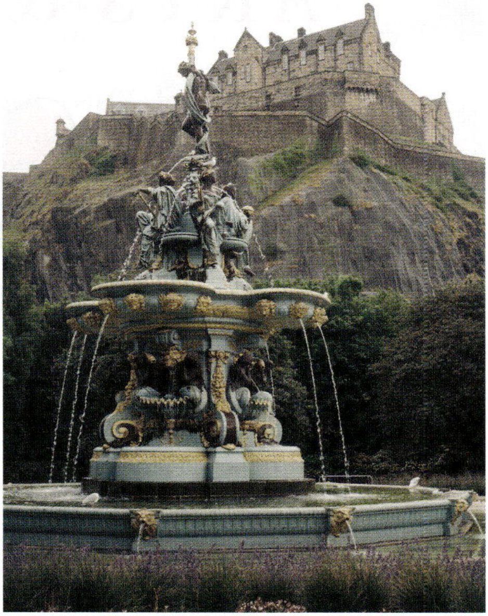

Edinburgh Castle from Princes Street Gardens

After using one of these for a while, you might want to move onto something a bit more sophisticated, but it'll give you a fantastic grounding in the basics of film photography, and they're absolutely delightful cameras to own.

Resources

tripman.co.uk – a site selling serviced and customised Trip 35s with a 12-month guarantee

casualphotophile.com/2016/10/03/olympus-trip-35-camera-review – excellent review with some example shots

fabioardito.com/olympus-trip-35-instruction-manual-with-photos – instructions, tips and tricks

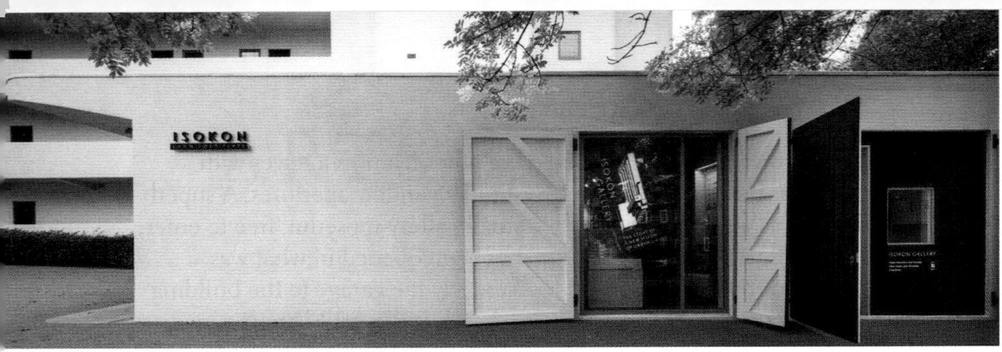

plywood furniture for the tiny, identikit apartments as well as for the bar and restaurant which served the residents and their friends. In its way the Isokon building was a socialist and urbanist riposte to the garden-suburb movement pioneered in places like northern Hampstead and Letchworth. To radical eyes, those half-timbered experiments seemed backward-looking and unashamedly bourgeois in aspiration.

In the event, however, the general tone of life inside the Lawn Road Flats was not thrillingly proletarian (as advertised) but decidedly upper-middle-class. Apartments

Proles apart: life at the Isokon was more upper-middle-class than its radical architecture suggested

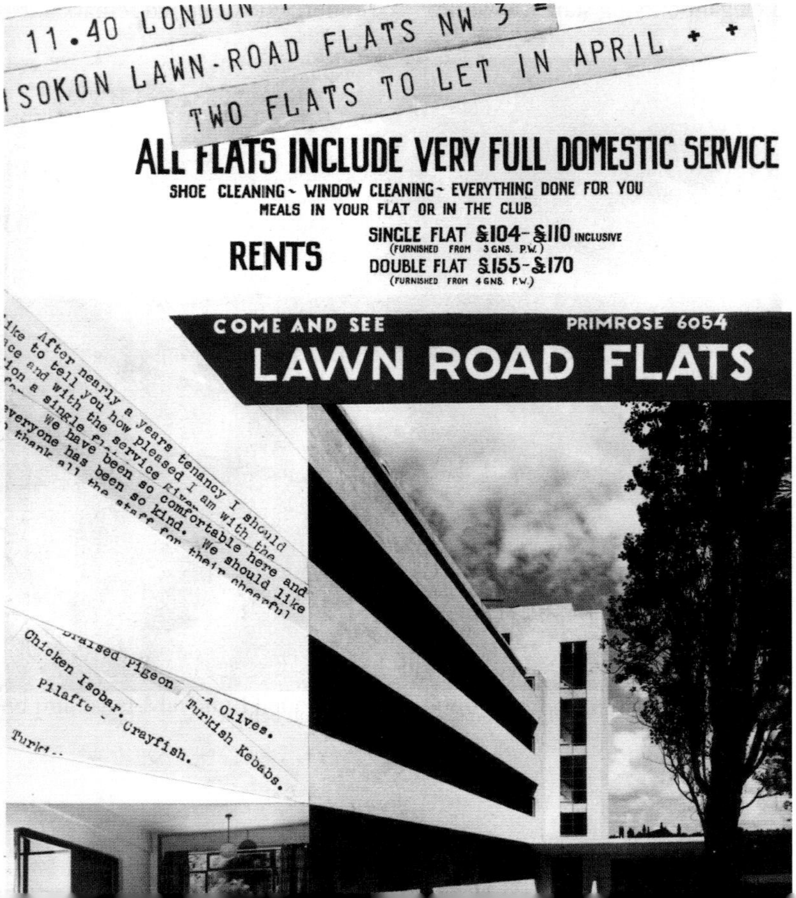

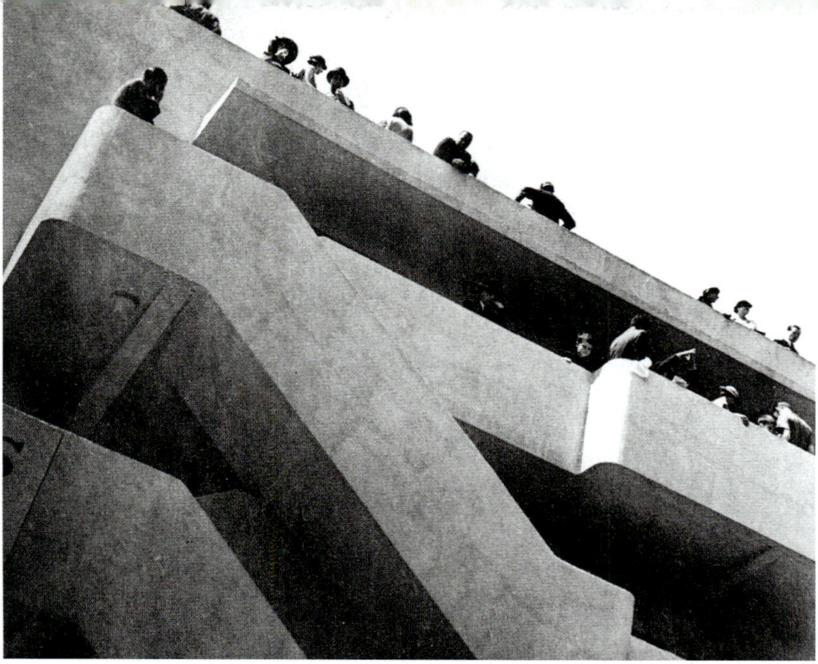

Spy camera: opening day at the flats, captured by photographer and Soviet agent Edith Tudor-Hart

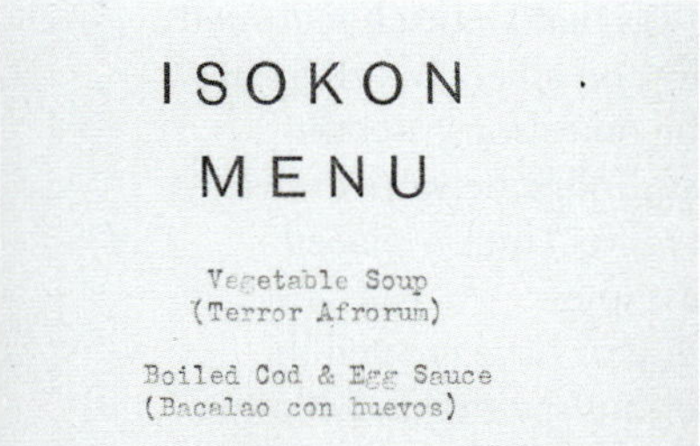

ISOKON

MENU

Vegetable Soup
(Terror Afrorum)

Boiled Cod & Egg Sauce
(Bacalao con huevos)

Stewed Rabbit & Potatoes
(Lapin ivfe; Jamaica Potatoes)

Port Wine Type Jellies
(Just so)

Camp Coffee or none at all
(None at all, of course)

Wines
Rainwater
Chambertin 1923 bottled 1927
Tokay

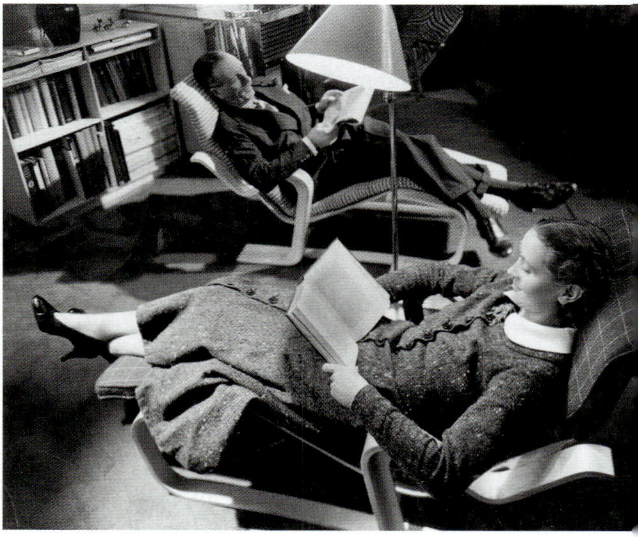

[left] A 1937 menu from the restaurant; [right] Marcel Breuer Long Chairs, designed for the flats and photographed by Philip Harben, also Isokon's chef

were serviced daily by cleaners and a cooked breakfast could be delivered each morning if required. The frankly luxurious Isobar and restaurant was presided over by Philip Harben, one of the first celebrity chefs, who appeared regularly on television clutching his trademark frying pan, his tie tucked under his apron. There were regular themed dinners, some of which were political – such as a week of Republican Spanish food, for example, or a dinner intended as a show of solidarity with the Chinese proletariat. The latter repast consisted of "a plain bowl of rice and a simple vegetable dish flavoured with meat juices".

All kinds of interesting people lived in the flats – mainly journalists, civil servants, artists and writers who might be described as "progressive" in their views. Agatha Christie rented a flat, as did the sculptor Henry Moore and the painter Laszlo Moholy-Nagy (Nagy is pronounced "nigh" –though his new neighbours in Hampstead simply dubbed him "Holy Mahogany").

Moholy-Nagy was a communist, which provides a clue to another identity for the building: it was the epicentre of Soviet spy activity in Britain in the 1930s and forties. Seven known Soviet agents lived in the flats at this time, with some 25 other sub-agents visiting regularly for meetings and rendezvous. Since there were only 32 apartments in the block, this makes for quite a high espionage ratio. The Isokon building, Lawn Road Flats, or simply Isokon – it seems fitting that this building went by several different names, as any good secret agent might.

Arguably the most successful of the Isokon spies was Arnold Deutsch, an Austrian who arrived in Britain in 1934 with his wife, a trained wireless operator, later taking a ground-floor flat in the building. Deutsch's instructions from "the Centre" (Soviet spy control) were "to cultivate young radical high-fliers from leading British universities before they entered the corridors of power". And so it was that Deutsch recruited Kim Philby, on a bench in Regent's Park, going on to construct the whole Cambridge network of five (or was it more?) highly placed communist spies.

Deutsch may have created the most notorious spy ring in Britain, but of far more use to the Russians was the data coming from Klaus Fuchs, a nuclear scientist and committed communist who was being run from the summer of 1942 by Ursula Kuczynski, one of the two women featured in Maryam's novel. Codenamed "Sonya", Ursula came from a veritable dynasty of spies – her father and mother were German communists and she, her two sisters and brother were all active Soviet agents; two of her sisters lived in the Isokon building while the rest of the family lived at 12 Lawn Road, a large Victorian house almost opposite. It was information provided by Fuchs, and duly passed on by Ursula, which enabled the Soviets to keep abreast of Britain's progress on its atomic-bomb programme, codenamed "Tube Alloys".

The other female spy in *Parallel Lives*, Edith Tudor-Hart, also came from a radical background (her very English surname came courtesy of her husband, a doctor and militant communist who went off to the Spanish Civil War). In pre-Nazi times, Edith's father and uncle had run a political bookshop in a working-class district of Vienna, where she drank deep of the writings of not only Marx but Wilhelm Reich, who – adding Freud to Marx – viewed sexual liberation as intrinsic to political activity. Edith's cover as a spy was her career as a photographer – she took the official pictures of the opening of the Isokon building, when the feminist Conservative MP Thelma Cazalet smashed a bottle of champagne against the wall, ocean-liner style. It was Edith who first befriended Philby and introduced him to Deutsch.

The great strength of Maryam's book lies in the way the emotional lives of these spies are brought to the fore, in an atmosphere of fear, pressure and paranoia – but also idealism and a profound sense of purpose. And yet *Parallel Lives* is not a normal novella. There are poetic interludes. It is never clear how much is fact and how much is fiction. The text has a documentary feel, but we never know how much is accurate or true, how much is speculation or even fiction. The story concerns two people who never met, so the focus constantly switches between two lives, running in parallel without touching. There is an intriguing void at the centre, in this space where the two women never met.

At the launch party for the book, I knew no one, however Maryam introduced me to a Swiss national whom I shall call "Bruno". It soon transpired that Bruno and I operate in the same world and have several mutual acquaintances; I was able to gather some useful intelligence – which I am not at liberty to divulge here. I spent most of the evening observing and drinking champagne.

Returning home, I took a circuitous route and doubled back on myself several times. This was not solely due to my champagne intake, but was in fact a carefully honed technique of tradecraft designed to identify and/or throw off anyone who may have been tailing me.

Some weeks later I made contact with an individual in order to gather intelligence related to this article. This led to a meeting at the Lawn Road Flats, one hot and muggy August morning. It was a Saturday – a good day for a rendezvous, since patterns of human behaviour are more randomised at the weekends. I planned my route and timed my journey with care.

On leaving home I took a complex route to the railway station, stopping once or twice to surveill the scene, in case I was being followed. I was also careful to check whether I was being "tailed" by someone who was in fact in front of me. Nothing suspicious. Near the station I abruptly halted to look in at the window of a butcher's shop, using the reflection to check whether any passers-by were acting unusually, or stopping for apparently no reason. All clear.

I made sure I got to the platform moments before "my" train departed, and climbed aboard. But just as it was about to leave, I quickly stepped back onto the platform. I watched the train depart – along with anyone who had been tailing me. They would now be travelling in completely the wrong direction, because I had faked my intentions by initially heading to the wrong platform. Now I doubled back via the station subway and a few minutes later boarded the correct train. I chose the quietest carriage and was able to assess my fellow passengers. A young couple who looked like tourists, a lone male in his late twenties nodding to his earbuds, a folksy middle-aged woman holding a small dog. Any of them could have been observing me; it was simply not possible to guess who. In my peripheral vision I checked to see if any of them stole a glance towards me at any time. If that were to happen, the mission would be aborted immediately and I would go into my exfiltration drill. But nothing.

Two stops later I exited the train and, going in the opposite direction to the exit signs, I changed carriages. No one followed. If they had, it would have been obvious, and a disastrous failure of tradecraft. But training is not what it was, and such mistakes do happen. Yet still there was no obvious tail on me. The mission could continue: I re-boarded the same train.

There was now an opportunity to make a few adjustments to my appearance. I made for the train's toilet cubicle. The small cloth bag I was carrying contained a complete change of clothes, a wig and false moustache – and so I was transformed from a slightly dishevelled middle-aged man wearing t-shirt and Vans, into a long-haired guy in his thirties wearing sports shorts, a singlet, stacked trainers and a baseball cap. The discarded clothes were bundled into the bag and pressed down into the bin between carriages. I consciously changed my posture so that I lounged and nodded as I walked or leaned.

I got to Lawn Road in time for the rendezvous. My instructions were to buy a hardback copy of David Burke's book, *The Lawn Road Flats* (the source of a lot of the information deployed in this article). I asked for the book in the specified manner, hesitating as I did so, as if unsure of the author's name. The USB stick was dropped into the carrier bag along with the book. It contained the images accompanying this article. I hope readers will appreciate the risks taken by myself and others to ensure that these photographs have seen the light of day.

I have to accept that this may not be the end of the story for the Spy Flâneur. It never is, in this line of work. On returning home, there were one or two discrepancies – I can't say what, exactly. My suspicion is that I have been exposed, or betrayed. Whatever happens, I would like it to be known that I understood the risks and believed in the cause.

ART PREVIEW

Flâneur Recommends

Michael Craig-Martin
Until 10 December
The "father" of the YBA scene gets his own tribute, documenting a career that spans painting, sculpture, installation and digi-art.
Royal Academy of Arts,
Burlington House, Piccadilly,
London W1J 0BD

Phyllida Barlow
Until 5 January
Expect giant textural interventions at this tribute to the artist who died last year, having scored a major hit in the British Pavilion at the Venice Biennale.
Hauser & Wirth Somerset,
Durslade Farm, Dropping Lane,
Bruton BA10 0NL

Monet and London: Views of the Thames
Until 19 January
A selection of Monet's extraordinary paintings, many of which he created from near the Savoy Hotel.
The Courtauld, Somerset House,
The Strand, London WC2R 0RN

Van Gogh: Poets and Lovers
Until 19 January
Unashamedly a "greatest hits" show of perhaps the 20th century's most celebrated artist – sunflowers, starry nights and all.
The National Gallery,
Trafalgar Square, London WC2N 5DN

Scent and the Art of the Pre-Raphaelites
Until 26 January
An intriguing premise – how artists such as Burne-Jones and Millais managed to conjure up scent from images alone. (Really?)
The Barber Institute of Fine Arts,
University of Birmingham,
Edgbaston, Birmingham B15 2TS

Electric Dreams: Art and Technology Before the Internet
28 November – 1 June
A trip back to the good old days, when artists had to make their own entertainment…
Tate Modern,
Bankside, London SE1 9TG

Alexander Pope as the "Darth Vader" to Wordsworth's "Luke Skywalker" is a bit of a stretch).

If it reads like a charismatic teacher delivering an undergraduate lecture series, that's because it kind of is (in the final chapter George even talks us through the slides he usually uses). But once you embrace that, then on those terms it's a success, offering up a lively, witty poetry primer. To use Frank O'Hara's verb it's a very charming "trot" through the form.

Buy this for a teenager you know who's doing A-Level English Lit; for the avid reader who has always considered poetry too hard; for yourself instead of that costly creative writing degree. Dai George distils a lifetime's poetic thinking and reading into this warm, accessible book. Like the poet Virgil in Dante's *The Divine Comedy*, he is volunteering to be our guide. I hope many readers take him up on his generous offer.

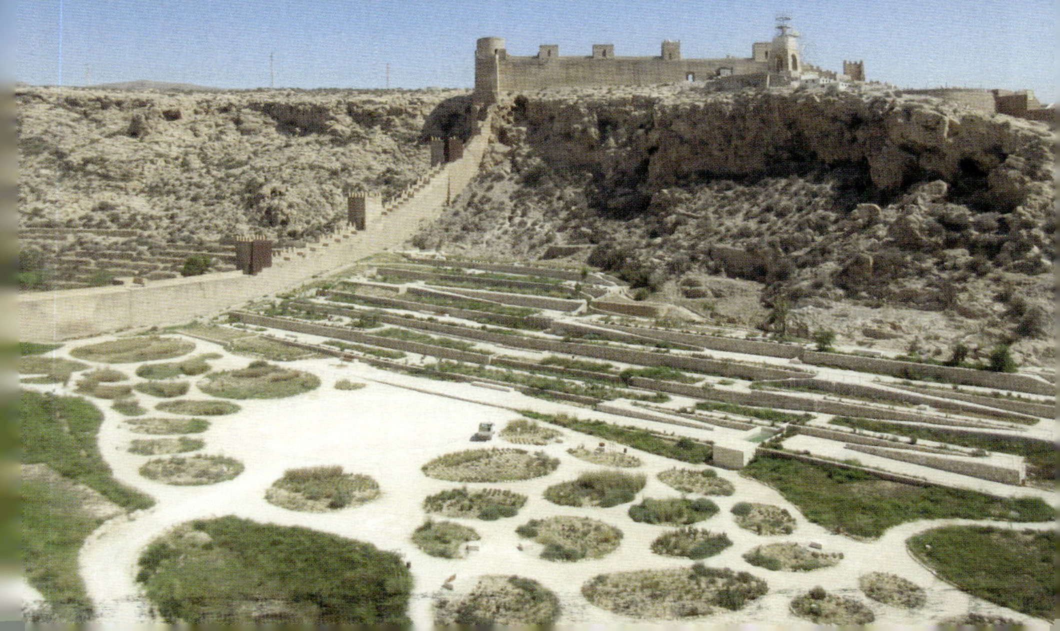

Books: Style & Design

Mind Your Manors

Two books on country homes with a difference, to linger over at a leisurely pace

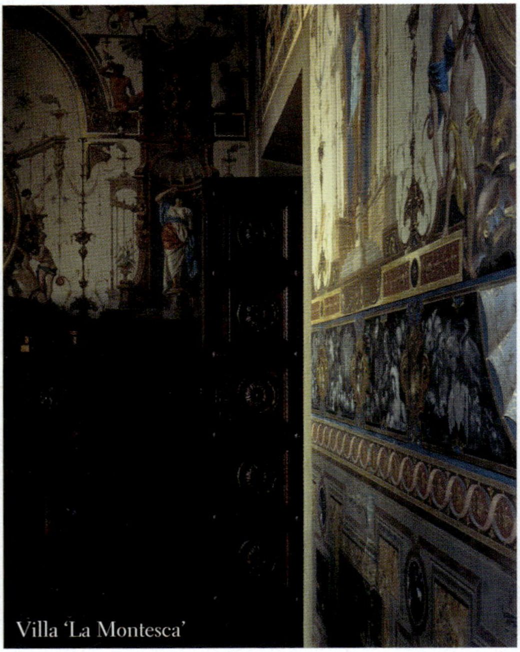
Villa 'La Montesca'

Villa Kérylos

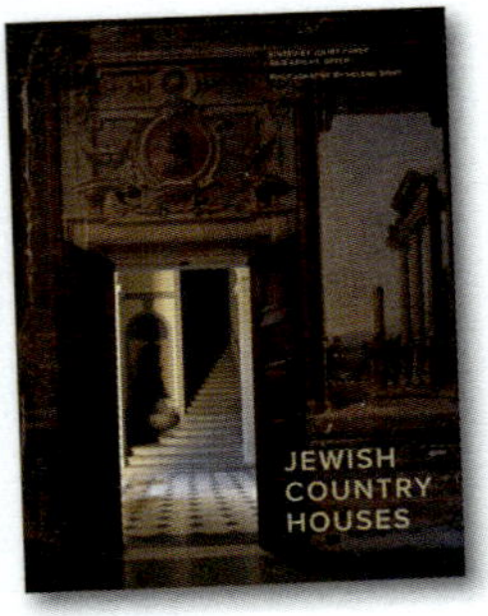

Jewish Country Houses **Juliet Carey** (editor) **Abigail Green** (editor) **Hélène Binet** (photographer) (£45, Profile Editions)

An essential tour of properties owned, built or renewed by Jews in the UK, Europe and America, *Jewish Country Houses* is so much more than a coffee-table book. A highly original approach to country-house history, it combines a scholarly understanding of its subject with beautiful new photographs of their rich interiors, bolstered by historical images. A nuanced story of prejudice, identity and assimilation that's also stunning to look at, this is a book with a head as well as a heart.

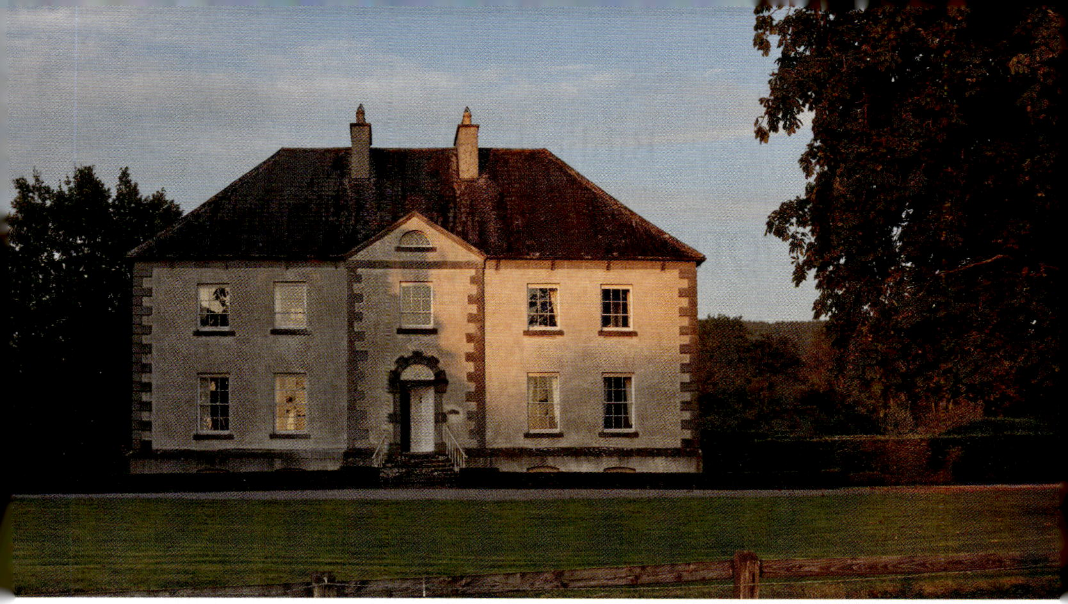

Ballysallagh House

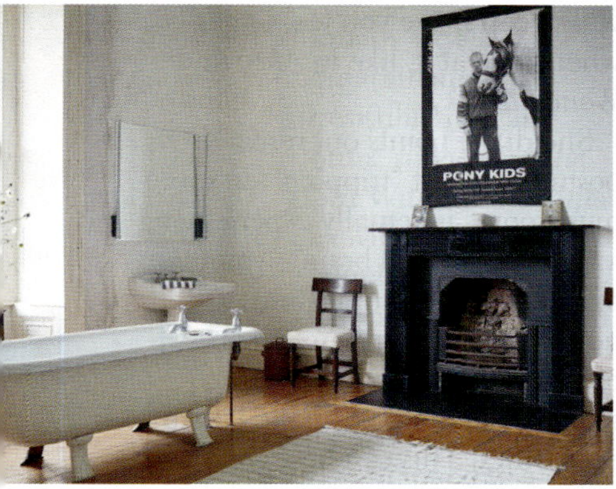

Turbotstown

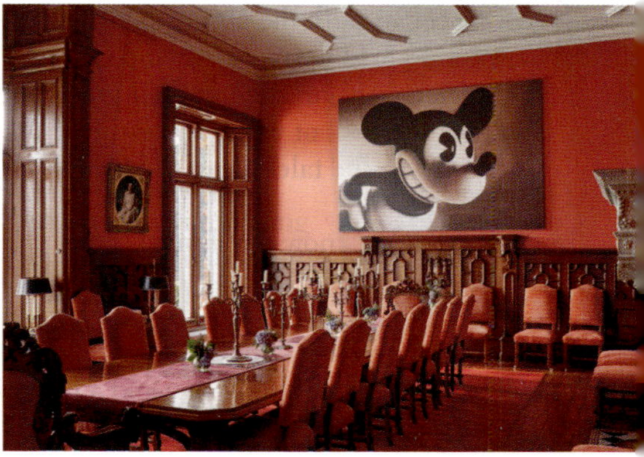

Gurteen

The Irish Country House: A New Vision **Robert O'Byrne** (writer) **Luke White** (photographer) (£50, Rizzoli)

Well-written and beautifully photographed, *The Irish Country House* celebrates some of the country's most characterful houses – not just the usual suspects of well-preserved historic estates, but also exciting new renovations. Each of these extraordinary homes – including a historic hunting lodge, a Gothic fantasy abode, and an ornately refurbished castle – reflects a new vitality in contemporary design. A joy to peruse.

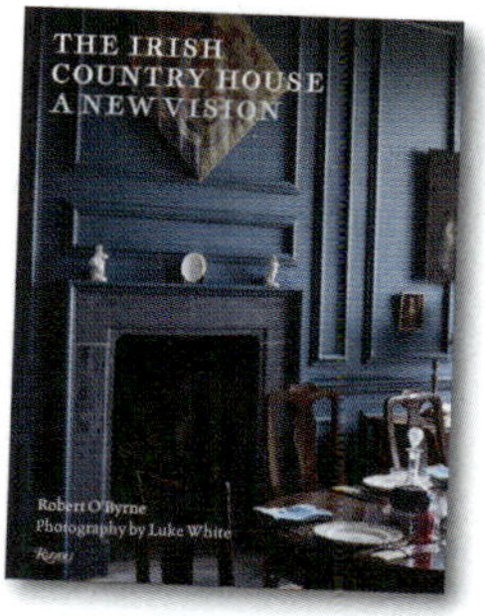

year-old Jaakko Kaunismaa is told he is dying from prolonged exposure to toxins connected with his own mushroom business. This is a book with dark humour and unexpected twists that endears you to the world of Nordic mushrooms.

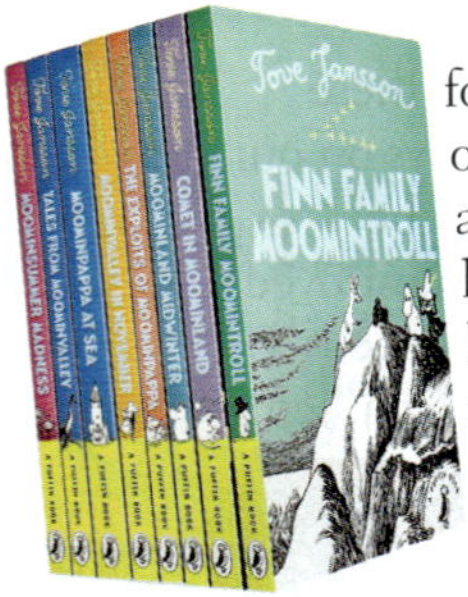

The Finns' reverence for the woodland organisms is infectious, and it's interesting to look at their children's books too, in which mushroom-hunters are frequently portrayed as part of daily life, such as in the Moomin books by Tove Jansson, in which Moominmamma is often drawn with a basket full of *champignons* over one arm.

In *Swimming in the Dark* by Tomasz Jedrowski, anxious Ludwig meets confident Janusz on a summer camp in Poland in the 1980s, and they spend an idyllic time swimming in lakes and picking mushrooms. When the summer ends, they are separated by the reality of life in Warsaw, and their gay love affair is tested to its limits. This is a tale of youth, love and desire. The mushrooms bring them together in a common purpose, and perhaps symbolise the brief but potent strength of their desire.

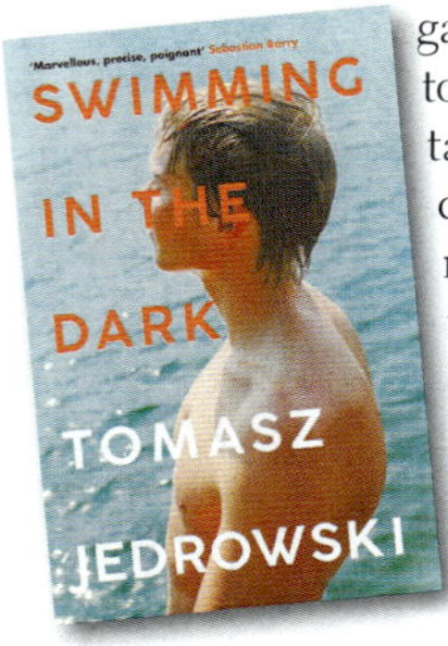

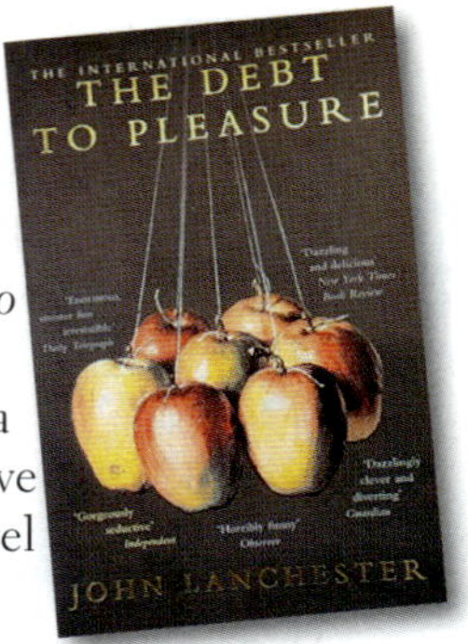

Another great favourite of fungal fiction is *The Debt to Pleasure* by John Lanchester. This is a surprising, ruminative and compelling novel in which the hero is obsessed with cooking all meals to perfection. Recipes are included in the book, which is a mouth-watering journey from London to the south of France, in which narrator Tarquin Winot reveals increasingly shocking facts about his life, leaving the most shocking until the end. Read it for a tour-de-force of surprises and delicious prose – and mushrooms whose uses vary according to the culinary purpose.

All of these books will make you want to seek out and savour fungi of all kinds, but also to treat them with a healthy hesitation. For a final blast of mushroom appreciation and fear, read "Mushrooms" by Sylvia Plath, which sends a shiver down your spine but also fills you with wonder.

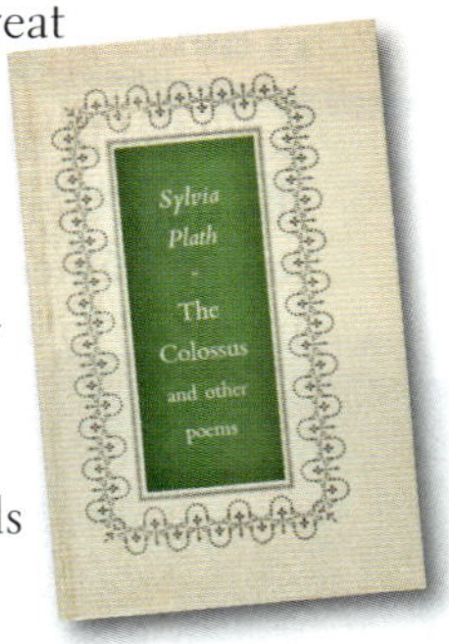

Ella Berthoud is a bibliotherapist. Go to ellaberthoud.com to book a one-to-one bibliotherapy session with her. Find her on Instagram @ellaberthoud

Music

In Memoriam

Stewart Lee *finds lost friends, kosmische dreamers and cowboy drifters through a post-punk Scotch mist*

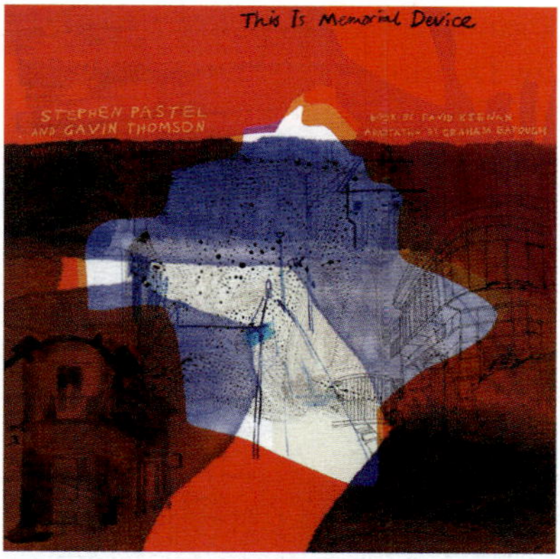

FINISHING DAVID KEENAN'S 2017 novel *This Is Memorial Device* I was bereft, exiled from my friends in the vividly realised eighties Airdrie post-punk massive that I now loved. I approached Graham Eatough's 2022 stage adaptation trepidatiously. How would he render the music of the band Memorial Device, which readers had only heard in our heads? But eventually I saw the brilliant play four times, trying to imprint its disappearing moment onto my mind before it evaporated forever, which I suppose is what Keenan's novel is about. In the end, Glaswegian veterans Stephen Pastel and Gavin Thompson, of The Pastels, delivered an understated soundtrack, some sounds harvested from home recordings of the period, here interwoven with actors' recitations, the music of the era remembered through a haze, without compromising readers' relationship with the work. Oddly the closing track, "The Morning of the Executioners", a pivotal moment in the novel, was just as I had imagined it, an elegiac unwinding of Velvety strums and floating horns, as if a ritual had conjured a music already there but merely awaiting discovery.

I think one of the typically Scottish indie faces that flashed up in *This Is Memorial Device*'s back projections was Alex Taylor, frontwoman of Shop Assistants and The Motorcycle Boy, who shone insouciantly at us from pallet stages in Birmingham and Oxford in the mid-eighties. Taylor passed away, unbeknownst to those who admired her, in 2005. An expanded double CD of Shop Assistants' oeuvre

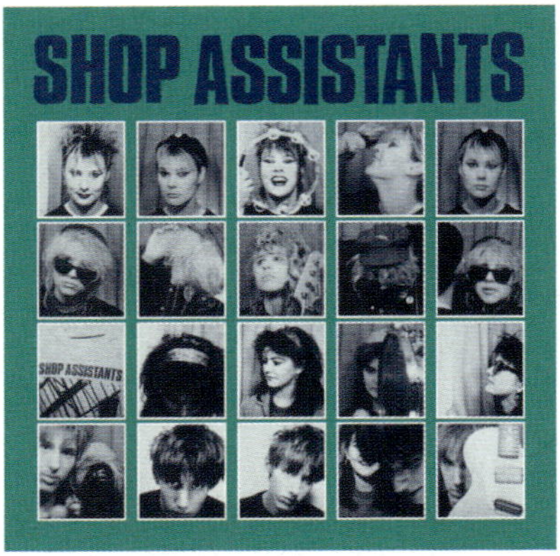

1984–1986, *Will Anything Happen*, memorialises the moment Scottish punks discovered girl-pop melody and gnarly fuzz pedals, with Peel sessions, demos, live tracks and production work from The Red Krayola's Mayo Thompson intact. Only the Jesus and Mary Chain made it through this maelstrom, but Shop Assistants could have been bigger than The Breeders.

The mighty Kosmischer Läufer, aka DDR-era state-approved sound editor Martin Zeichnete, is

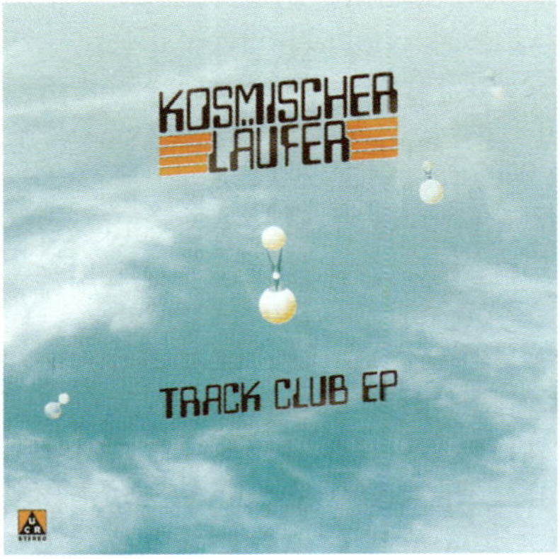

re-exhumed once more as tracks by his own late-seventies teenage band, Die Weißen Taube – as opposed to his inspirational work for the East German Olympic squad – emerges intact from the vaults. *Track Club EP* looks adoringly back to the sleek autobahn hum of Neu! and Harmonia while anticipating the assimilation of the Deutsche kosmische musik's pulsar waves by Joy Division and Ultravox! Yet it also sounds like the work of the kind of modern Scottish hoaxer

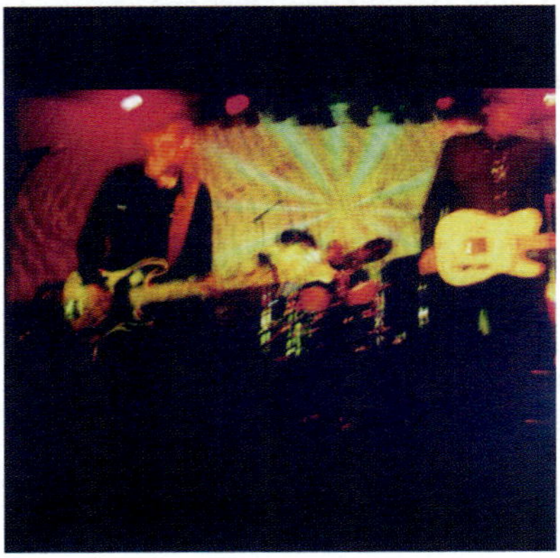

Memorial Device might have welcomed. Either way, I'm now nostalgic for a socialist utopia that never was.

Due to emotional cowardice, I lived the last months of the 20th century on an office sofa in an industrial estate, with three CDs for company, including *Seven Fathoms Down and Falling* by the enduring power-pop classicists The Green Pajamas, and was enamoured in isolation. In 2000, I flew to Seattle

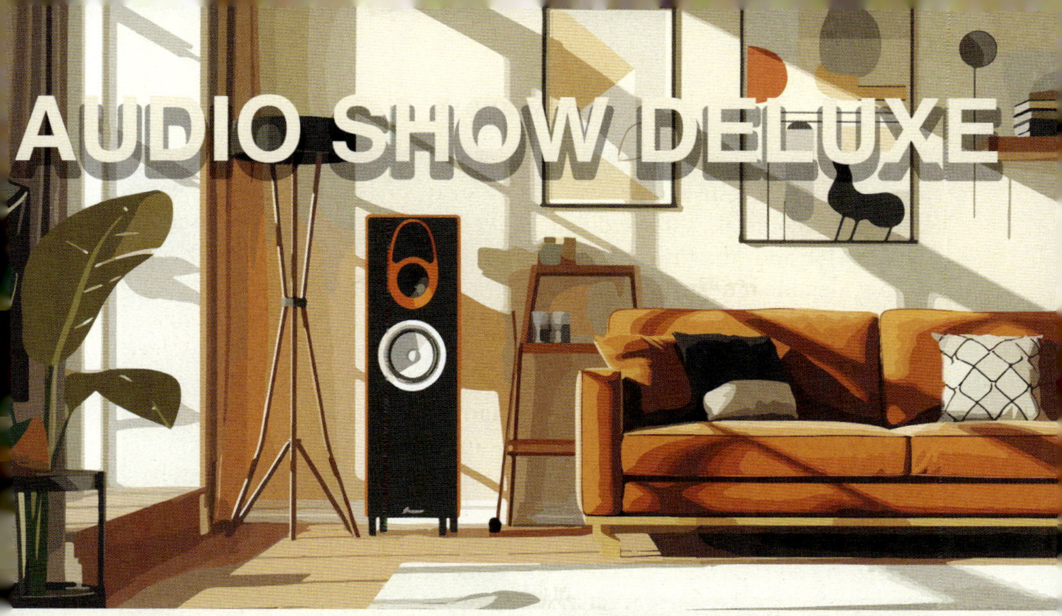
AUDIO SHOW DELUXE

to see them in an era-spanning psychedelic rock festival. Immigration officials, surprised that Country Joe and The Fish were still a thing, detained me for interrogation. *Live at Terrastock 4* documents that very show, an unexpected acid flashback to the cascading Byrdsian arpeggios of "She's Still Bewitching Me", the surging hooks of "Emily Grace", and the sunset comedown of "Autumn Leaves". It's a memorial device.

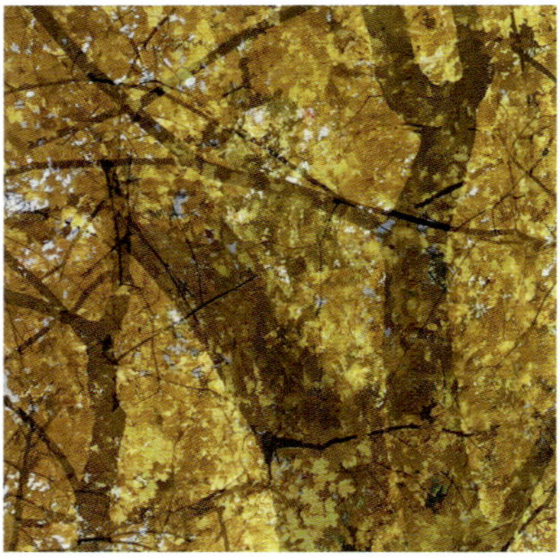

One of those other three CDs was a burn of Tucson's cussed country rock band Giant Sand's imminently career-defining *Chore of Enchantment*, which had been rejected by Virgin, who then invited mainman Howe Gelb to leave the label and buy his masters back. Having canvassed enthusiastic fan opinion, he sold one salvaged track to a lucrative Coke commercial, and repaid us with a quarter century of quirk. In the last six months

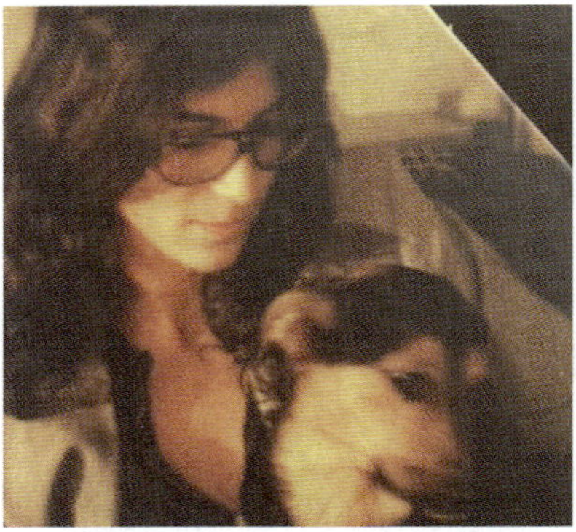

alone, Howe's unearthed an album's worth of stringy new-wave demos from 1977–79 entitled *ZEQE 24.088*, a perpetually nervous sci-fi synth-punk suggesting Devo in the desert and Giant Sand in embryo. He's also recorded *Weathering Some Piano*, 13 sepulchral solos from an adobe room, Thelonius Monk sobering majestically in the corner of a cowboy saloon.

Sid Griffin, Steve Wynn and Chuck Prophet are survivors from the West Coast wing of the same revivalist school that gave us Giant

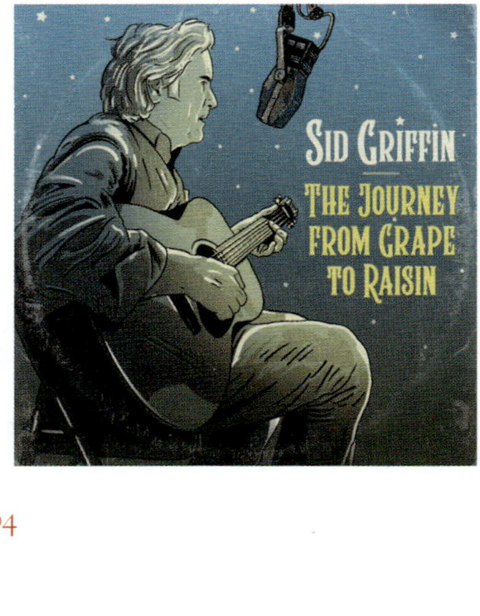

Sand. Griffin's country punk pioneers The Long Ryders are fully revivified, allowing him to deliver, from a Nashville studio, an unashamedly downhome solo album. *The Journey from Grape to Raisin* sounds like something sleek from the same seventies songwriter circle as John Prine and Guy Clark, with banjo-bejewelled vamp on The Velvets' "Femme Fatale" to boot.

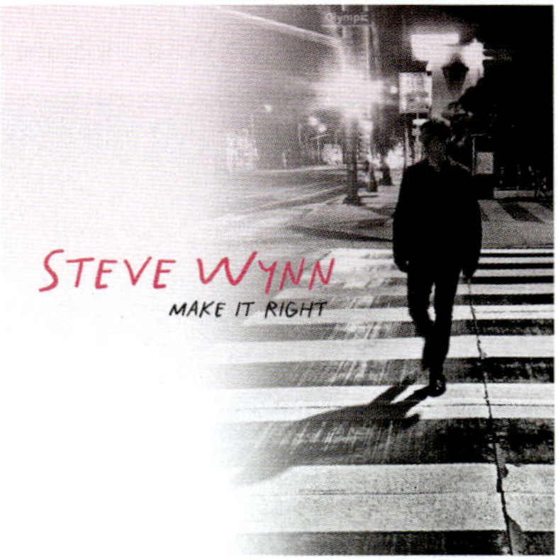

Steve Wynn's retooled LA firestarters Dream Syndicate can deliver the explosives, so his new solo album, *Make It Right*, plays with plangent pedal steel-suffused balladry and cavernous sonic silos of electronically enhanced reflections, as he mines memories triggered by writing his recent autobiography, *I Wouldn't Say It If It Wasn't True*.

When Crazy Horse-inspired roots rockers Green on Red split, guitarist Chuck Prophet turned down a Rolling Stones slot, and their loss was our gain. His latest album, *Wake the Dead*, pairs his parched

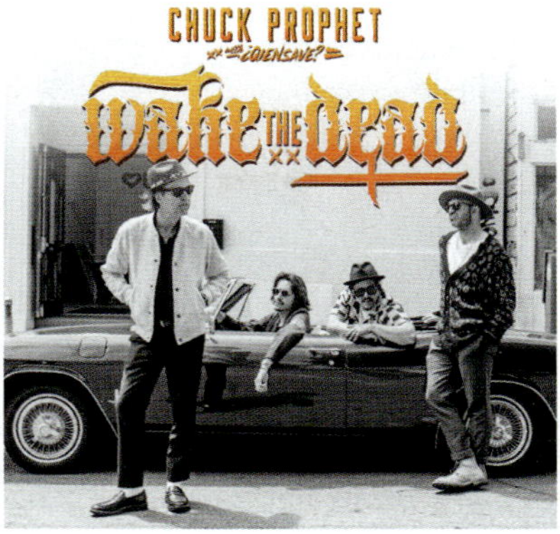

vocals and razorclam Telecaster work with Salinas, California band ¿Qiensave?'s loping cumbia grooves, and finds time to eviscerate the tech-ruination of Prophet's San Franciscan home on "In the Shadows (For Elon)". An elegant reassertion of the value of cross-cultural fertilisation, the album is yet another musical reinvention from Prophet, who always pushes forward creatively while remaining the consummate showman.

The eighties American underground's inelegantly wasted Australian counterparts had a much higher mortality rate, but The Go-Betweens' drummer Lindy Morrison, The Blackeyed Susans' singer Rob Snarski, and The Triffids' pedal steel player Graham Lee, have survived to form the Indian summer success story of SnarskiCircusLindyBand, who turn up like outlaws in Australian country towns and rob record collectors with long memories.

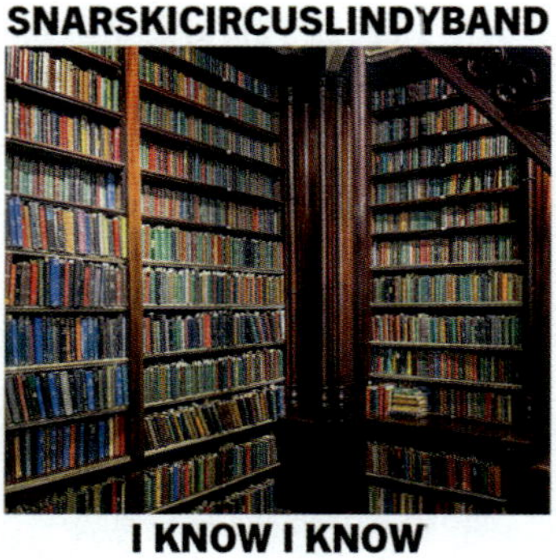

Their second album, *I Know I Know*, opens with the propulsive New York literary-punk push of "I Don't Think I'll Ever Sleep with You Again", goes country-funk on "Parapet", and deploys Lee's plaintive signature sound definitively on the elegiac "My Sweetheart Always Comes Back".

After answering an online ad for a Lindy Morrison-style drummer, the 68-year-old Morrison found herself behind the traps of The Girl with the Replaceable Head, featuring the strident sixties chanteuse vocals and

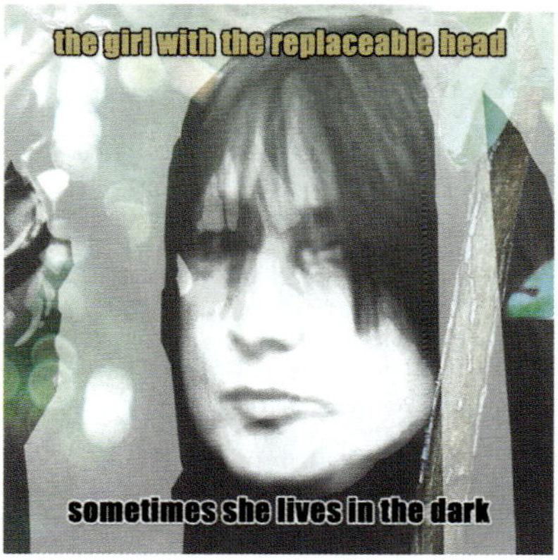

jangling guitars of Sylvia and Dave Hughes respectively, the latter distantly familiar from the brief bright burning of Newcastle's Hurrah! Their fourth album, *Sometimes She Lives in the Dark*, is the kind of classy, thoughtful, immersive, plaintive timeless adult pop people like me tell you they don't make any more.

The bar manager at a book event this summer told me to listen to his band, and so I did. 40 Watt Sun are

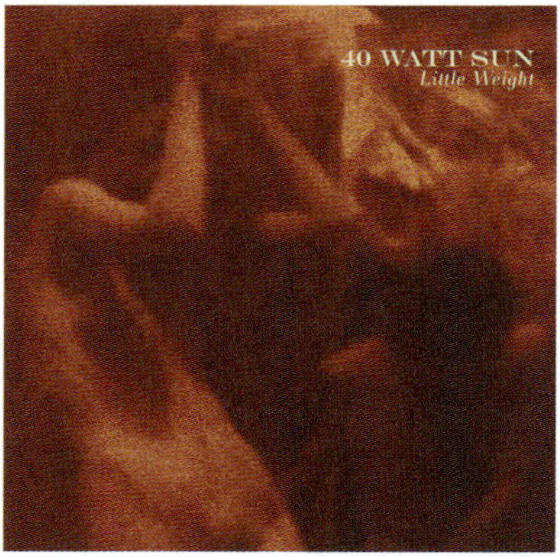

something of a legend in the extreme metal circles I don't understand, but to me Patrick Walker's cracked folksinger voice filters the familiar closing-time country rock consciousness of Marks Eitzel or Kozelek, but through a heavier and more pronouncedly contemplative soundscape, as great cosmic slabs of guitar and drums shift like tectonic plates around mournful memories. *Little Weight* is a keeper, and 40 Watt Sun are my new favourite band, the sudden surge of my enthusiasm connecting me with the boy who would have followed Memorial Device doggedly around a small town 40 years ago. So maybe nothing's changed.

Stephen Pastel & Gavin Thompson *This Is Memorial Device* (Geographic)
Shop Assistants *Will Anything Happen* (Chrysalis)
Kosmischer Läufer *Track Club EP* (Unknown Capability)
The Green Pajamas *Live at Terrastock 4* (Bandcamp)
Howe Gelb *ZEQE 24.088* (Bandcamp)
Howe Gelb *Weathering Some Piano* (AKP)
Sid Griffin *The Journey from Grape to Raisin* (Label 51)
Steve Wynn *Make It Right* (Fire)
Chuck Prophet with ¿Qiensave? *Wake the Dead* (Yep Roc)
SnarskiCircusLindyBand *I Know I Know* (Teardrop)
The Girl with the Replaceable Head *Sometimes She Lives in the Dark* (Bandcamp)
40 Watt Sun *Little Weight* (Fisher's Folly)

Classical Music

White Noise

From Schubert's ice-bitten Hurdy Gurdy Man *to Ramin Djawadi's terrifying* Winter Walkers, **Georgia Mann** *conjures a classical winter concert to chill you to the bone*

'TIS THE SEASON for being annoyed at yourself for forgetting your gloves, for considering purchasing an electric blanket, for really not enjoying the process of scraping thick frost off the windscreen and - in my mother's case – for taking three hot-water bottles to bed with you. Yes, the wintery weather is upon us. As Christina Rossetti so beautifully put it: "Frosty wind made moan, Earth stood hard as iron, Water like a stone".

At this time of year not only do I always feel deeply grateful for the invention of central heating, but I also feel a particular appreciation for the music that so perfectly captures this season of intense beauty, and more than occasional discomfort. So grab a hot toddy and some ski socks – here's my roundup of some of the finest winter music ever written, from the 17th century through to the 21st.

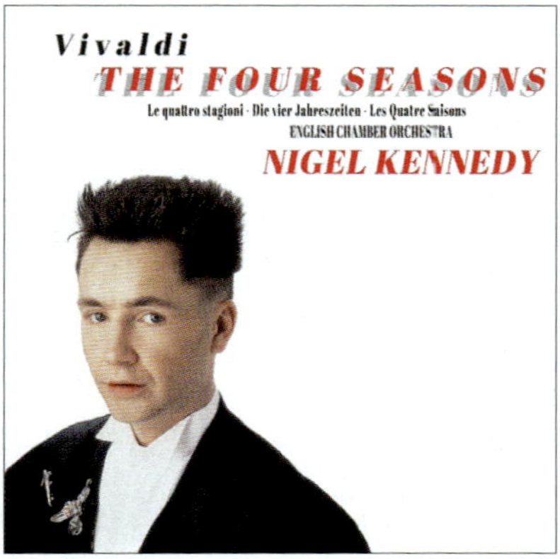

Vivaldi's "Winter" from *The Four Seasons*

All the way back in 1720 the man who came to be known as the Red Priest set about writing a series of violin concertos inspired by the seasons of the year. He accompanied each one with a sonnet on the score, and on this one he wrote:

> "To tremble from cold in the
> icy snow,
> In the harsh breath of a
> horrid wind ...
> Our teeth chattering in the
> extreme cold"

You won't find finer word painting

in music than this; listen to the staccato bursts of the opening chords, then the sprinkling of icy harpsichord on top, perfectly capturing the sound and feel of chattering teeth.

Chill factor: 10/10.

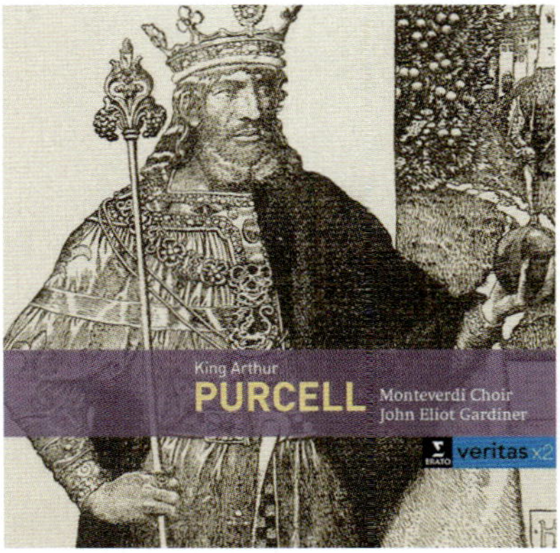

Purcell's "The Cold Song" from *King Arthur*

Like Vivaldi, Henry Purcell dates from the era of big wigs and baroque grandeur. This aria is from his 1691 semi-opera *King Arthur*. John Dryden wrote the libretto and, in it, the spirit of Winter, woken by Cupid from his slumbers, sings:

> "What power art thou,
>   who from below
> Hast made me rise unwillingly
>   and slow
> From beds of everlasting snow?"

And he sings it like a man desperately in need of a defrosting, halting and menacing, as if struggling to catch his breath in the icy air. An ensemble with a liberal dusting of harpsichord sparkle provides a spectral accompaniment. For a sensational modern-day update of this piece, I strongly recommend an album called *Hush* by the singer Nora Fischer and guitarist Marnix Dorrestein. The combination of breathy vocals and shards of electric guitar make for even more sheen than the original.

Chill factor: 8/10.

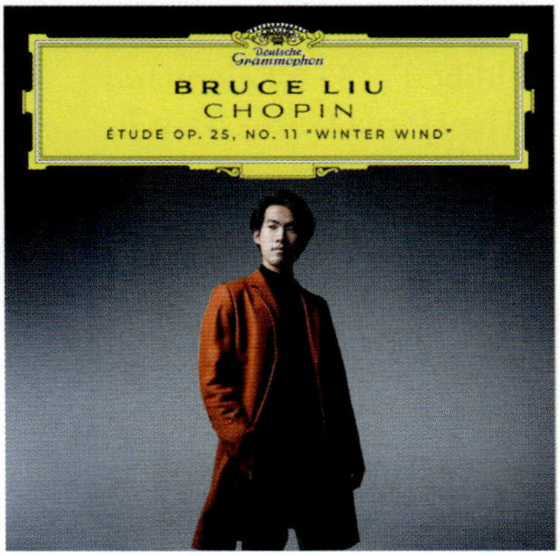

Chopin's "Winter Wind" Prelude

Thanks to its percussive qualities, the piano can do "icy chill" very well. Chopin was the 19th-century Pole who reinvented how the piano could sound. He created this prelude in 1836 and it requires absolute dexterity and stamina to play. A soft opening introduction establishes the melancholy melody, then it breaks into a pianistic blizzard, flurries of tumbling, blindingly white notes subsuming pianist and listener.

Chill factor: 7/10.

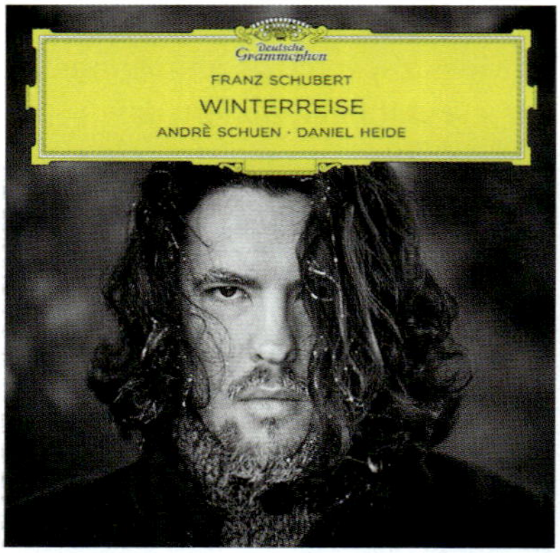

Schubert's "Der Leiermann" ("The Hurdy-Gurdy Man") from *Winterreise*

OK, this isn't the cheeriest of winter soundtracks, but Schubert wasn't out for laughs when he created this particular song cycle, setting 24 poems by Wilhelm Müller; in fact he was dying from syphilis at the time. *Winterreise* tells the story of a betrayed lover who steals away from home at night, broken-hearted, embarking on a winter journey. In this final song of the cycle, our wanderer witnesses a lone street performer, putting on a sad show:

> "There, beyond the village,
> Stands a hurdy-gurdy player;
> With numb fingers
> He plays as best he can"

A painfully pared-back piano accompaniment throughout gives the same feeling of winter bleakness that you get in Thomas Hardy's poem "The Darkling Thrush", with its lines about leaning "upon a coppice gate, When Frost was spectre-grey".

Chill factor: 8/10.

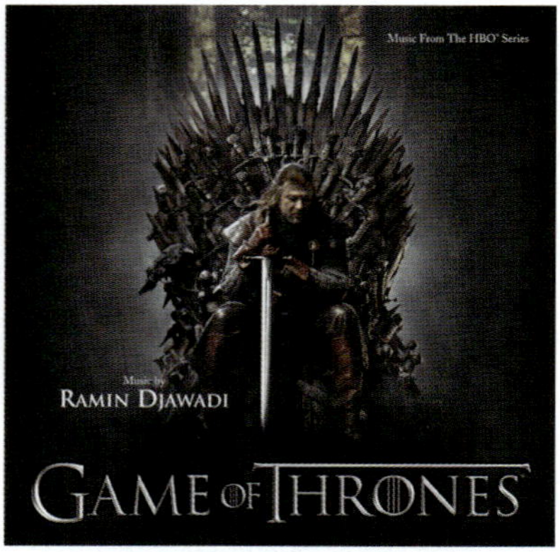

Ramin Djawadi's "Winter Is Coming" from the soundtrack to *Game of Thrones*

Has there ever been a greater representation of winter on screen than *Game of Thrones*, the HBO television adaptation of George R R Martin's book? I think not. In that first episode, rangers of the heavily-cloaked Night Watch scout the forest beyond the Wall, the massive ice barrier to the north, and discover terrifying White Walkers in the snow-covered wastes. The music which accompanies this nightmarescape is what really makes your skin creep, and it's the creation of Ramin Djawadi, a German composer and producer of Iranian heritage. The dark sweeping layers of strings Djawadi uses, coated in ghostly reverb, brilliantly ramp up the threat that winter can represent.

Chill factor: 9/10.

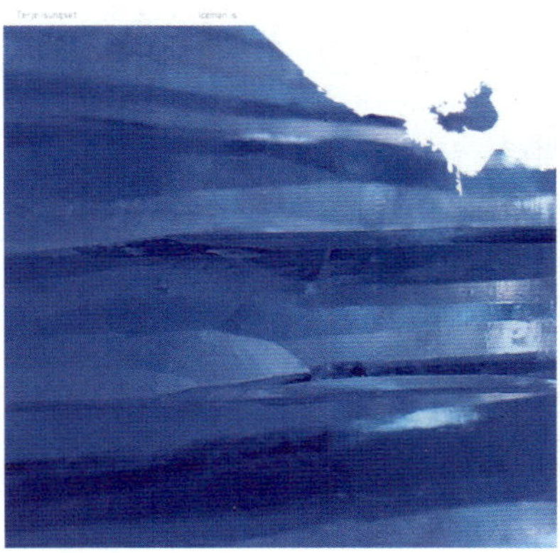

Terje Isungset's "Frozen"

Terje Isungset is a Norwegian percussionist. He's also the world's first "icemusician". In 1999 he was commissioned to perform amid a frozen waterfall, and that sparked his fascination with carving instruments out of ice. Terje has created an ice harp and an ice trumpet, both making their first appearance on record on his 2002 album *Iceman Is*, recorded in an igloo where the temperature outside was 37° below zero. Terje's track "Frozen" uses ice percussion that takes your body temperature down several degrees, all the whites and blues of winter coming gloriously alive. Listen while close to heat.

Chill factor: 10/10.

Scan for Spotify playlist:

IDLE PURSUITS

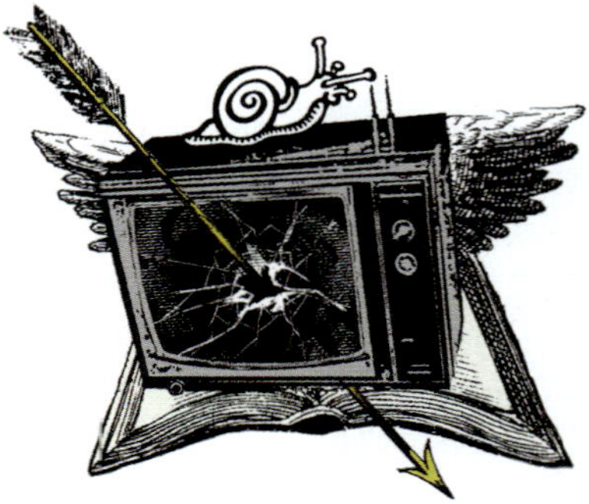

Pilgrimage

Misty Mountain Hop

The brooding border landscape of the Black Mountains has attracted mystics, musicians, poets and knights from time immemorial. **Guy Hayward** *guides you through its misty magic*

THIS PILGRIMAGE meets three very remote valleys that embrace the Welsh-Herefordshire border and the Black Mountains. Local tradition has it that the landscape here was Tolkien's inspiration for Mordor – and when viewed from the spine of the Malvern Hills in his native Midlands, it's easy to see why. It's a wilderness that has long called out to the visionary mystic, and this journey illustrates why. Named the Ewyas, Olchon & Monnow Valleys Way, it's a detour into our ancient past that's only 16 miles

Ty Mawr

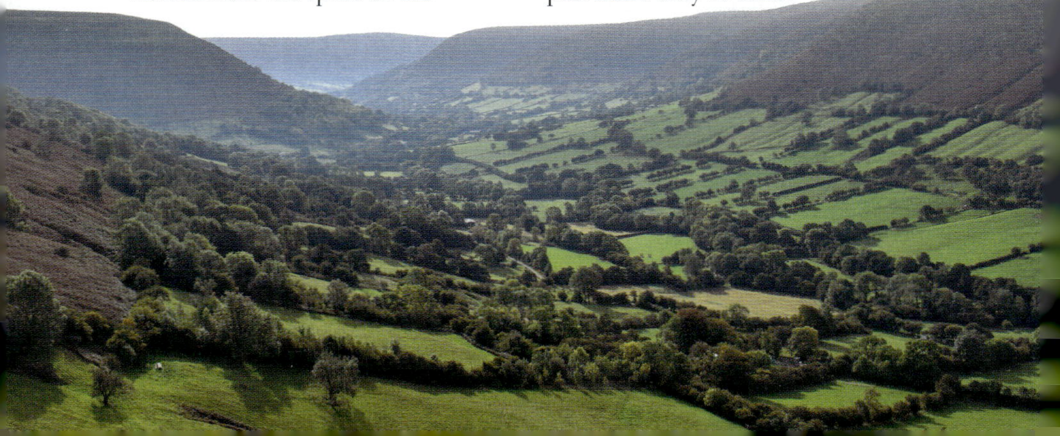

long, and so can be comfortably traversed in two days.

You start in the small village of Partrishow, Powys, at St Issui's well, a sacred structure from at least the sixth century, when a Celtic Christian hermit named Issui founded a cell next to it. The well, said to have healing powers, became a place of pilgrimage after the saint was robbed and murdered by a traveller who asked for shelter but refused to be converted by St Issui to Christianity.

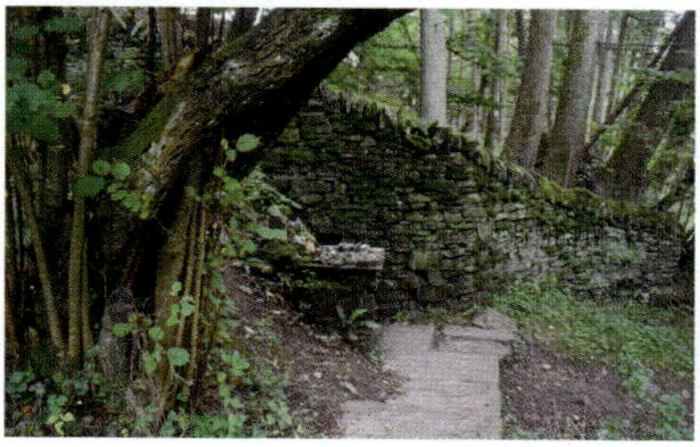

St Issui's well, Partrishow

Just up the hill nearby is the Church of St Issui, which overlooks a beautiful valley and contains several treasures: an astonishingly intricately carved 15th-century wooden screen, arguably one of the finest pieces of medieval art in

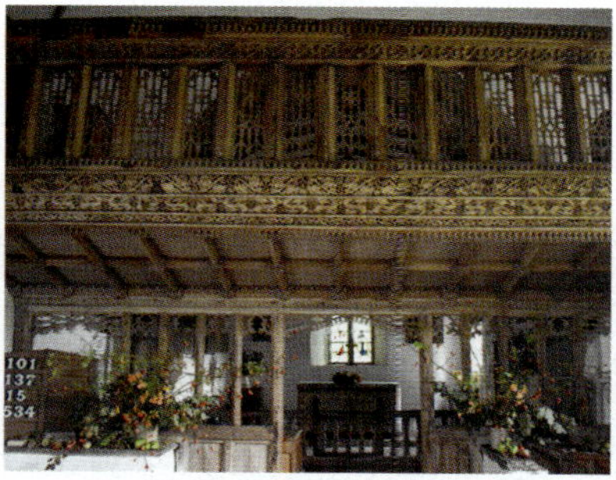

The 15th-century screen

Wales; a wall painting of a "Doom" figure – a skeleton holding a scythe, hourglass and spade; and the "chapel of the grave" of St Issui, a rare example of a saint burial place in Britain.

From here you walk a wiggly path past the Tabernacle Baptist Church and over the moorland ridge of Ty Mawr to a view of the wonderfully wonky Church of St Martin in Cwmyoy, perched on a Shire-like hillside. All the different elements of the church building are at strange angles to one another, due to it being built on a hillside made of unstable debris from an Ice Age landslide, yet its structure remains stable.

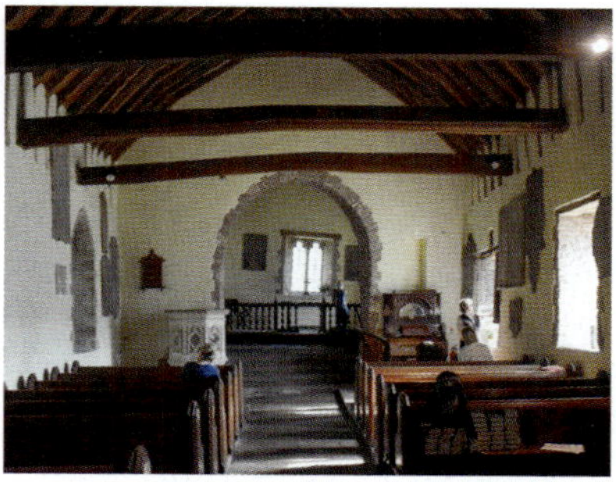

The splendidly lopsided Church of St Martin

Then you descend into the Vale of Ewyas following the River Honddu to the majestic ruins of Llanthony Priory. The 12th-century traveller Gerald of Wales described the priory, nestled amid elegiac mountains, as "truly suited to the monastic life... in a wilderness far removed from the bustle of mankind". Indeed, before the priory

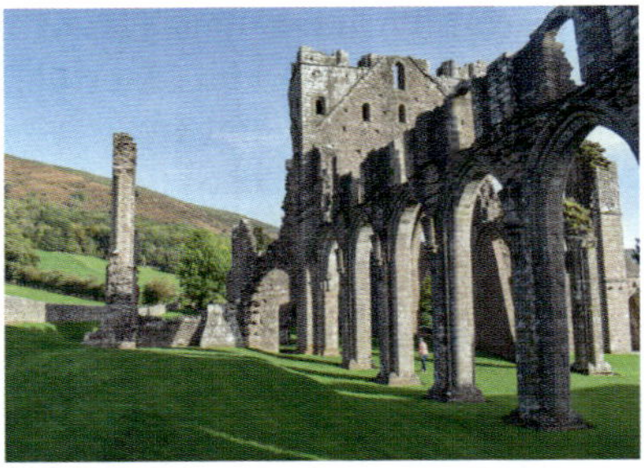

Llanthony Priory

was built, the local Norman knight and landowner William de Lacy was so inspired by the remote tranquillity of this spot that he took the very unusual decision to found a hermitage here, eschewing the life of a soldier for one of religious contemplation – not the done thing in that age.

Llanthony also has a 13th-century two-voice polyphonic carol associated with it. Written in Old English and called "Edi Beo Thu Hevene Quene" ("Blessed Be You, Heavenly Queen"), several versions of it can be found online. Perhaps listen and spend the night here while enjoying the exceptional stargazing potential the area offers.

From Llanthony you can either ascend straight up to the Hay Bluff ridge with panoramic views (a route which shaves off a couple of miles too) or continue along the valley floor towards the hamlet of Capel-y-ffin. Here in a circular churchyard, which often denotes Bronze Age burial sites, you'll find the magical St Mary's Chapel "squatting like a stout grey owl among seven great black yews" as the diarist Francis

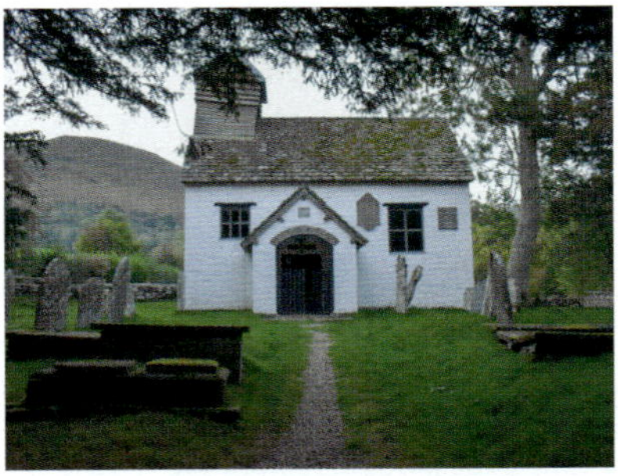

St Mary's, Capel-y-ffin

Kilvert relates. Capel-y-ffin was an ancient place of pilgrimage, its name meaning "chapel at the border", and the chapel itself is one of the smallest in Wales at just 13 by 26 feet. Visitors have included Dorothy and William Wordsworth, Allen Ginsberg, the travel writer Bruce Chatwin, the poet and artist David Jones and Eric Ravilious, who celebrated the chapel in his 1928 painting *Wet Afternoon with*

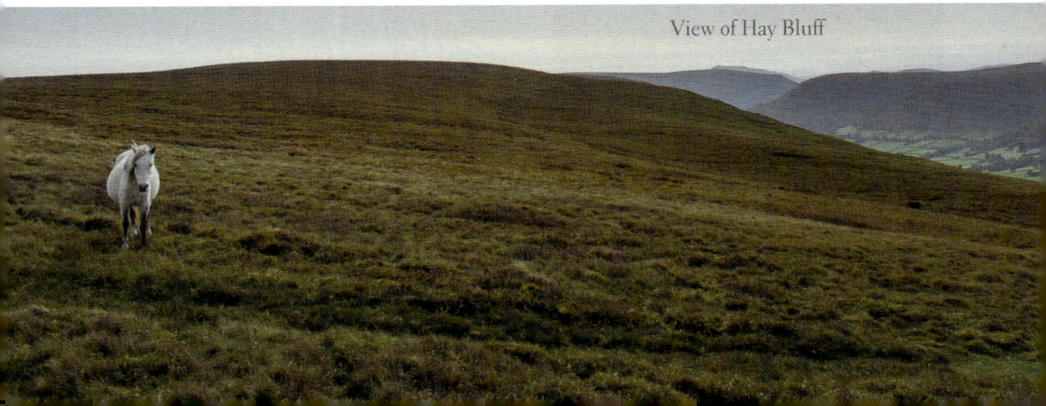

View of Hay Bluff

View of the Church of St Mary, Capel-y-ffin. Also in the 1920s, the artist Eric Gill and his family lived in the former monastery nearby, where he designed the typefaces Perpetua and Gill Sans.

From Capel-y-ffin, you retrace your steps to the bottom of the ascent up Hay Bluff at Nant Vision, where a vision of the Virgin Mary was seen by monks and local farm boys. The way is steep but rewardingly breathtaking. When you reach the top of Hay Bluff, you quickly start descending towards the enchanting Olchon Valley, another Tolkien-esqe feature, to Cae Thomas Well, which is an oasis of

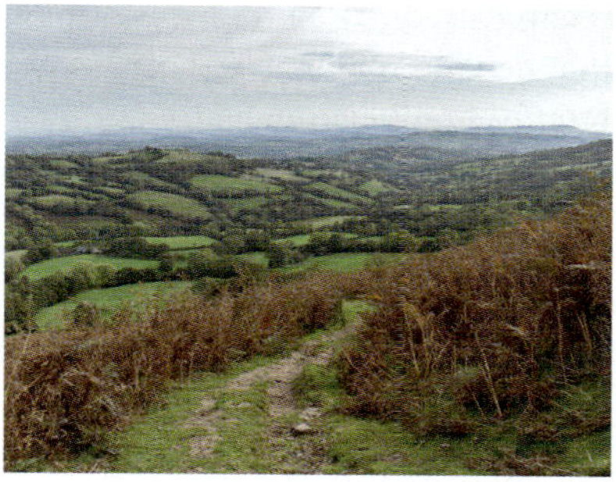

Olchon Valley

crystal and sparkly waters bubbling up from the roots of an old tree, permeated by an angelic energy of peace. Spend good time here before walking along the low ridgeline overlooking the Monnow Valley, where you approach foodie favourite pub the Bull's Head at Craswall, Herefordshire. Then perhaps visit Chapel House Farm to buy some local perry and other delicious produce, and onto St Mary's Church with its own "Sanctuary" yurt tent for low-cost pilgrim accommodation.

After a moment of silence in this working church, take the final stage of this journey, up to Craswall Priory, the oldest, highest and remotest Grandmontine Priory in

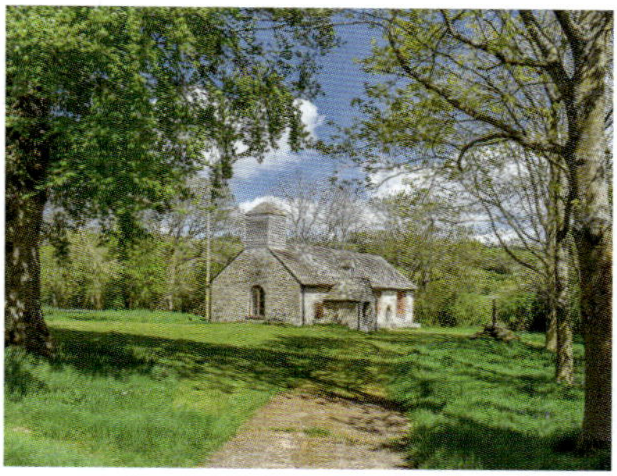

St Mary's Church, Craswall

England. Now in ruins and nestled within a valley delta of springs that form the source of the River Monnow, it must have been an austere place to be a monk, but feels a fitting end to this remote pilgrimage route – one also regularly travelled by *Idler* favourite Rowan Williams.

Dr Guy Hayward is the Director of the British Pilgrimage Trust, which he co-founded in 2014. He has been leading guided pilgrimages since 2016. Guy co-founded the Choral Evensong Trust with Rupert Sheldrake to promote Britain's sacred choral tradition, and is half of comedy singing double act Bounder & Cad.

Gardening

From Tiny Acorns

Britain's woodland is in steep decline. But you can help reverse the damage by building your own micro-nursery. **Graham Burnett** *shows you how*

A 2021 REVIEW BY the Woodland Trust found that only seven per cent of Britain's native woods and trees are in a healthy condition, with wildlife habitat declining along with the UK's ability to tackle extreme weather events caused by the climate crisis.

Growing trees from seed is thus a great way to think globally while acting locally, and potentially one of the most radical forms of direct action anybody can take. You don't need lots of specialist knowledge or much space – at least for the first couple of years – so it's easy to start your own micro tree nursery in the smallest garden, or even just a window box.

The best time to collect tree seeds from local parks and woodlands is during autumn when they're mature and ready to disperse. This is a great activity for children and gets them out into nature, but make sure they don't cause any damage by breaking branches or throwing sticks or stones into the tree. Look for healthy trees, preferably in groups of the same species. Gather seeds that are fully formed and without cracks or blemishes in small paper bags or envelopes, and make sure they're clearly labelled.

Many tree seeds go through a period of dormancy before they will germinate, usually caused either by growth-inhibiting chemicals, or by hard seed coatings that need to soften. These will require stratification, a process which mimics the cold winter temperatures seeds would experience under natural conditions. Cold stratification is necessary for seeds like acorns, beech nuts, and the fruits of the ash, known as "keys". Indoors, you can place the seeds in a plastic bag with moist sand or peat and store them in the fridge for two to four months. Other seeds, like those from Scots pine, benefit from a warm stratification period. Store these seeds at room temperature in moist sand for a few weeks before moving them to cold stratification.

The following guidelines are for a selection of native species to get you started.

Illustration by Graham Burnett

Oak
Collect acorns from September to November. Look for acorns that have fallen to the ground, as these are more likely to be mature, and discard any with holes that indicate insect damage. Plant immediately after collection in pots, about 25mm deep in a soil/peat mixture. Firm down pots, water and place outdoors. Young shoots could emerge as soon as April.

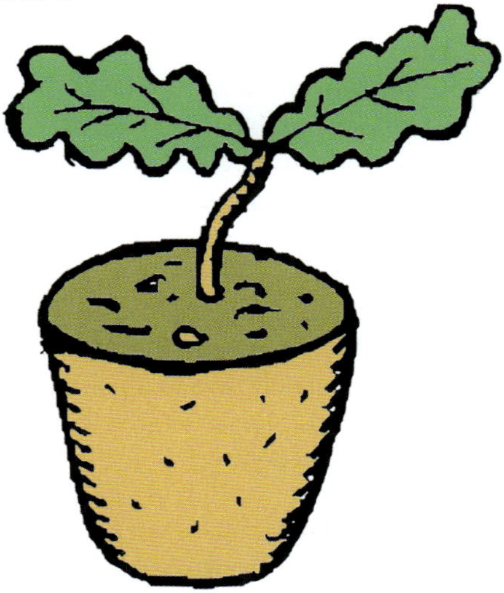

Beech
Gather nuts (or "mast") from the ground beneath the tree in October/November. They should be brown and fully formed, with no signs of insect damage. Break open some specimens to make sure there's something inside the nut. Sow immediately into pots outdoors, although special care should be taken to protect emerging beech seedlings from frost.

Silver Birch
A pioneer species that will grow readily and quickly on poor soils and in exposed positions, providing shelter for more demanding species such as oak. Birch seeds are very small and hidden in the catkins which ripen from September to October. Place an envelope over the ripe catkins and tap lightly to dislodge the seed. Sow immediately in a sandy peat-free compost mixture in trays by sprinkling them over the surface. The trays should then be watered and covered with cling-film. Germination should occur within four weeks, although germination rates can be erratic and vary from year to year.

Rowan
Collect fruit from July to September. Store in a polythene bag until the fruit is slightly rotten. Clean off the flesh in water, with the seeds that sink being more likely to be viable. Sow seeds in trays in a peat compost. Any seeds not germinating the following spring can remain dormant for up to two and a half years, so are probably not worth the bother.

Hawthorne
Berries should be collected from October to November although only about five per cent of seeds collected will germinate that season.

Ash
Either collect the keys green in August for immediate sowing or when ripe during October-November for stratification.

Crab Apples
Collect the ripe apples in autumn. Extract the pips in the winter and sow immediately, five to a pot, in seed compost. Leave to grow for a year before repotting.

Growing Tips
Tree seeds can be planted in large plastic lemonade bottles or fruit juice tetra cartons with the tops cut off and drainage holes made in the bottom, or recycled margarine tubs, again with drainage holes in the bottom, and will grow in any decent seed compost. Some species, like birch, will need some sand added to the mix.

Place in a sheltered spot outdoors and keep moist by watering regularly to ensure proper germination. Never allow the compost to dry out while the young seedlings are getting established, watering at least daily during hot, dry weather. But avoid overwatering as this can lead to root rot.

Growing on
When seedlings are large enough to handle – usually after one growing season – they can be transplanted into larger pots or directly into the ground in nursery beds where they can grow on. Be careful not to damage the roots during this process.

After one or two more years your young trees will be ready for planting out in their permanent location. Choose a suitable site with the right soil conditions, light, and space for the tree to grow to its full size. Dig a hole twice the width of the root ball and slightly deeper than the pot it was grown in. Loosen the soil at the bottom to help roots establish. Place the tree in the hole, ensuring the root collar (where the roots meet the stem) is level with the soil surface. Backfill with soil, firming it gently around the roots. Water thoroughly after planting and apply a mulch of organic material around the base to retain moisture and suppress weeds.

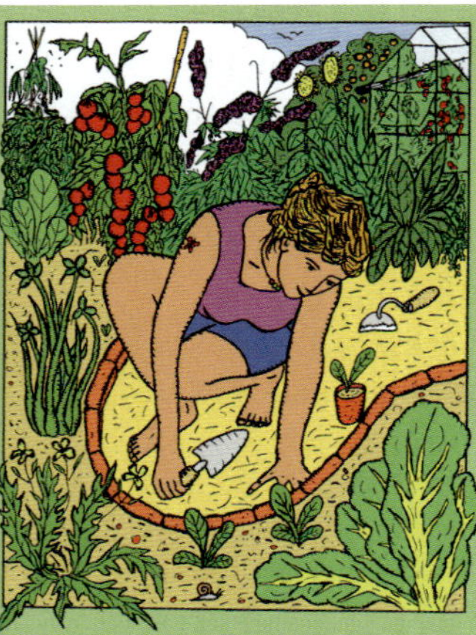

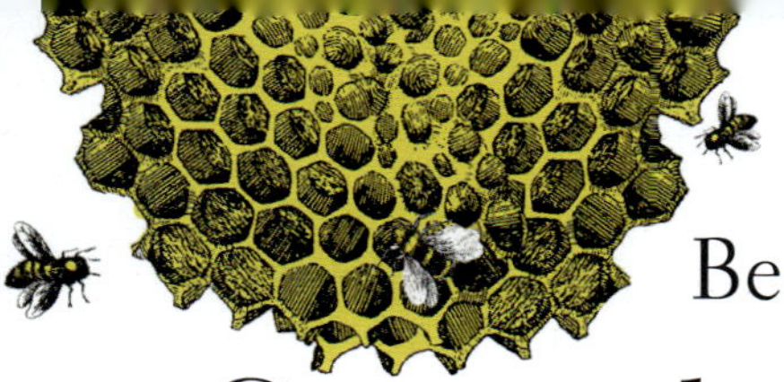

Beekeeping

Gunpowder, Pollen and Plot

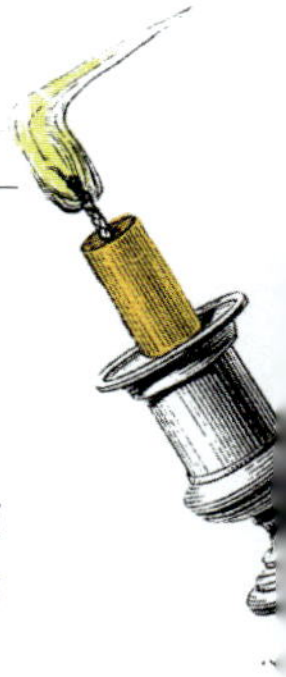

What do fireworks and honeybees have in common? Quite a lot, explains **Bill Anderson**

"REMEMBER, REMEMBER the fifth of November, gunpowder, treason and plot." Thirty-six barrels of gunpowder hidden in the basement vaults of the House of Lords were primed to blow the place off the face of the earth – timed to kill King James as he presided over the State Opening of Parliament in 1605.

We've been remembering the exact date this audacious plot was foiled for over 400 years, with effigies of Guy Fawkes, the plotter arrested just before he could light the fatal fuse, still burnt atop bonfires today.

As a terrorist and member of a persecuted religious minority, Fawkes was given an all too familiar send-off: tortured and executed by a Protestant government, which then presumably repurposed those handy 36 barrels in the increased persecution of Catholics that followed the failed coup.

But at almost exactly the same time in Japan, the art of turning the explosive power of gunpowder into something very creative, and very beautiful, was born. Named *hanabi* – literally "flower fire" – we know it as fireworks.

And today, gunpowder is used annually to celebrate the arrival of the New Year in a dazzling display of "fire flowers" over the river Thames (outside, rather than underneath, the Houses of Parliament). One hundred thousand people gather in the winter darkness to be thrilled by the beautiful illuminations democratically available to all by just looking skywards – and millions more watch live on television.

Like gunpowder, nuclear energy can be used in both creative and destructive ways, having the ability to provide our homes with electricity – or to utterly destroy them.

But there's one source of highly concentrated energy that has never been used for damaging purposes: honey.

Honeybees have evolved a highly sophisticated system of democracy. In it, not only is debate crucial, honest and rigorous, with voting always transparent, but the resulting democratic decisions are more than 90% in alignment with what we would humbly perceive as being in their best interests. (For more on this subject, read *Honeybee Democracy* by Thomas D Seeley, available from hive.co.uk.)

As the flowers of fire bloom over the crowds on the chilly banks of the Thames each New Year's Eve, inside hives all over the country thousands of honeybees are clustered, sweetly nourishing and gently heating themselves with honey they have previously collectively – laboriously gathered from flowers lit by warm summer sunshine.

We can smell and taste the difference between honey gathered from particular flowers: lavender, chestnut, acacia and heather to name but a few. Bees not only have infinitely more sensitive senses of smell and taste than us, but they had to fly to the individual flowers to collect the nectar they distilled down to the honey. Smell and taste are such powerful triggers of memory for us, it begs the question – do bees remember the flowers the honey came from when they eat it? Within the profound darkness of the hive, does the taste of the honey from a particular flower trigger the bees' synapses into generating in their minds' eyes flashes of its dazzling, radiant blooms?

This bonfire night, scan this QR code below and savour a spoonful of your favourite honey while watching and listening to the one minute video it links to. See what you think …

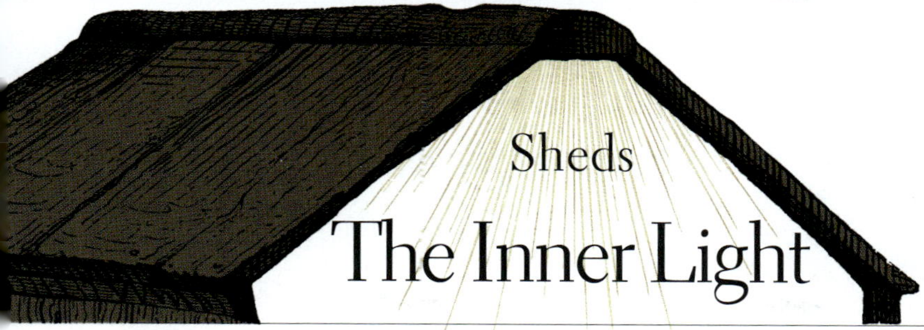

Sheds

The Inner Light

When it comes to beauty – with sheds as with people – it's what's on the inside that counts. **Alex Johnson** *looks at four spaces whose individuality shines once you step inside . . .*

LET'S BE HONEST, many garden buildings look pretty similar from the outside. Of course you can bespoke them up to an extent, but mostly you're looking at a fairly standard cuboid. When it comes to the inside, however, the world is your oyster.

How you decorate the interior is up to you – and I'd strongly recommend two books by Sally Coulthard, *Shed Chic* and *Shed Décor,* which both offer marvellous inspiration as well as listings information for where to source the items showcased – but one possibility is simply to bring the greenery indoors, perhaps painting it green and bringing the vegetation inside with colourful plant pots and flowers. I've also seen nice examples of garden offices that have fairly straightforward traditional office furniture, but are then finished off with garden benches, patio chairs and even hammocks.

Julian Wormald's shepherd's hut-style haven in Carmarthenshire fits into this category. Looking out onto his wildflower hay meadow, it's a peaceful and relaxing off-grid build (a solar battery powers some tasteful LED lights) with a big open window allowing spectacular views. You can also enjoy Julian's pride and joy since he opens it up for charity as part of the National Garden Scheme.

Inside, it's painted a soothing light blue, with Julian's photos discreetly displayed along the walls, and furnished with a simple table, and a couple of chairs and cushions, finished off with a Green Man head on the far wall. It has a lovely

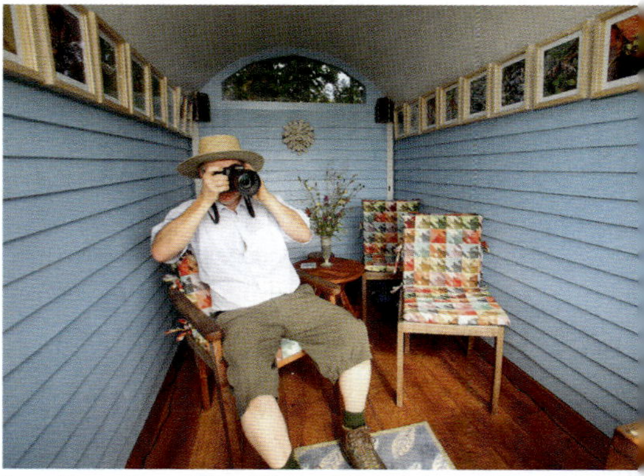

Something blue: Julian Wormald in his azure oasis

photos: Cuprinol Shed of the Year

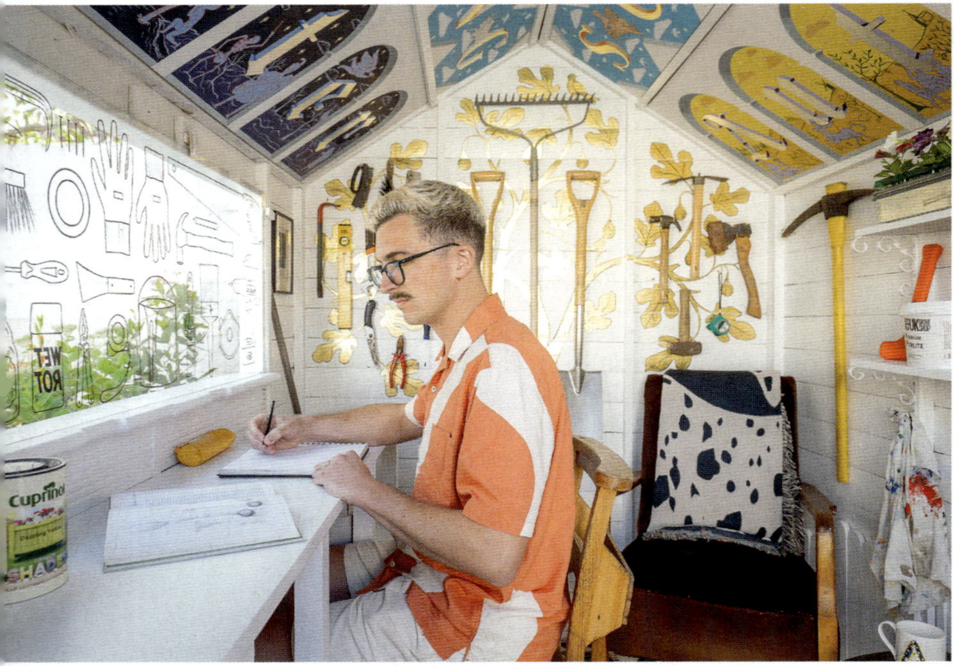

Frankly fantastic: Archie Proudfoot's Frankenshed

summery atmosphere, though carefully built-in insulation means it remains at a nice temperature even when it's a little nippier outdoors.

Meanwhile, Frankenshed, which scooped the Cuprinol Shed of the Year competition in 2023, has a similarly light and airy vibe. Built and owned by London-based artist and sign-painter Archie Proudfoot, it was originally a basic 8ft x 4ft timber shed that had become rather dilapidated and was rebuilt using recycled timber, including old fence posts and an unwanted bed frame. Whitewashed inside, the shed now boasts windows featuring Archie's own reverse-gilding designs of his best-loved tools. One wall has a 23-carat gold leaf Tree of Life, with all his tools "hanging" from its branches, while the ceiling is painted with signs of the zodiac and celebrations of the four seasons.

"What started as a bored attempt to save a rotten shed turned into the most elaborate and enjoyable piece of artwork I've ever created," says Archie. "The Frankenshed is now a beautiful place to escape and enjoy an afternoon sketching, writing, tinkering or potting plants for the garden."

Founder and Head Judge of the competition, Andrew Wilcox, says:

photos: Cuprinol Shed of the Year

"The Frankenshed is unlike anything Iv'e seen before in the decades of running this competition. Archie's artistic flair takes centre stage, but the way he transformed his sorry shed into something so elegant has to be seen to be believed."

The key to both these designs is that they reflect the idea of the shed being a "me space", somewhere that's very personal to the owner's individual interests. A particularly good example is The Yawning Portal, a shed owned by Wayne Haskett from Staffordshire, which he uses as a room for his role-playing gaming. Reminiscent of medieval England, there are plenty of ale flagons, skulls, and weaponry on show to give it a genuinely unique feel.

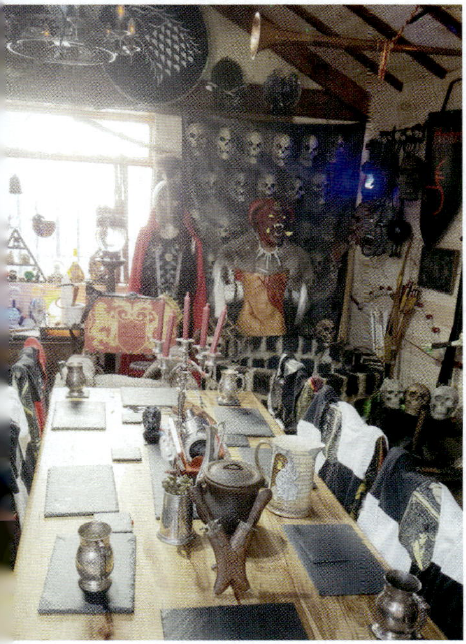

Getting medieval: The Yawning Portal

Louise Mayoh in Devon has gone rather less far back in time for what she calls her Retro Retreat. Outside, there's a large deck area with seating, while the shed exterior has been spruced up with Cuprinol Sweet Sundae and Muted Clay paint shades. Inside, it's a

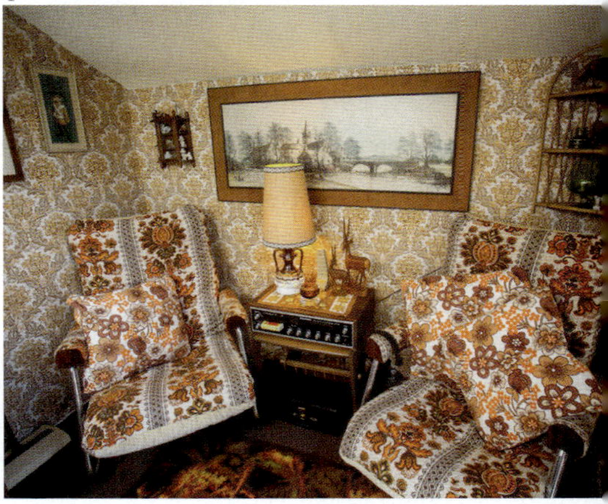

The kitsch is back: Louise Mayoh's Retro Retreat

spectacular celebration of a 1970s sitting room, built by her boyfriend from two creaking sheds which otherwise would have gone to the local dump. It boasts quite a busy pattern on the wallpaper and chair fabrics. Features include a bar, drinks trolley, vintage wireless, and an old gas fire.

Alex Johnson runs Shedworking (shedworking.co.uk). The co-author of the Haynes Shed Manual, *his latest book is* Studios of Their Own, *published by Quarto.*

Travel

My Week Without WiFi

Is it possible to enjoy a holiday in a secluded beauty spot without WiFi access? **Kate Morris** *took her husband and friends on a trip back in time to find out*

I DEVOURED Enid Blyton's *Malory Towers* books as a young girl, gripped by the lashings of ginger beer, potty pranks and secret midnight feasts that took place at a jolly boarding school just after the Second World War. So when my husband and I arrived at the Hartland Abbey estate in north Devon to find a large BBC crew in the grounds filming an adaptation of the books, it was thrilling. It also seemed apt to be transported back to a previous era, since we were on our way to a secluded 15th-century seaside cottage that had deliberately been kept unmodernised and was situated at the end of a treacherous one-mile track. We were at the Abbey to collect the keys to the holiday home from the landlady, Angela.

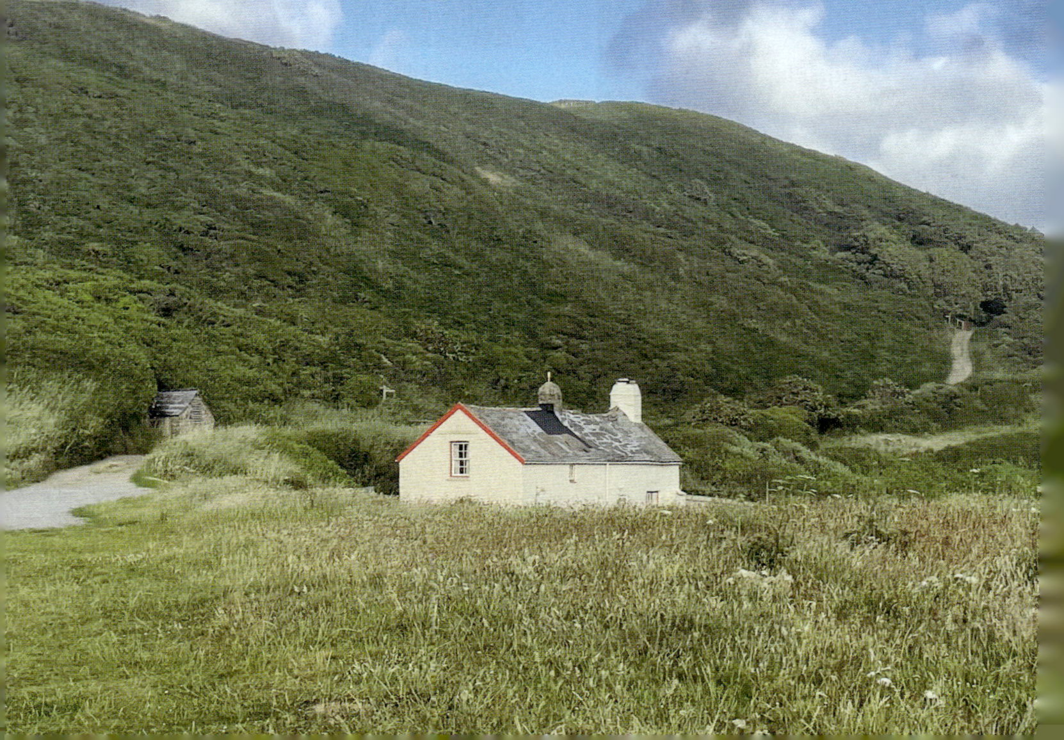

There was no WiFi, television, radio or phone signal at the cottage, so on the six-hour drive up from London I'd frantically used my mobile to move money, download some articles, scroll through Instagram, read emails, check the weather, the news, and say goodbye rather dramatically to our children on the family WhatsApp. Our messages are mostly banal, so I hoped there would be no emergencies.

We were welcomed by Angela, who was watching the filming and came to our car window worrying about whether there was loo paper and soap at the cottage. She was also concerned that the filmmakers were using boys *and* girls to film a scene of a "lax" (lacrosse) game. That certainly wouldn't have happened in the 1940s she said, scoffing.

I'd decided to rent the cottage on a whim, not considering the lack of WiFi or phone signal. I'd been there 20 years before when WiFi wasn't such a big thing. I couldn't remember there being a problem – in fact, all I could remember was making porridge. But as we manoeuvred at 5mph up the drive, I began to worry: what if one of us had a heart attack? How would we call an ambulance in time? How would an ambulance even get down the drive? Our daughter was away in Greece – how would she get hold of us if something happened? What if our house burnt down?

My use of phone time had been inching up, sometimes averaging six hours a day. Shocking. It is true that I keep my phone by my bed, with the excuse that it's to check the time. In the morning, I inevitably find myself reading the *Times*, emails and scrolling through Instagram all before 8am. My part-time job as a community manager for a large charity means I have to be vigilant on social media for signs of how the public are reacting to the paid adverts on Facebook and responding to their comments. I'm on my computer for several hours a day, seven days a week. In between times, I have meetings with work colleagues on Teams or I'm writing a book on my laptop. So now, getting away for a while, the thing I was most looking forward to was having a break from moderating all those intolerable right-wing trolls on Facebook.

As we inched down the track, the clouds burst and rain fell (lashings of it) across the windscreen. The white cottage stood all on its own tucked into a valley, a coastal path behind the back door, a rippling river below the front lawn, rising cliffs on both sides and a view of the raging Atlantic sea. We dumped our bags and made our way down to the rocky beach. The wind tore through our clothes. The waves were enormous, the edges of the rocks sprouting from the sea like jagged sculptures.

Back at the cottage, we discovered we'd locked ourselves out and left the car keys in the cottage. We had friends coming to stay and they were due within the hour. Horror! The wind howled and the rain blasted. I wondered how we could get another key without a phone signal or our car? We'd have to walk the tricky road back to the Abbey and locate Angela. Except, I had the distinct memory that she didn't actually live at the estate. Or we could brace the storm and walk up the cliff chasing a phone signal. But I wasn't even sure we had her number. The situation felt really desperate until my husband managed to hurl himself through a partly opened window.

On day two, as we languished lazily in the sunshine, our friend Vic volunteered to set off up the steep cliff with our four phones so we could get news downloaded. She also bravely agreed to do my husband's Spanish Duolingo lesson – not that she understood a word, but so long as she logged on for him, he wouldn't lose his streak (a measure of how consistently you use the app). It does seem odd for a grown man to be worried about losing his streaks, but anyway…

As the days rolled on, I became more and more chilled. It was liberating not to get the hourly WhatsApp messages from my daughter recording her various ailments – bruises, sunburn, a new blemish. The four of us noted that when we were the same age as our children, our parents didn't hear from us from one year to the next, practically. If we needed something, we just sorted it out.

Instead of waking up and straightaway checking the *Times*, the weather and Instagram, I read articles from the *London Review of Books*, which I'd downloaded. This was far more edifying and interesting and a less stressful way to start the day. I read two novels in four days and we played Uno, Irish Snap and backgammon in the evenings, which we never do at home. It was really enjoyable.

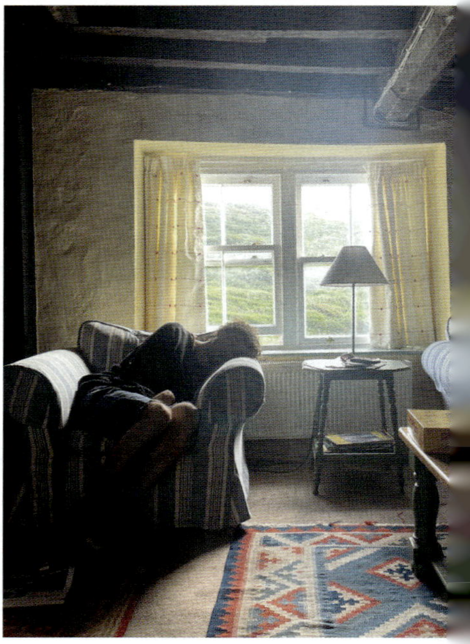

Escape room: our tech-free retreat was also very styl

We walked on coastal paths past an exceptionally beautiful landscape – waterfalls, wildflowers and ancient dwellings. We walked to the pub, which took about 40 minutes up and down really steep hills, and if I'd had a TV or internet I probably wouldn't have bothered, but the walking made it all the more enjoyable. Other times, I would sit on a bench above the beach just looking at the waves and listening to the cascading ripples as they drew back and forth across the stones. It was meditative and so peaceful.

One day, I even left my phone in a café and forgot all about it. We just spent our time idly doing nothing much, going down to "our" beach at low tide to swim or lie around staring at the sky.

By day seven it had started raining again, so it wasn't such a wrench to pack up and leave the cottage. But, as soon as we got a phone signal, I'm afraid I couldn't resist the urge to check everything straightaway – WhatsApp, emails, the news, the weather. All of it, despite pledges to myself to stop using Instagram so obsessively, to cut down on my phone time and not to scroll.

It was pleasing, at least, to note that while I was away my phone time decreased from six hours daily to something like three. I can't think what I was doing on it, except taking photographs or reading the newspaper when it happened to download after a cliff-top climb. I really enjoyed not being so up to date on everything – Trump, Israel, Putin. I want to go back to the house by the sea every year now, just to be jolly and wholesome and quiet. Two weeks rather than one. Once a month would be ideal.

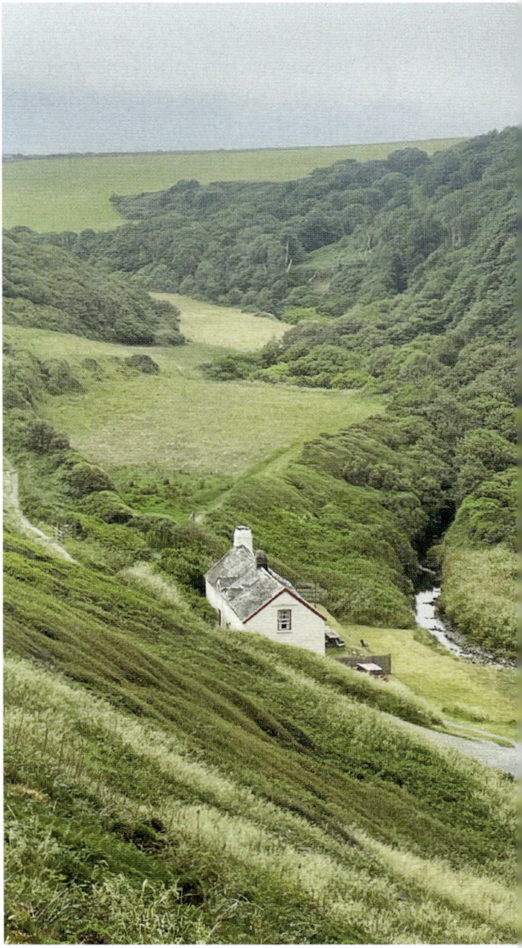

Peace in the valley: the remote cottage, with rippling river below and steep hills each side

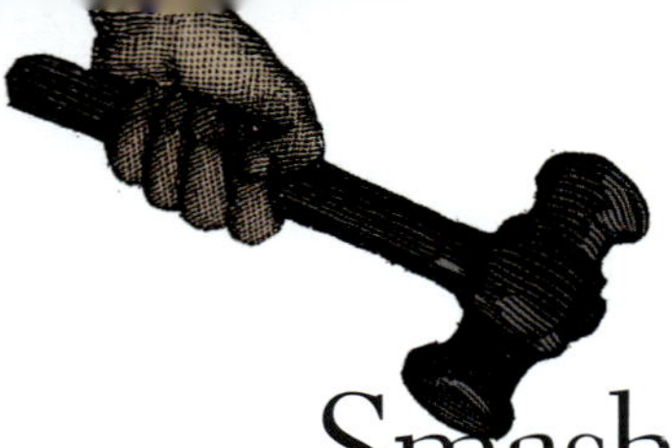

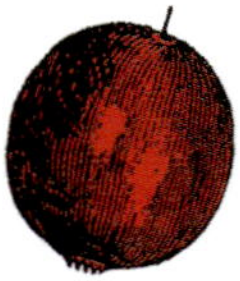

Recipes

Smashing Cranberries

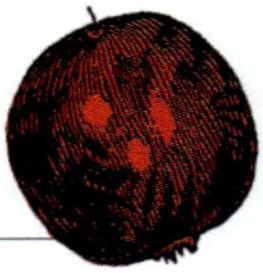

There's more to cranberries than garnishing a turkey.
Lindsey Bareham *makes merry with them*

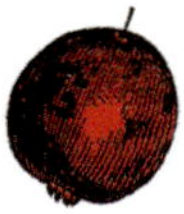

Cranberries are forever associated with cranberry sauce and have their moment at Thanksgiving in the US (a fifth of the annual crop is consumed then) and here at Christmas. But did you know that these sour little berries should be on our radar all year round? High in nutrients and antioxidants, cranberries are a superfood – something you may know if you've suffered from a urinary tract infection.

They're native to northern America and Canada and grow on low-lying vines in freshwater bogs. Farming them is big business and involves flooding the plants twice – the second time they float to their September harvesting, in time for Thanksgiving. The little berries take 16 months to mature, the next crop already growing on the vine behind the ripe fruit.

They start off green, then turn white and end up red, but under the skin they're white and crisp like apples. They never sweeten as they ripen. The pigment in the skin dominates when cooked.

Fresh cranberries are usually sold in larger packs than we need to make cranberry sauce, but they freeze well, like peas. A few added to mincemeat for mince pies brings a welcome sharpness. I also add some (from the freezer) to gravy, to give it a fruity astringency, which goes well with chicken and game. I'm not keen on cranberry sauce and prefer cranberry and orange relish, which I make at Christmas. Everyone loves it, so it's a good gift. Try it with cold cuts and cheese. Or use up leftover cranberries by cooking them with red cabbage. Be surprised, be very surprised. This is delicious with sausages, poached eggs and baked potatoes.

Cranberry & Orange Relish
This relish is so pretty, a vibrant deep red flecked with orange zest, the flavour as bright and lively as it looks. It's a huge improvement on dreary, sickly cranberry sauce, bringing a freshness to the meal. Adjust the quantities depending on how many cranberries you have to spare. Store in lidded jars.

500g fresh cranberries
100g caster sugar
1 large navel orange

Place the cranberries in the bowl of a food processor with the sugar. Quarter the orange, remove core and pith (if the pith is very thick, remove orange zest and discard pith), coarsely chop the orange (and zest) and add to the processor. Blitz in bursts to make a coarse relish not a mush. Transfer to jars and refrigerate for 2 days to mature. Will keep in the fridge for several days.

Red Cabbage & Cranberries

This juicy, fruity stew is also pretty, the bright berries contrasting with the purple cabbage. Every mouthful is slightly different, some with a smack of chilli, others with the aniseedy tang of fennel seed but all succulent with fresh orange juice. It's great with sausages or covered in thick scraps of mature Cheddar that melts in the heat. It's also good with poached eggs or cold cuts and baked potatoes.

Serves 2–4
Prep: 20 min
Cook: 40 min
1 onion, 150g
1tbsp olive oil
¼tsp crushed chillies
½tsp fennel seed
½ red cabbage, about 350g
1 juicing orange
¼ chicken or vegetable stock cube
150g cranberries
Knob of butter
Squeeze of lemon

Halve, peel and finely chop the onion. Cook, stirring often, in 1tbsp olive oil with a generous pinch of salt in a lidded, heavy-bottomed pan over a medium heat. Once it begins to wilt, stir in chillies and lightly crushed fennel seed. Meanwhile, slice the cabbage into short ribbons, discarding the thick core. Finely zest the orange then extract the juice. Stir the cabbage into the wilted onion, add orange zest and juice, crumble over the stock cube and add 150ml water and cranberries. Stir thoroughly, cover with a sheet of buttered greaseproof paper touching the food, fit the lid and cook over a low heat for 30–40 minutes until the cabbage is juicy with slight resistance to the bite. If very juicy, simmer uncovered for a few minutes to concentrate. Season to taste with salt and lemon.

You'll find more of Lindsey's recipes at lindseybareham.com and in her latest paperback One Pot Wonders *(Penguin/ Michael Joseph).*

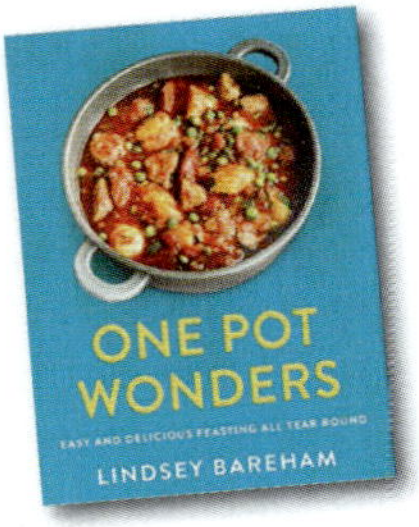

MERRIMENT

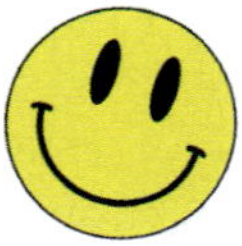

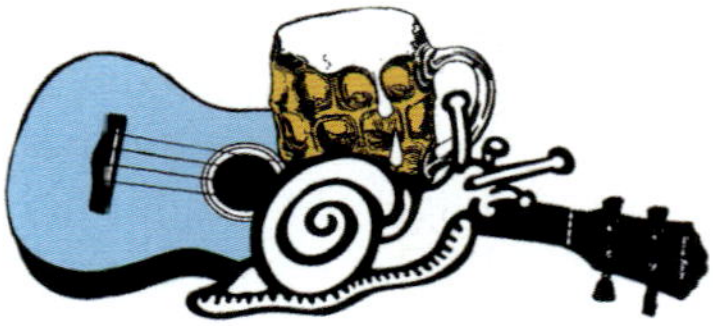

Eating Out

Local Heroes

Where to go to enjoy Florence's culinary delights? Where the locals eat, of course. **Victoria Hull** *heads for a treasured trattoria in the heart of the city*

DA ROCCO is a simple traditional trattoria inside Mercati Sant'Ambrogio, the oldest market in Florence. It's an easy ten-minute walk from Basilica Santa Croce, one of the must-see sites of the Tuscan capital, but this is the market for locals, stocked with traditional food and produce from local suppliers. Inside, there are three lines of stalls, sparkling stainless-steel counters of cheeses and meats, pastries, truffles, and a dried produce shop with more types of pulses and spice than you ever knew existed. Outside, tables are heaped with vegetables, seasonal and home grown, the tomatoes in different shapes and colours – ridged, oval, huge, tiny, yellow, green, reds. There are table cloths, crockery, bric-a-brac and clothes old and new.

The author Kamin Mohammadi wrote about this market in her book *La Bella Figura,* describing the friendly stallholders making a newcomer to Florence feel welcome, and helping her choose the perfect tomato for lunch. Kamin brought *Idler* editor Tom and me here a couple of years ago, on the

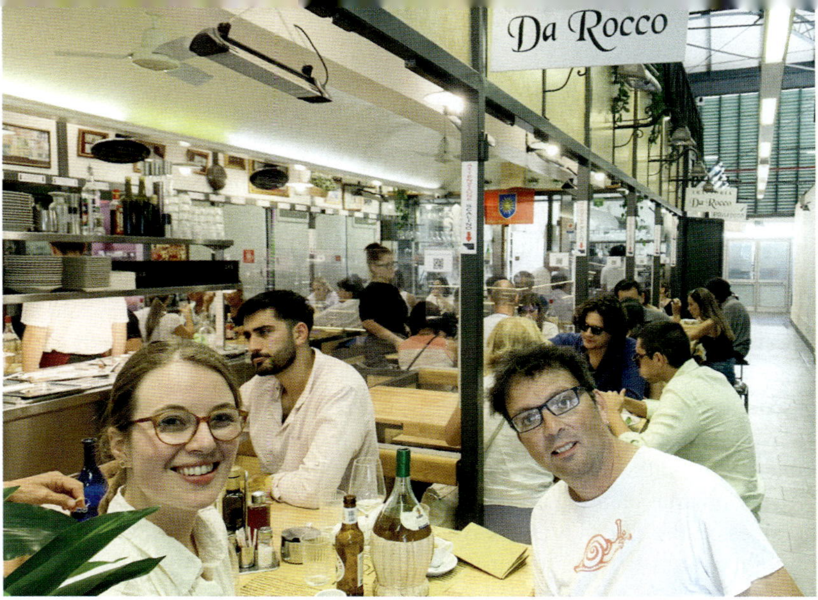

Simply perfect Cathleen and Tom at our stylishly unfussy table

Idler's Artisans of Florence Retreat, but today Tom and I are having lunch with Cathleen Mair. Cathleen worked for the *Idler* for many years, producing events and reviewing books. She was educated and grew up in Florence so she's the perfect person to show us places off the tourist track. Now she works for the British Academy having gained her PhD but she promises to continue contributing programmes for our retreats to Chianti and Florence.

Tom and I arrive late, having indulged in a map argument on the way, exacerbated by that arrow on Google Maps that points in the wrong direction half the time. Cathleen is sitting at one of the simple caff-like tables. Da Rocco is at the heart of the market, all open except for the occasional clear glass wall. There's a counter with hot dishes at one end and a chef with flame cookers at the other. Hung above him is the local team flag from Florence's brutal historical football game, *Calcio Storico Fiorentino*, the equivalent of Siena's *Palio*. Brown paper place mats list famous people significant to Florence including Boccaccio, Dante, Byron, Tolstoy, Tchaikovsky and Queen Victoria.

Rocco himself is here, buzzing around and charming the diners. After years serving as a chef's apprentice, he started his own trattoria in 1987. His son Paolo works with him and we are served by Rocco's red-headed granddaughter. The traditional menu includes the Florentine classic *lampredotto* – a rich, tasty stew made from the unlikely delicacy of the fourth compartment of a cow's stomach, served with salsa verde. Other specialities include *peposo* – a dark beef and pepper stew – and there's a little fish on Fridays and Saturdays including *spaghetti allo scoglio* – pasta with white wine and cherry tomatoes. Rocco is renowned for his baked pears drizzled with dark milk caramel.

Two jolly Florentines share our table, eating slithers of beef, simply served on white plates, with roast potatoes on the side. The steak is brought over by the neighbouring butcher when they order it. When they leave, I ask Cathleen what they were talking about. "They were asking Paolo if he's ever going to retire and making jokes with the staff about only wanting a light lunch but then ordering lots. They knew all the staff," she says. "One must be an academic or a teacher because they called him Professore."

There's a caddy on the table with olive oil, red wine vinegar, salt and pepper. A glass of red Chianti is the norm, brought in a two-litre straw-wrapped bottle that you help yourself from, and are then charged by how much you've gone through. I'm the only person drinking the house white from Cantina Lorini, near Siena, but nonetheless a whole bottle is uncorked and left on the table for me. It's light and easily quaffable but I resist temptation and stop at one civilised glass, feeling very Italian, actually stopping for lunch and hoping for a siesta afterwards.

Tom loves the spicy Spaghetti All'Amatriciana and Cathleen her Pappa al Pomodoro. Spelt Panzanella, the typical Tuscan bread and tomato salad, has sold out so I order the other local hefty classic – *ribollita*. It's solid and thick with cannellini beans and bread, less veg and juices than I would prefer, but nothing will deter me from the joy of eating someone's home recipe. This is what it tastes like – fresh, flavourful and real.

We sip an espresso before we leave. Even the coffee is an artisanal product, from a small roasting company in Lucca that uses manual grinders. Then we walk back into the famous city, sure that we have had an archetypal Florentine experience.

Ribollita: €7.50
Spaghetti All'Amatriciana: €7.50
Pappa al Pomodoro: €7.50
Water: €2
Wine glass: €4
Moretti: €2
Bread and cover charge: €3
2 coffees: €2
Lunch for three total: €35.50

Da Rocco's Trattoria
Mercato di Sant' Ambrogio, Piazza Lorenzo Ghiberti, 50122 Florence, Italy.
Telephone: 0039 331 838 4555
Monday to Saturday, 11.30am to 2.30pm

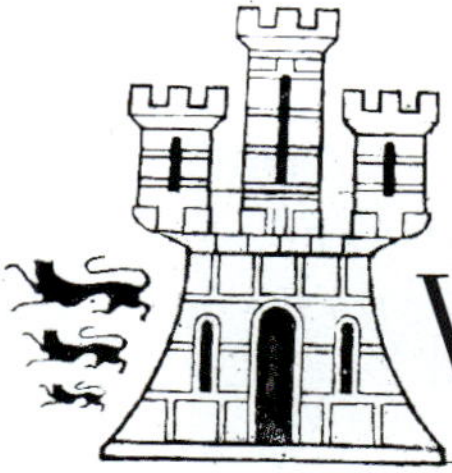

Beer

Windsor Wonderland

A walk and a brew – what could be more idling? **Oli Meade** *enjoys a beer amble through a town you might not think of as a craft mecca*

I'M ALWAYS SEARCHING for beer inspiration – ideas for where to find new and unusual brews and places to drink them – and recently my quest led me, somewhat surprisingly, to Windsor. With its amazing walks along the Thames, great shopping and castle, this historic Berkshire town is of course famous as a visitors' hotspot. But in recent times it's also become something of a must for beer tourists, with a collection of hip new kids on the block creating a trail of quirky taprooms and pubs that's well worth checking out.

The scene's beginnings can be traced back to 2019, when Windsor locals Dave and Naomi Hayward set up independent micropub A Hoppy Place, bringing independent craft beer to the town for arguably the first time. Then in 2020 the Windsor Trooper pub reopened as a freehouse, serving craft beer from the likes of The Kernel and Arbor (both among my absolute favourites) alongside fantastic traditional ales.

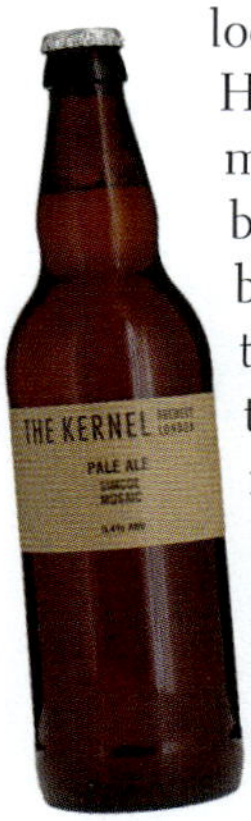

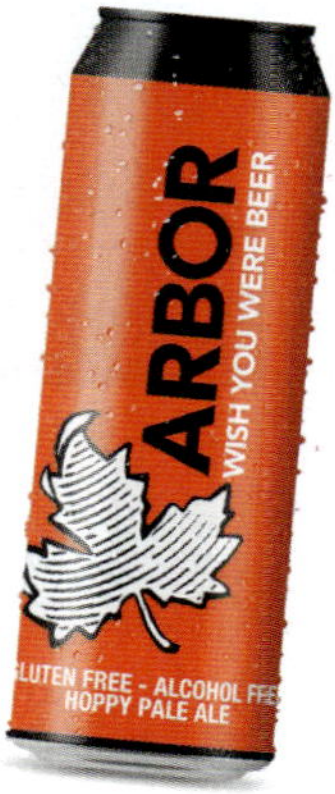

It was post-Covid, however, that Windsor's beer world really took off. Seeing the benefits of regeneration in areas such as Bermondsey and Brixton, small businesses landlords The Arch Company kicked off a project to renovate railway-arch spaces in the town, and opened their doors to independent breweries to set up shop there. One of these was the awesome Two Flints Brewery, whose beers I've stocked for ages and rate very highly. Two Flints opened their shutters at 25–26 The Arches in late 2022, and were joined at number 27 the following August by Indie Rabble, this year's SIBA award-winner for the UK's Best New Independent Craft Brewery. These four venues, along with the nearby and more established Windsor & Eton Brewery, comprise my Windsor Beer Walk.

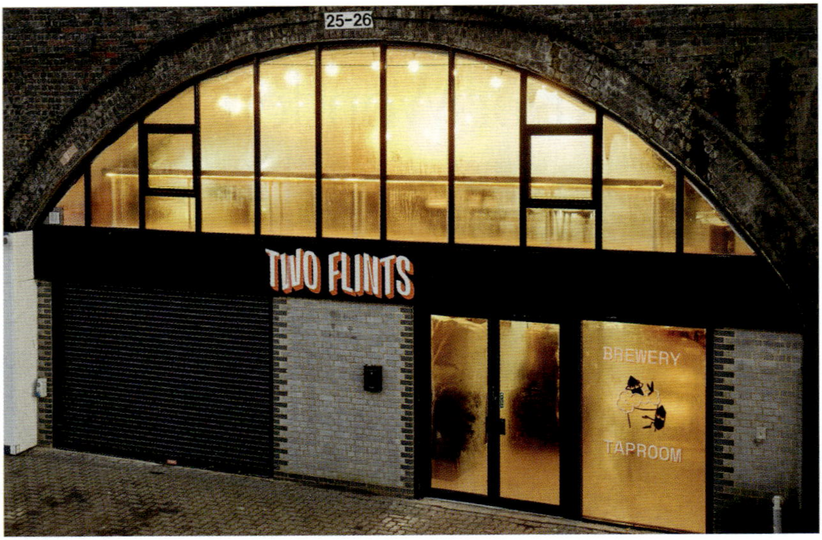

Underneath the Arches: Two Flints and Indie Rabble (engine room shown below) are your first beer stops

Your beer odyssey begins at The Arches, a two-minute jaunt from Windsor & Eton Central station (itself a mere 35 minutes from Paddington), where you'll find your first two stops, Indie Rabble and Two Flints. Open Thursday to Sunday, these very different yet extremely welcoming venues both offer 12 lines of their own beer plus a wide range of wines, spirits, cocktails and soft drinks – inclusivity being a key priority here. So much so, in fact, that you'll regularly see a Two Flints glass at Indie Rabble or vice versa, with customers of both breweries mixing together among the traditional table

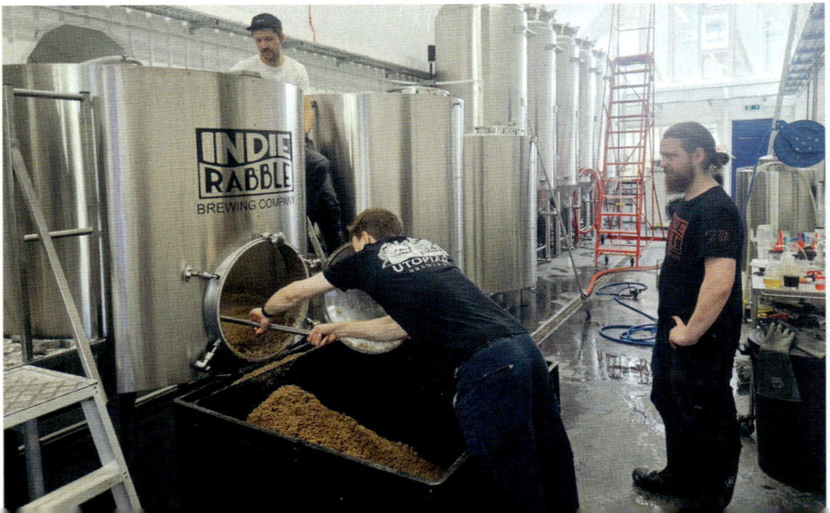

seating outside.

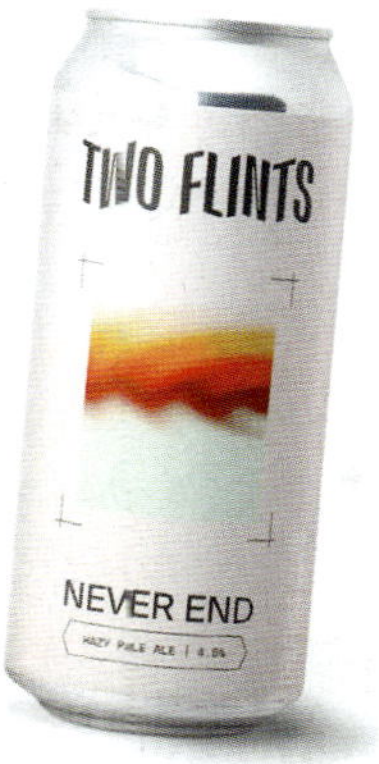

Actually, the collaboration goes even deeper than that: as well as brewing a beer together to celebrate Indie Rabble's launch, the two breweries share a forklift and canning line. It's a beery love fest and the results are tremendous, both sides boasting award-winning ales. With pop-up street food vendors nearby, as well as empanadas served at Indie Rabble to complement their beers, this spot makes a grand double-start to your Windsor Walk.

Five minutes away is venue number three. Windsor & Eton Brewery's new taproom, renovated during Covid, is mega, with beers offered on cask and keg. Split over two stories, plus outside space, and hosting regular live events, this is the brewery's flagship bar and is well worth a visit.

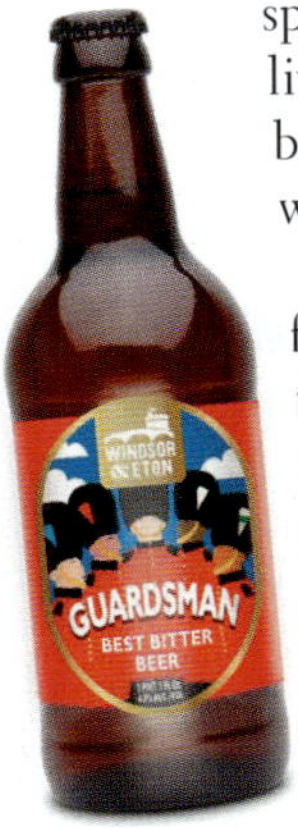

Perhaps a 10-minute walk from here is venue number four, A Hoppy Place, which offers 13 keg lines, two cask, and over 200 cans or bottles in the fridges. It's cosy, with seating inside for about 30, plus an extra 15 in the rear "secret garden". Regular beers include Two Flints and Indie Rabble, but also a range of national and international craft beer. You're just as likely to find a fantastic local pint of cask here as a crazy double-digit American fudge-laden stout. I was very much in hog heaven. It's a venue for all-comers and carries one of the widest ranges of cans and bottles in the country – almost as good a Craft Metropolis.

Finally the Windsor Trooper, five minutes further afield, features a huge beer garden, great food, regular events, and great beer – fantastic cask ale in particular. Their Belgian beer fridge isn't to be sniffed at either, with stone-cold classics everywhere you look.

Ten years ago it would have been inconceivable for such a beer scene to exist in a town like Windsor. But now it really is a worthwhile trip. Five great beer destinations within minutes of each other. It's genuinely a cracking day out. Oh, and there's the castle and river too, if that floats your boat…

Oli Meade owns and runs Craft Metropolis, a specialist online bottle shop and two taprooms in south London. You can support his business and the breweries mentioned by ordering beer from craftmetropolis.co.uk.

Ukulele

Two Ton Tessie

Cameron Murray *remembers a banjo-ukulele star who, in her heyday, rivalled George Formby and even shared a TV show with The Beatles*

WALES IS well-known for its entertainers – Dame Shirley Bassey, Sir Tom Jones and Sir Anthony Hopkins to name just a few. But have you heard of Tessie O'Shea? Sadly, most people these days haven't, despite a hugely successful career that spanned more than six decades and two continents.

Born in Cardiff on 13 March, 1913, Tessie was an accidental child prodigy. While convalescing in Weston-super-Mare after a serious illness, she heard the music of travelling troubadours near the beach and went to investigate.

"I crept underneath the tent and one of the men said, 'Oh, hello little girl! Do you want to come up?' And I said, 'Yes!'" Tessie revealed in a 1985 BBC TV show called *A Happy Return*. "In the meantime, my mother has gone mad because I've disappeared and she's got a policeman, and they're up and down the sands screaming and yelling when all of a sudden my mother said, 'Hold it – that's my Tessie's voice!' She came in with the

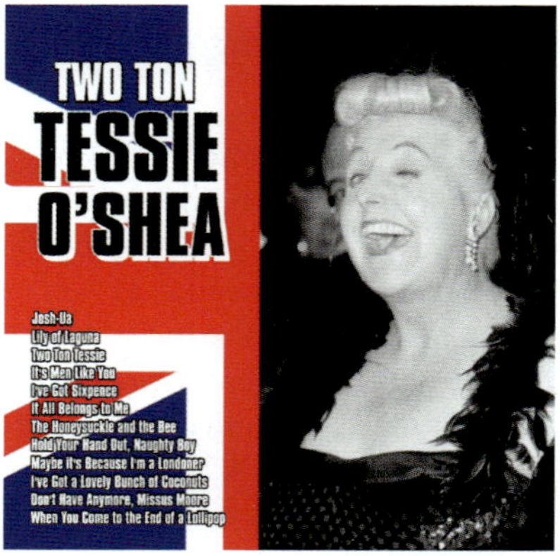

policeman and I was up on the stage singing a song that my dad taught me.

"They couldn't keep me quiet after that, once I'd smelt the stage. By the time I was six or seven, I was becoming 'The Wonder of Wales'."

Tessie was booked for a solo appearance at the Bristol Hippodrome aged 12. When she was 15, while starring in a revue in Blackpool, she first performed the song "Two Ton Tessie from Tennessee", which capitalised on her large physical size and eventually became her signature tune.

When people see or hear a banjo-ukulele, they usually think of George Formby, the English comedian with the naughty songs and the dynamite right hand. But Tessie was strumming up a storm during the same period as George.

"My mother loved banjos, so the first thing I ever did was learn how to play," she said on *A Happy Return*, before launching into a spirited performance of "Ain't She Sweet".

"Tessie was a powerful player," says Chris Jameson, the proud owner of the star's 1926 Gibson UB5 banjo-ukulele. "You probably wouldn't have lent her your favourite instrument, if not because of her enthusiastic fan stroke, then maybe for her habit of throwing her uke into the air at the end of a song and not always catching it!"

By the mid-1940s Tessie was topping the bill at the London Palladium, the queen of music hall. She earned a whopping £3,000 per week, received thousands of fan letters, and became the first woman to play the Palladium for an entire year.

Movie roles and hit records followed, and in 1963 Noël Coward created a part especially for her in his Broadway musical *The Girl Who Came to Supper*. Tessie's turn as Cockney fish'n'chips seller Ada Cockle garnered her a Tony Award and an appreciative American audience. She was a guest on *The Ed Sullivan Show* in 1963 and proved so popular that she was invited back the following year to share the spotlight with four lads from Liverpool called The Beatles. Broadcast on 9 February, the show attracted 73 million viewers, the largest TV audience in history at that point.

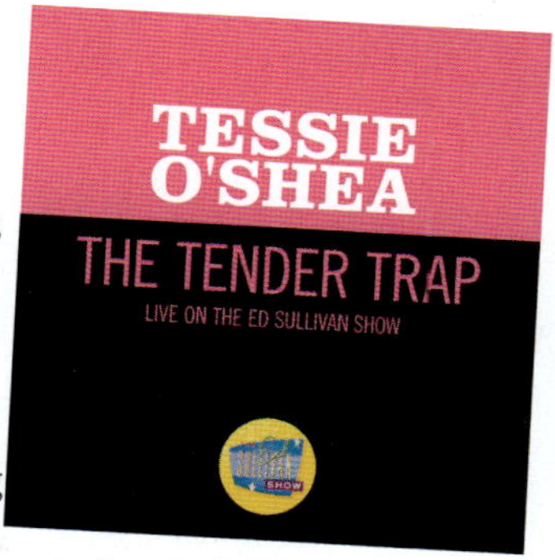

Tessie's zeal and love of performing was never dulled by age.

"I'm having more fun since I'm 60 than I had all the rest of my life," she said in her one-woman show *We'll Keep a Welcome*. "You can let the birthdays come and go, they won't leave me feeling glum. You know that the more candles I have on my birthday cake, the hotter I become!"

Later, Tessie moved to Florida, where she lived at the home of Ernest Wampola, a pianist and composer she'd met during World War II while entertaining the troops. Ernest welcomed her into his family and became her musical director and manager.

In 1995, Tessie died of congestive heart failure at the age of 82.

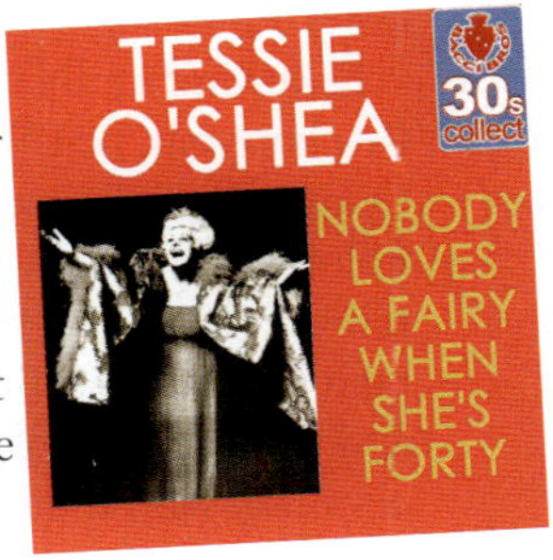

Making Spirits Bright

Surveying the plethora of booze-related Christmas gifts, **Joseph Piercy** *selects his top tipples – and steers you clear of the ones to avoid*

ALMOST UNDETECTED, creeping stealthily under the radar, Akvavit/Aquavit has emerged in 2024 as the owner of the slightly meaningless mantle "the new gin". Remarkably – and I'm sorry if this reads as a little boastful, but my claims to bragging rights about anything in life are such a rarity – I wrote a column for the *Idler* over two years ago about Bristol's ultra-hip micro distillery Psychopomp being the first producer of Akvavit in Europe outside of Scandinavia and predicting it was only a matter of time before other artisan distillers followed suit. OK, so the bandwagon took a little longer to get rolling than I may have initially forecast, but it's certainly rolling now.

Following trailblazers Psychopomp, first Scotland's the Orkney Gin Company, swiftly followed by Wales's Silver Circle, released their own small-batch, craft-style Aquavit. In a touching and rare example of cooperation not common within the UK's three largest regions, all three distilleries have joined forces, sharing expertise and resources to develop what they believe is a distinctly British version of Akvavit. So I thought a brief bluffers' guide to Akvavit / Aquavit would be helpful in understanding this most underrated of spirits.

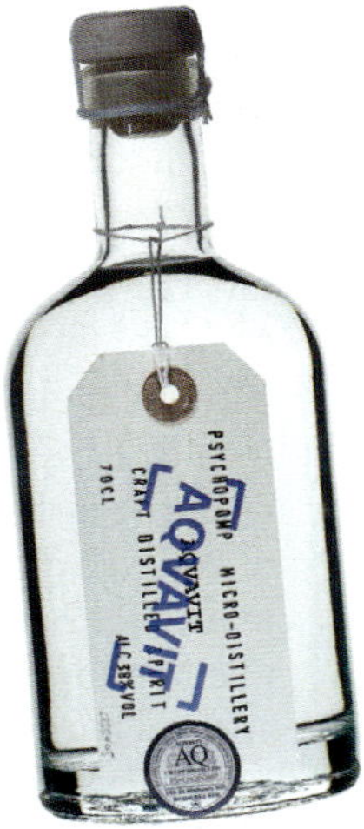

Akvavit (which roughly translates as "water of life") is a grain-based spirit typically flavoured with caraway, dill seeds and other botanicals that has been made in Scandinavia since the 16th century. Produced in Norway, Denmark and Sweden, there are marked differences in the individual styles of each region's drinks, which is a source of considerable competition and pride. Whereas Swedish and Danish Akvavit is clear or a very faint pale yellow, Norwegian Aquavit is a golden hue, as it's extra aged in brandy, whisky or port casks. Each country has its particular and peculiar production methods, ingredients and codes, none more eccentric than Norway's bestselling Linie Aquavit.

Legend has it that in 1805, at the height of the Napoleonic wars, Norwegian merchant ship the *Throndhiems Prøve* set sail with a cargo of Norwegian delicacies, including several barrels of Aquavit, bound for Batavia (present day Jakarta). Their journey required running the gauntlet of the blockade the British Royal Navy was imposing, under the command of Admiral Lord Nelson. When the ship finally arrived in Batavia, the Norwegian traders found little enthusiasm for the Aquavit among the locals and reluctantly transported the barrels back on the perilous voyage home. It was only on arriving in Norway that they discovered the quality of the Aquavit had markedly improved. This has led to the tradition of ageing Linie Aquavit by transporting it by boat across the equator and back in brandy or port barrels before bottling.

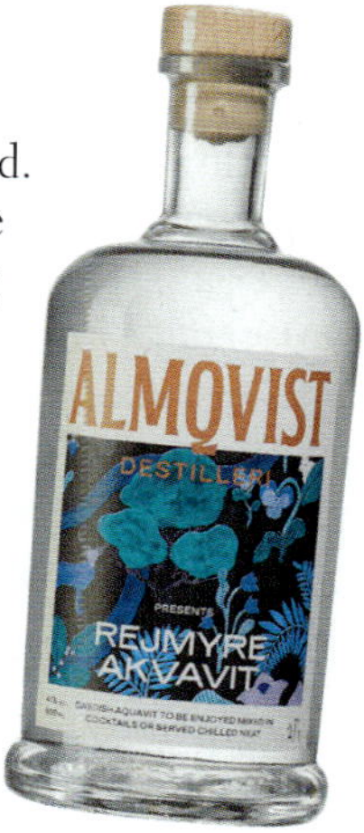

More contemporary Scandi peculiarity is personified by Bex Almqvist, maverick Swedish master distiller and former London cocktail bartending champion. Almqvist made her name as an innovative cocktail bartender, working in some of the capital's swankiest establishments in the early 2000s, before being head-hunted by Absolut Vodka. After returning to her native Sweden, Almqvist founded a micro distillery in the remote village of Rejmyre, with the mission to create the world's first entirely sustainably produced Akvavit and gin. Her Almqvist Distilleri was built inside an ancient glassworks and uses recycled and residual heat from the glass furnaces – which naturally produce the bottles – to heat the pot stills in the distillery. Virtually all the botanicals used are foraged from the dense surrounding forest or grown on site and even the quartz used in the glassworks is from local open mines and quarries. Almqvist's two flagship marques, Swedish Rejmyre Akvavit (be careful not to say Akvavit from Sweden – it's not the same thing according to Almqvist) and Nordic Dry Gin launched in the UK in July (see prices and details below).

I also wrote in the *Idler* last year about the absurd proliferation of celebrity endorsements of alcoholic drinks, initially confined to wine but rapidly spreading to the spirits market. Not content with his own brand of California blended wine – yes you read that right, *blended wine* – rapper Snoop Dogg has reunited with producer Dr Dre to enter the potentially lucrative RTD market. RTD stands for ready-to-drink, meaning pre-mixed cocktails and spirits with mixers of questionable quality and taste, sold at often eye-watering prices. The rappers' excuse for their reunion is to celebrate the 30th anniversary of the release of Snoop Dogg's single "Gin and Juice", by producing their RTD Gin and Juice.

The year the record was released, 1994, was also the time that the bubble burst on the alcopops market, sunk due to a mixture of market saturation, legislation and aggressive changes in taxation codes. One can only hope that RTDs suffer the same fate. Leaving aside the obvious emperor's new clothes trick these products somehow pull off – inexplicably sales have risen dramatically in the past five years – the joy of mixing drinks is either in the DIY element or in entrusting someone competent or skilled to do it for you. Would you really trust some disgruntled factory worker in Truro, Cornwall or Blazing, Kentucky not to urinate in the giant vats of Snoop Dog and Dre's Gin and Passionfruit Juice™? I know I wouldn't. The lines of brand sponsorship and artist merchandising are starting to get very blurred.

Speaking of disgruntled factory workers, at the time of writing, Whyte & Mackay distillery workers have voted to go on strike over pay and conditions at three Highland distilleries. Other distilleries currently planning to ballot members over strike action include Edrington, the makers of the Famous Grouse brand. Over the last decade there have been an increasing number of such disputes in the drinks industry across the world, driven by the inevitable results of aggressive corporate takeovers by global multinational drinks conglomerates.

The result is a marked deterioration in working conditions, renegotiation of contracts, zero-hours contracts, and attempts at banning unions. This makes the admirable efforts of the people at Psychopomp, Bex Almqvist, Silver Circle and others in preserving the integrity and skill of craft distilling something to cherish and support.

Stocking Fillers

- A British Aquavit tasting set (3×5cl) is available from the Orkney Gin Company's online shop (orkneygincompany.com) priced at £16.
- Almqvist Distilleri's Rejmyre Akvavit and Nordic Dry Gin can be purchased via the Whiskey Exchange (thewhiskyexchange.com) priced at £32.95 each (50cl).

SELF

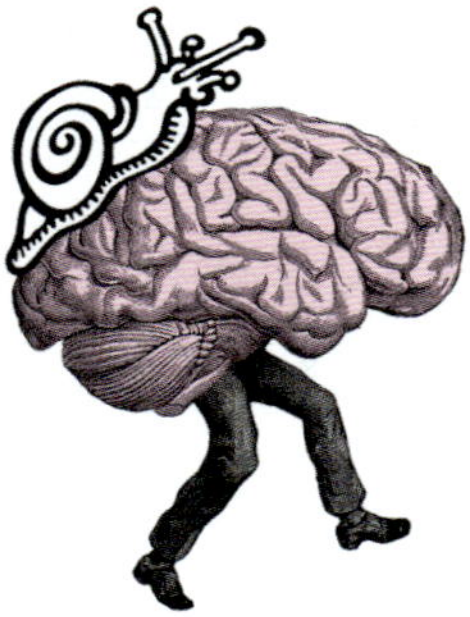

Being Well

Cut the Crap

Ultra-processed foods aren't just bad for your body – they're increasingly being linked to psychological disorders too. **Rachel Kelly** *on how to ditch the junk and eat yourself happier*

WHEN I WAS working as a journalist at the *Times* in the 1990s, there was still something called a cuttings library. We hacks could phone the library and order the file on whatever we were writing about. A messenger would arrive at our desks with a pile of neatly assembled pieces in date order on the topic in question. Bliss!

Now a freelancer, I laboriously maintain my own cuttings library on different aspects of mental health. One topic has seen a vast increase in coverage in the last few years: the links between mood and food. In the last few months alone, headlines have included "Ready Meals Linked to Anxiety and Illness" (*Telegraph*, February); "Lonely Women Crave Sugar" (*Times*, April); and "Ultra-Processed Foods Kill Millions Each Year" (*Telegraph*, June). The gist of all the articles is that anything that can't be made in your kitchen can lead not just to physical health problems but to psychological ones too.

Given my own history, these pieces strike a big chord. I first became intrigued by the idea of using diet to manage my tendency to anxiety-driven depression at least a decade ago (long before the topic became mainstream, I add smugly). I'd been having a long-running battle with racing thoughts, low moods, and insomnia. I'd also suffered two serious depressive episodes in my thirties that had led to spells in hospital. Visiting my GP for a check-up, the doctor told me there was compelling evidence about the links between mood and food. She wrote on her prescription pad a list of "happy foods" that might keep me calm, including her top three picks: green leafy vegetables, dark chocolate and oily fish.

She also suggested it made sense to cut out ultra-processed foods, or UPFs, though the acronym wasn't so common then; she talked about "convenience" and "pre-packaged ready meals". I remember being surprised. It wasn't commonplace back then to link diet with psychological well-being. Indeed she was the first person I can remember doing so, despite the fact I'd seen lots of mental health professionals. (Actually, given how little training NHS doctors are given in nutrition, perhaps this isn't so surprising. Figures vary, but even now it's only around 11 hours of teaching in a seven-year course.)

My curiosity piqued, I enlisted the help of a nutritional therapist, Alice Mackintosh, who holds degrees in nutritional therapy as well as biomedical science. Together, we began to develop recipes for my symptoms – some to comfort me when I felt low, some to boost my energy levels, and others to help when I suffered from a "foggy brain", another symptom of my anxiety. It's not the most elegant of acronyms, but I found cutting the CRAP (carbonated drinks; refined sugars; additives and aspartame; processed food and meats) a handy reminder to steer clear of the dangers of ultra-processed foods.

Almost immediately, I began to see an improvement in my symptoms, and have been an evangelist ever since about the power of food to help with anxiety and depression, to the point that I co-wrote a book with Alice on the topic and now run Good Mood Food workshops, including one for the Idler.

Today it's very common for conventional psychiatrists to recommend dietary changes for those suffering from anxiety: there's growing evidence that some forms of depression and mood imbalance may be linked to low-grade, chronic inflammation in the body. Adopting an anti-inflammatory diet, as well as other mood-boosting nutritional interventions, can therefore help improve our mental health.

The psychiatrist Dr James Arkell practises at London's Nightingale Hospital. "I'm increasingly aware that the brain, as the most sensitive organ in our body, is vulnerable to general inflammation and metabolic issues," he says. "Spikes in blood sugar from UPFs increase inflammation as our system struggles to handle them."

Arkell continues: "Recent research illustrates how people who eat UPFs are more likely to die earlier and more likely to get depressed. I talk to patients much more about food and gut health and lifestyle and less about pills these days."

Changing your diet can be tricky. I certainly find (*ahem*, found) it hard to abandon my favourite cheese-and-onion crisps, Cumberland sausages, Diet Coke and fruit yogurts. The whole point with UPFs is that they keep us coming back for more because they're made with delicious combinations of refined carbs and fats – combinations you won't typically find in nature.

My answer has been to fight back against the lure of UPFs by adding delicious new foods to my meals. The three main ingredients in my anti-inflammatory, mood-boosting diet are plants (vegetables in particular but fruit too); healthier fats; and fermented and gut-loving foods.

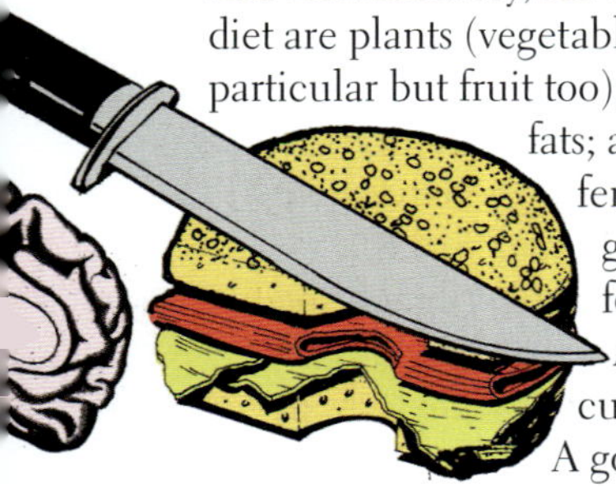

And finally, I cut the CRAP. A good tactic to avoid these temptations is a trick of Dr Arkell's, which is to have an alternative to hand should old cravings reassert themselves. My go to is a handful of almonds to help with snacking. By keeping the refined sugars at bay, I can improve my blood sugar balance, and keep my mood nice and steady.

Which, most of the time, it is. I use other approaches too. Mindfulness, plenty of therapy, exercise, and the healing power of poetry all play their part in my improved mental health. But if I had to recommend one tool, it would be the power of a very particular acronym – though it's not one I've yet seen in any newspaper headline. You read it here first.

Rachel Kelly's The Happy Kitchen: Good Mood Food *is published by Short Books, £14.99.*

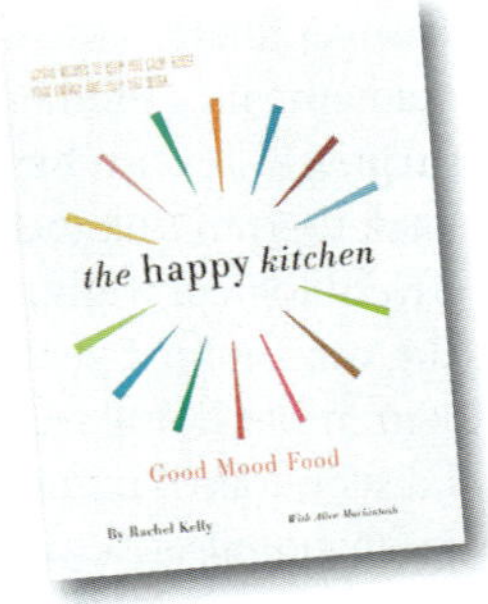

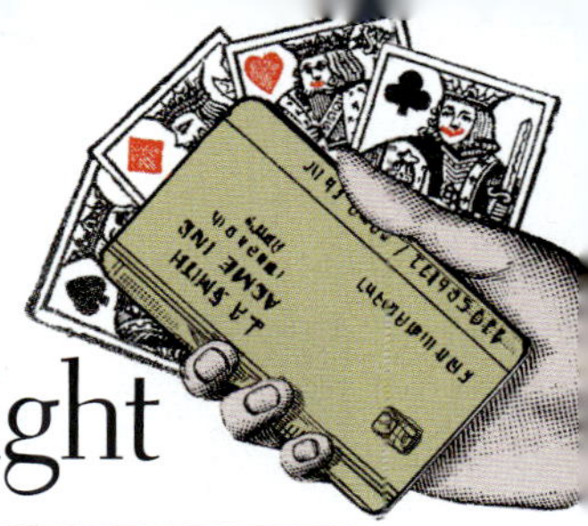

Fun and Frugality

Play Your Cards Right

The **Money-Saving Amateurs** *on why the credit cards are always stacked against you*

One of the most irresponsible credit card slogans ever was, "Don't put it off, put it on!" which featured in Barclaycard ads in the 1990s. In our view such encouragement to take out loans at very high rates of interest to buy things you can't afford should never have been allowed.

The temptation to "put it on" the credit card at Christmas is mighty. But should be resisted. The word "credit" sounds vaguely positive, like a gift. Credit cards should be renamed "debt cards" or "high-interest borrowing cards".

Interest rates are generally in the region 25-30% per annum. Credit cards are a method for transferring wealth from a large number of poor people into the pockets of a small number of rich people.

The *Guardian* recently reported that 13% of adults in the UK had missed three or more credit or bill payments in the last six months. For younger people it was worse: 29% of 18- to 24-year-olds had missed three or more payments. This means big bucks for the shareholders of the banks that run the credit card business. In the old days these people were called usurers and were generally despised for taking advantage of the poverty of others.

For around ten years we M-SAs decided to live without a credit card altogether. This simplified life very well, and of course there was no credit card debt and no temptation to spend money we didn't have (and would have to work to get).

Recently we've decided to get one because it makes hiring cars abroad much easier. But we never use it for everyday spending. We pay it off very quickly – within a few days. The advice generally is to pay it off within the month – but if you leave it a month you might miss the deadline, and see little bits of interest creeping in.

If you do have a big credit card debt, then the thing to do is cancel the card and take out a bank loan over five or ten years to pay it off.

And never splurge on a credit card in the hope some magical windfall will appear next month – it won't.

Easy Money

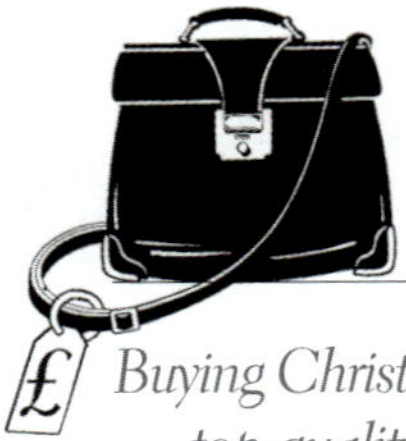

A Thriftmas Carol

Buying Christmas presents can be an expensive nightmare – or you could get top-quality bargains while aiding good causes and helping the planet, says **Michael Gilmore**

LAST CHRISTMAS my younger daughter, who's still in college and therefore essentially living off my money, bought me two Jermyn Street shirts. One Hilditch & Key, one Hawes & Curtis. One check, one stripy. One with button cuffs, one needing cufflinks, but both beautifully wrapped in tissue paper and ribbons, without any nasty plastic wrappers or weird little clips that new shirts usually come with.

That's because neither was new, but both were freshly washed and pressed, and I was delighted. They were exactly what I wanted – for two reasons. I'll explain the second in a minute, but the main reason is that with no money to spare, my daughter used different "assets" to buy me the perfect present: she knew where to find the best clothes bargains, and had the good taste and spare time to buy me things I probably would never have purchased myself, or even discovered.

What's more, this was a gift that didn't contribute to landfill or resource usage – and it supported charity.

She followed this up later with a bonus present: a tour of her top charity shops in central London. A couple of visits later and my wardrobe had been boosted by a Huntsman tweed jacket that fit perfectly, and a three-piece suit that didn't, but a little side-street tailoring put just right.

My daughter insists that central London is the second-best place for second-hand clothes (and she knows her stuff: she's dragged me around places like Tokyo's vintage mecca Shimokitazawa before now). Areas like Marylebone, Mayfair and Fitzrovia have enough well-heeled residents to provide their charity shops with a never-ending supply of high-quality items. Given how much footfall there is in these areas, the good stuff goes quickly though, so quick, regular visits are the key.

She used to like provincial cities more, with a special fondness for Hillhead in Glasgow – but too many student shoppers and

specialist vintage buyers (as well as an influx of fast-fashion items) have made the locale a tougher hunting ground.

Her favourite is now smaller but posher towns or suburbs, one of which is within easy reach of central London, on the way towards that polar opposite of thrift-shopping, Bicester Village. Sorry for the obfuscation but I can't tell you the exact location because she'd kill me. The treasure at the end of this hunt is probably more valuable than Kit Williams' golden hare, and much of it the same vintage.

And that's another unique joy of thrift-shopping. Some of the older finds are just so much better made than the modern equivalent – sometimes even when compared with the same item by the same company. I know how old-fashioned this sounds, but standards have fallen so far that a couple of years ago, the heel fell off a brand-new pair of my supposedly Northampton-made shoes, suspiciously soon after the company had been purchased by a global (but mainly Italian) fashion brand. Oldies but goodies don't do that – another reason to love them.

Now, as to the second reason why those shirts were exactly what I wanted, it's because, well, they were exactly what I'd asked for – and the very fact that I now ask for specific presents has become a sort of little Christmas gift to my family. This is actually less self-serving than it sounds. Let me explain…

A few years ago, my wife made it clear to me (in as nice a way as possible) that I'm very difficult to buy Christmas presents for. I don't want anything particularly, and if I do but haven't bought it, that's probably because I've decided it's too expensive, and I don't want her to change that decision. She's right, that is annoying.

So she told me I had to give her and the kids a list of things I wanted. And I had to think about it properly. Which I did… and I couldn't think of anything. It was inordinately difficult. So instead, I decided to stop buying myself anything from about June onwards. After that point, if anything caught my eye, be it a book, a gadget, or even a pair of new-to-me shirts, I didn't buy it. I wrote it down and told the family.

Obviously if my laptop breaks I'm allowed a new one, as I don't think Oxfam would have one that meets my requirements, and my editor may want me to file my copy a little more timely than such shopping around would allow. But for anything less urgent, I have to wait until Christmas.

It stops waste, it helps the people buying presents for me, and it means that when I actually get something, I've genuinely been looking forward to receiving it for some time. It makes for a merrier Thriftmas all round.

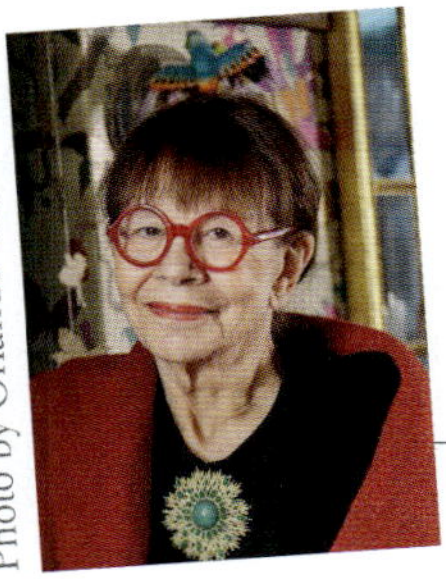

Photo by Orlando Gili

Problems

Virginia Ironside

Our agony aunt sorts you out

Bully Beef

My boss is a complete jerk. He runs me down, focuses on tiny mistakes and never praises me for good work – instead he takes the credit for it. I've tried remaining Stoic and I've tried to blame myself and my own attitude. But nothing seems to improve the situation.

Jane Green, Glasgow

I'M AFRAID you sound rather passive. So before you run, screeching, understandably, to HR and unpleasant tribunals, if you want to stay in your job and not leave – which to me would seem the most sensible move – have you taken steps to make your job better? Have you had a word with your boss and asked how you could improve? Try disarming him? Ask him directly if he'd like to get rid of you? Say you're trying to do your best but it seems you can't do anything right. Don't just sit there, taking it. Your boss sounds pretty grim, but he's only a human being like you. If you really try to make things better for him, he'll appreciate your efforts even if they don't always work out. Suggest a weekly chat about how your progressing and be prepared for criticism. Try to make your presence in the office a positive one – smile, offer to make coffee, turn up on time (or even early!) and be more pro-active.

My Girl's Mad at Me

My wife constantly runs me down and says I'm an idiot. She seems to disagree with me on absolutely everything, almost as a matter of principle. Is this normal?

Jack B, London E10

WELL, IS IT? In some couples it is, in others it's not. Many people have bizarre and apparently dysfunctional ways of carrying on behind closed doors. Nothing in any relationship is "normal". As Tolstoy said at the beginning of *Anna Karenina*: "All happy families are alike; each unhappy family is unhappy in its own way."

If this is unusual behaviour for your wife, there are two reasons why she might be carping. One is that she's very unhappy and the other is that she really has just discovered irritating aspects about you that she's never noticed before. Perhaps you've recently retired and she's spending more time in your company than she has for decades? Whichever is the case, you need to take a deep breath and ask her – in a completely calm, non-judgemental way – why she's behaving like this. Explain that it makes you feel horribly small and put-down, and you're at a loss to know what to do. Is there anything that could help change her opinion? Be enquiring and nurturing, not blaming and resentful – whether you feel like it or not.

Absent Friend

I'm 32 and my best friend died a year ago. I'm just about managing with life but I find I break down in tears every week or so, and I think about my friend every day. Will I ever get over it?

Anonymous

THERE'S NO "right" time to get over a bereavement but as you seem to be a bit stuck in a very unhappy cycle, now might be the moment to look for help. Think about contacting a Cruse bereavement counsellor through cruse.org.uk. They have helplines all over the UK and you can talk to experienced staff on the phone or see one face-to-face, if you'd prefer. These are people who have not only been there themselves but, because they talk to bereaved people all the time, know many of the familiar pitfalls – and strategies to help to come to terms with your loss. They've got useful book lists and offer workshops with other bereaved people – there's nothing they don't know about the grief business. The intensity of your grief right now is perhaps related to an earlier issue in your life that will need a bit more conversation to properly understand, but reaching out is the best way to proceed, and these are the right people to help you.

Security Blanket

I'd like to quit my job and devote myself to idling and philosophy, but I'm worried about money. What do you think would be a safe sum on which to retire?

Jim Bartlett, Cornwall

YOU DON'T GIVE me much information! Are you 25 or 70? Are you ill or well? Are you married or single? Do you have dependents? Are you extravagant or thrifty? Where do you intend spending your retirement? Though, even if you gave me this information, I still couldn't give a proper answer. Life is not like that. You might go out this afternoon and be run over by a bus with no life insurance …

Idling doesn't mean doing no

work whatsoever, you know. It means taking responsibility for your life now, so that you can work out how to better your future. To start with, get down to the business of working out exactly what you need to live on – and factor in a surplus for accidents and economic slumps and disasters. Maybe talk to an insurance broker and find out if there are any schemes you could sign up to that you can presently afford.

Do you actually want to spend the rest of your life loafing or are you looking to make what is presently a hobby into an income that will help you get by? Unless you're rolling in readies, now's perhaps not the best time to drop out completely – but if you can monetise the work you like doing somehow, then maybe you can do less of the drudge and more of the meaningful, creative enterprise? Only you can know – so take charge and make steps to finding out!

Readers' Letters

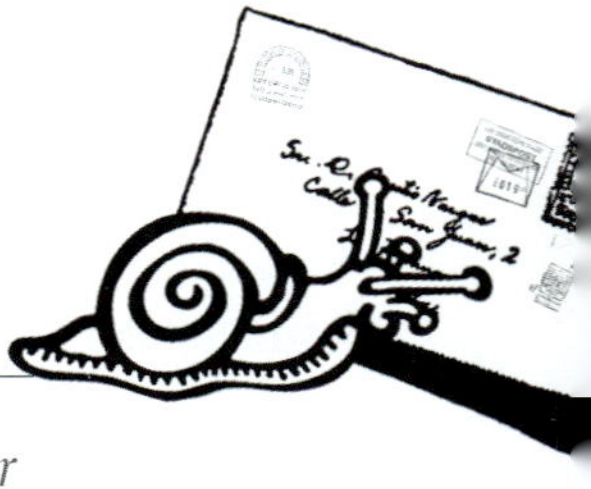

Send your letters to us at mail@idler.co.uk *or*
The Idler, Great Western Studios, 65 Alfred Road, London W2 5EU.
Please stay within a 200 word limit. Letters may be edited.

★★★ Star Letter ★★★

Manhattan Transfer

Sir: Having been very fortunate in my working life, I'm at an age of earning less and idling more. My current idling involves a cycle tour in the Netherlands. Active idling. A small collection of travel essays is in my pannier. It's Jan Morris in a 1979 essay called "The Islanders: Manhattan" (published by Penguin) writing about an unnamed business corporation "which seems to me to be run entirely, from top to bottom, by people off their balance … They have all been driven off their heads, I suppose, by the needling and hallucinatory pressures of Manhattan, the prick of ambition, the fear of failure: and in their eyes I see, as they contemplate the future of their lunatic careers, just the same fierce but loveless passion that one sees in the eyes of brain-washed cultists – a blend of alarm and mindless dedication, dimly tinged with tranquillisers."

Keep up the good work.

Angela Bailey

Back to Schole

Sir: John Davie's essay "School for Slackers" (*Idler* #98) relates to a theme that all idlers should revive. The ancient Athenians made two crucial distinctions that our modern age has obliterated. First, they distinguished between labour, which was arduous and deforming of mind and body, and work, which was activities done for reproduction and for strengthening the sense of *philia*, civic friendship. Second, they distinguished recreation, done to keep mind and body fit, and leisure, as captured by the word *schole*, which really meant a combination of education and public participation in the life of the polis. A citizen tried to maximise time spent in *schole*, combined with recreation and work in and around the home. But in addition a proper place was reserved for *aergia*, literally meaning idleness, needed for contemplation, reflection and balance. They also began the appreciation of commoning, in the idea of *eranos*. I have taken these distinctions through history in my new Pelican book *The Politics of Time: Gaining Control in the Age of Uncertainty*, which I presented at the Idler Festival in July. I believe every idler should wish to revive the ethos underpinning *schole*, *aergia* and commoning. Ending the jobs fetish would be a good place to start.

Guy Standing, Geneva

Fools Rush Out

Sir: I had to write to say well done *Idler* for publishing, and Griff Rhys Jones for writing, the hilarious Odium piece on outdoor dining in the May/June issue (*Idler* #96). I have many a fond memory of my parents and I walking the filthy and "aromatic" sidewalks of the Upper West Side of Manhattan decades ago when it first became a thing for every restaurant to have outdoor space – the better to provide food infused with bus exhaust and accompanied by the audible indignation of rushed pedestrians inches away and none too pleased to be denied two thirds of the width of their walkways. Not to mention presumptuous pigeons with low startle points. My dear departed mother's reply to the server's "Inside or out?" was always a dry "This isn't Paris." And she'd been there and found that even Paris isn't Paris. She would have loved this article and laughed out loud at its bold and necessary truth. I don't know what she would have made of the Covid era heated dining tents (aka rat spas), now slowly disappearing. I don't eat out much these days, but the persistent folly of urban al fresco dining has one benefit: with all the fools outside, it leaves more room, peace and quiet inside for me to enjoy food free of particulates, clamour and the unwanted attentions of local wildlife. Thanks for a great read and a good laugh.

Gabriella Mirollo, Rutland, Vermont

Crocodile Tears

Sir: I cannot be the only be reader to have noticed that in the Odium column (*Idler* #98) "Why I Hate Whale Watching" Griff Rhys Jones, no doubt driven to distraction and struggling to see through his somewhat disingenuously generated froth and spittle, inadvertently labels

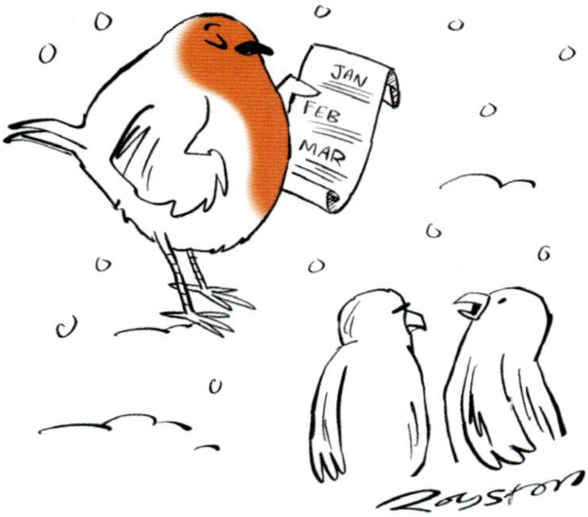

"Here we go, another tedious round robin."

crocodiles as "socially nervous amphibians". Sure, I get the brief – disingenuousness is all part of the schtick – but, blimey Griff, take a breath, mate …

Andy Gunn

Clean Machines

Sir: Electric cars are no longer "out of the reach of most budget buyers" (Slow Tech, "Get Your Motor Running", *Idler* #98), as I recently found out. Circumstances have curtailed long-distance travel for my wife and me, and instead we do lots of short journeys every week. This just felt a bit wrong in our large diesel estate car. Having looked into the second-hand electric car market, we bought a nice blue electric Renault Zoe a couple of months ago. It was under three years old, in perfect condition, with just 15,000 on the clock and so was, frankly, a new car with slightly worn tyres. The Zoe was one of the very earliest electric cars and so has steadily improved and had all the niggles ironed out of it (including battery issues, as I happily told a chap who is suffering with a new electric Jag that has already had cells fail in the battery – twice). In fact it seems so reliable now that Renault have just discontinued it in favour of sexy new models, making the second-hand value drop nicely. It appears capable of doing more than 200 miles on a full charge (not that I can be bothered to work it out exactly – and I also haven't bothered to spend up to a grand on a home charging point when the slow three-pin plug charger is fine for our purposes). Having the good fortune to have solar panels, I'm probably "filling it up" in daylight hours for next to nothing. The whole thing is a delight, and the feeling of passing filling stations thinking, "I'll never *ever* have to stop there" is still a minor thrill. Intrigued by the price I paid, warrantied, from a large reputable dealer? £10,000.

Geoff March, Stroud, Gloucestershire

I have driven a Nissan Leaf for the last nine years and consider it *ideal* for the idle motorist. The car needs almost no servicing (no combustion engine, no gearbox) and is showing few signs of age even after eighty thousand miles. The only major work you will have to do to an electric car is to change the tyres when they start perishing after five years or so. And I don't bother going to petrol stations anymore because I can simply "fill up" at home. EVs are more idle than you'd think: you don't even have to change gear! You are missing out.

John Tuffrey, by email

Beer Goggles

Sir: Coming across that regular *Idler* column featuring beer again, I've decided I'm absolutely up to here with beer monikers. Definitely. Each time I traipse into my local supermarket seeking out this week's wine bargain buy, I'm assailed with row upon row of designer beers given ridiculous names. "Tiger Brew", "Badger Whisperer", "Cheeky Chappie", "Lovers Leap" and so on. What has hops, water and God knows what else some young buck brewer has put into it, got to do with a tiger or a badger? The preponderance of names that adorn cans of beer nowadays staggers the imagination. Which comes first, the beer or the name? I've not seen "Sexy Sauvignon", "Cheery Chardonnay" or "Risque Riesling" looking for buyers. Never. When I began my alcohol journey 60 years ago, supping beer, "Grahams Ale", "Dorset Brew" and "Eldridge Pope Best" were the beers of choice. No highfalutin' trade names to be seen anywhere. Not "Gas Fuel", "Power Keg", "Dynamite" or "Brewers Droop". Those were the days when glitzy graphics splashed all over a beer bottle or can was deemed unnecessary. A contrivance. Well, just imagine stepping up to a pub bar 50 years ago and asking the landlord for a pint of "Brewers Droop"? Or maybe a pint of "Nitro"? You probably wouldn't get out of there alive.

Ray Howes, Weymouth, Dorset

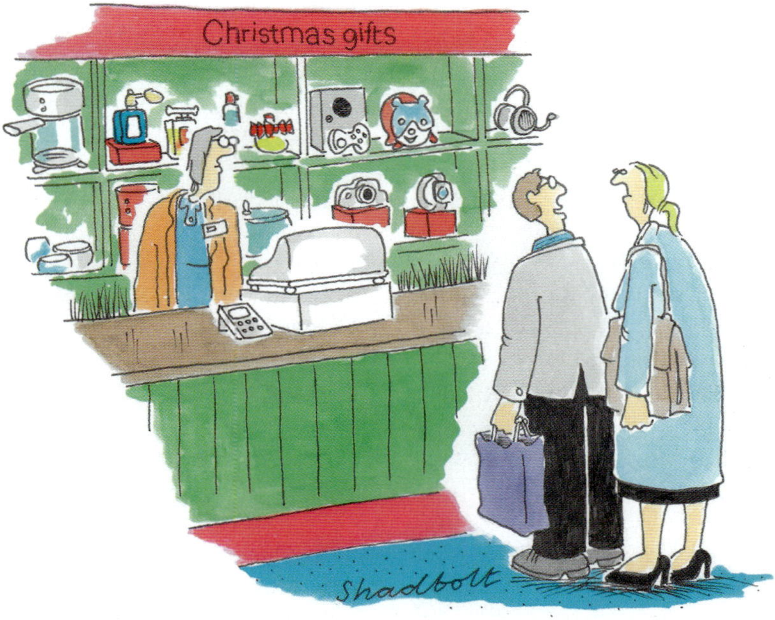

"Let's instil some festive cheer and hope by pretending to be interested in buying something before ordering it online"

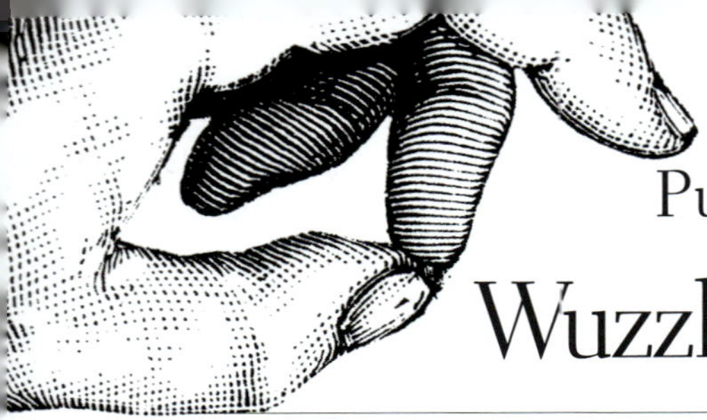

Puzzle

Wuzzling Fun

By Alex Bellos

A PORTMANTEAU WORD is one that's made up of two separate words. Examples include "brunch", "mansplain" and "hangry".

Are you familiar with the portmanteau words below? Can you work out which of the options is closest to their meanings, and what the constituent words are for each one?

1. PHUBBING
a) massaging
b) ignoring
c) crying
d) dancing

2. FLUMPET
a) woman
b) obese person
c) instrument
d) Disney character

3. BROZILIAN
a) beauty treatment
b) surfer
c) Bros superfan
d) parasol

4. JORTS
a) medicinal plant
b) item of clothing
c) exercise
d) skin ailment

5. CRONUT
a) old person
b) avian genitalia
c) widget
d) pastry

6. SNICE
a) frozen water
b) compliment
c) rodents
d) grain

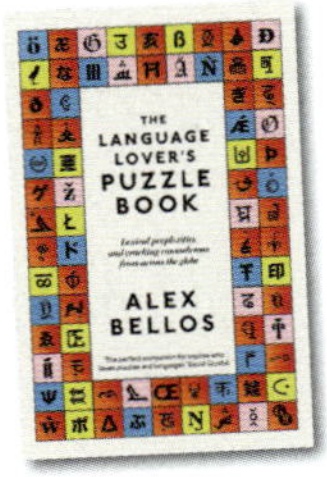

Answers on page 160.

Alex Bellos is the author of The Language Lover's Puzzle Book.

JOIN AS AN IDLER ACADEMY MEMBER

GO TO IDLER.CO.UK OR CALL 01442 820 580

ENGLISH LANGUAGE

How to Write Your Life Story *with Simon Petherick*
How to Write *with John-Paul Flintoff*
How to Write a Poem *with Clare Pollard*
Punctuation *with Harry Mount*
Elocution *with Sir Timothy Ackroyd*

LITERATURE

The Idler Guide to Paradise Lost *with Professor Anna Beer*
Dante's Divine Comedy in 100 Images *with Mark Vernon*
What Matters in Jane Austen *with Professor John Mullan*
An Introduction to Medieval English Literature *with Henry Eliot*
The Life and Works of Charles Dickens, Series One: Young Celebrity, *with Henry Eliot*
The Life and Works of Charles Dickens, Series Two: Dark Genius, *with Henry Eliot*
The Life and Works of Charles Dickens, Series Three: Social Critic, *with Henry Eliot*
An Introduction to Borges *with Henry Eliot*

PHILOSOPHY

How to be Idle *with Tom Hodgkinson*
An Introduction to Ancient Philosophy *with Mark Vernon*
An Introduction to Plato's Dialogues *with Mark Vernon and Tom Hodgkinson*
An Introduction to Modern Philosophy *with Mark Vernon*
A History of Christianity in Eleven Short Chapters *with Dr Mark Vernon*
Romantic Philosophy *with Mark Vernon*
Eastern Philosophy and Alan Watts *with Tim Lott*
A Brief Introduction to Anarchism *with Tom Hodgkinson*
How to Build Your Own Utopia *with David Bramwell*
Introduction to Psychotherapy *with Mark Vernon*
The Idler Guide to Imagination *with Mark Vernon*
How to be an Anarchist *with Ruth Kinna*

MUSIC

The Idler Guide to Bach *with Sandy Burnett*
An Introduction to Classical Music *with Sandy Burnett*
The Idler Guide to Jazz *with Sandy Burnett*
The Idler Guide to British Folk *with Will Hodgkinson*
How to Write a Song *with Chris Difford*
How to Sing *with Diana de Cabarrus*
Ukulele for Beginners *with Danny Wootton*
Harmonica for Beginners *with Ed Hopwood*
Intermediate Harmonica *with Ed Hopwood*

WELLBEING

How to Meditate *with Sister Jayanti*
How to Cope with Grief *with Julia Samuel*
How to Live and Eat like an Italian *with Kamin Mohammadi*
The Happy Kitchen: Good Mood Food *with Rachel Kelly and Alice Mackintosh*
A Guide to Modern Manners *with Mary Killen*
How to Read the Tarot *with Daisy Waugh*

HISTORY

A Brief History of Iran *with Kamin Mohammadi*
The Seasonal Festivals of Britain *with Ronald Hutton*
A History of London *with Dr Matthew Green*
Eminent Victorians *with John Mitchinson*
A History of British Buildings *with Harry Mount*
An Introduction to the History of Wine *with Anne McHale MW*

CLASSICAL STUDIES

The Idler Guide to Classical Civilisation *with Harry Mount*
Learn Latin *with Harry Mount Part One*
Learn Latin *with Harry Mount Part Two*
Learn Latin *with Harry Mount Part Three*

FASHION

How to Dress: A Guide for the Modern Gentleman *with Gustav Temple*

Idle Pets

Ketz the cat

Owner **Maggie Rosier**

Ketz doing some cat yoga on his favourite rug

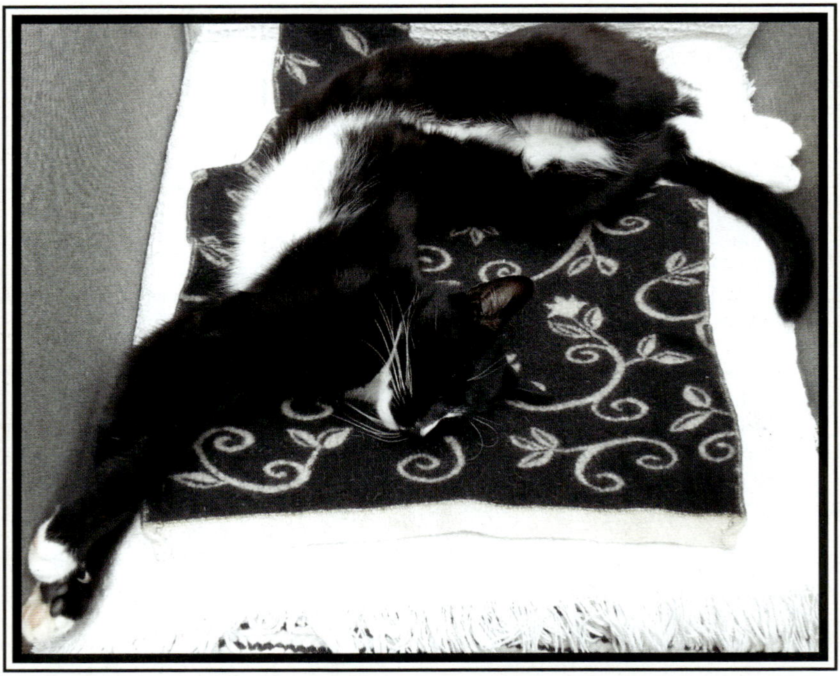

Puzzle Answers:

1. b) phone + snubbing, 2. c) flugelhorn + trumpet, 3. a) bro + Brazilian wax, 4. b) jeans + shorts, 5. d) croissant + donut, 6. a) snow + ice